CONTENTS

D1739428

KEY TO SYMBOLS

	no dogs please
	dogs on leashes only
	supervised children only
	no children please
	no smoking
	wheelchair access
	no wheelchair access
	toilet available
	no toilet available
	picnickers welcome
	morning and afternoon teas available
	lunches available
	accommodation available
	New Zealand Historic Places Trust classification

Map note: There are full-page maps at the beginning of each region to assist the traveller. The location of every garden is marked on these maps by a white numeral in a black rectangle. These correspond to the numeral at the top of each garden page.

© New Zealand Gardens Open to Visit – Friars

Friars' Guide
to
New Zealand

Gardens

Open to Visit

2001–2002

5th Edition

Written, photographed, compiled and typeset
by
Jillian and Denis Friar

Hodder Moa Beckett

*We dedicate this fifth edition to all
those kind garden owners, friends and relatives
who offered us hospitality
on our travels around New Zealand,
and to our teenagers
for their help with the typesetting
Daniel (19), Joy (17) and Sarah (15)*

Front Cover:
Miyazu Japanese Garden, Nelson City Council, Nelson, South Island (*see page 174*).

Back Cover:
Atholbrae, Norsewood, Tararua, North Island (*see page 138*).

ISBN 1-86958-833-9

© 2000 – original text, Jillian Friar, and original photographs, Denis Friar, FRIARS
The moral rights of the authors have been asserted
© Concept – Jillian and Denis Friar and Hodder Moa Beckett Publishers
© 2000 – design and formatting, Hodder Moa Beckett Publishers Limited

Published in 2000 by Hodder Moa Beckett Publishers Limited
[a member of the Hodder Headline Group]
4 Whetu Place, Mairangi Bay, Auckland, New Zealand

Typeset by Jillian, Joy & Daniel Friar, FRIARS, Auckland & Wanganui

Colour Separations – Microdot, NZ
Printed by Toppan Printing Co, Hong Kong

INTRODUCTION

Denis and I are pleased to present this fifth edition of *Friars' Guide to New Zealand Gardens Open to Visit*. This edition showcases over 200 gardens, including many new ones not included previously, as well as a garden tour. In addition to the private gardens, the book includes public botanical gardens throughout the country. The gardens cover a diversity of styles, terrain, ages, and sizes, ranging from smaller urban to large rural: "medium" is defined as from one to four acres (0.4 to 1.6 hectares); less than an acre is "small"; more than four acres is "large".

Unlike other garden guides, our book is accurately updated and comprises only gardens that are reliably open according to the times and conditions listed. The owners have paid for their gardens to be featured, ensuring a commitment to the visiting public, and reducing the retail price of the book. Each garden is professionally photographed, some owners choosing a double-page spread to do justice to their large or varied gardens. A location map enables visitors to find each garden readily, and regional maps assist in planning itineraries.

The gardens are arranged in approximate geographical regions, from north to south. As the climate varies, from subtropical in the far north to alpine in the high country and further down the South Island, so do the garden styles and content change as you travel through the country. New Zealand gardens display a huge range of flora, both native and introduced. Many of the gardens have nurseries attached, often specialising in plants that grow well in that particular region. For most an entrance fee is stated, but this is subject to change.

As most of these gardens are privately owned, the privacy of the owners needs to be respected at all times. If a garden is open by appointment, visitors must phone ahead to arrange a mutually convenient time. Those gardens that allow children to visit do so on condition that they are kept under strict supervision at all times. Children are admitted free of charge unless otherwise stated. If morning and afternoon tea or lunch are by arrangement, you will need to phone ahead. If there is a picnickers symbol displayed, visitors are welcome to picnic, sometimes by arrangement. Hot water is often available.

If you visit a garden at a different time of year from when it was photographed, it may look different from its photo. Gardens are never static – they change with the seasons and years, so although one feature may have peaked, there is always something new to see.

As with the previous editions, I have endeavoured to describe each garden in neutral language, avoiding superlatives and "flowery" adjectives, in order to give the visitors an accurate idea of what to expect and to leave them free to form their own judgments and opinions. I have avoided excessive use of botanical names and have used Maori names with the plural the same as singular, eg nikau, ponga, rimu, tui. All garden owners have checked their text and map, but any improvements or suggestions are welcomed.

Again we spent many weeks travelling throughout the country gathering new material for this book. We trust you will enjoy the privilege of visiting these gardens as much as we did. We would like to thank the garden owners for their hospitality in offering us refreshments, meals and accommodation – we do appreciate their kindness. Those we missed this time we hope to catch up with for our next edition in two years' time. If you, or anybody you know, would like to be included, please contact us as detailed over, on page 6. Happy visiting!

Jillian Friar

INVITATION

Would you like your garden to be featured in the next edition of
Friars' Guide to New Zealand Gardens Open to Visit
to be published in the year 2002?

This book is produced to highlight glorious gardens that are open to visit
throughout New Zealand. If you would like to have your garden promoted
with full-colour photography, a location map and descriptive 200-word text,
then contact the authors, or photocopy and send the form below.

There is a fee for each garden to be included in the book,
which helps to reduce the retail price.

Jillian and Denis Friar
44 Western Line
R D 1
Wanganui 5021
NEW ZEALAND

Phone 6-4-6-345 9702
Fax 6-4-6-345 9703
Mobile 6-4-21 453 867
Email gardens@friars.co.nz
Website http://friars.co.nz/gardens

I am interested in the 6th edition of
Friars' Guide to New Zealand Gardens Open to Visit.

Please contact me at the following address:

Name: ....

Address: ....

....

....

Phone/fax: ....

Email: ....

NORTH ISLAND

New Zealand

North Island

Auckland

South Island

Wellington

Christchurch

Dunedin

Kaitaia

Kerikeri   Russell

Paihia

Kaikohe

WHANGAREI

Dargaville

Orewa

AUCKLAND

Manurewa

Thames

HAMILTON

TAURANGA

Whakatane

ROTORUA

Te Kuiti

Tokoroa

GISBORNE

Taumarunui   **TAUPO**

NEW PLYMOUTH   Turangi

Wairoa

Hawera

Waiouru

Taihape   **NAPIER**

HASTINGS

WANGANUI

PALMERSTON NORTH

Paraparaumu

Porirua   Masterton

Lower Hutt

WELLINGTON

NORTHLAND

This northernmost region of New Zealand enjoys a balmy climate: warm, humid summers and very mild, frost-free winters, with a good rainfall. Tropical and subtropical species thrive under these conditions, and the citrus centre of the country is located here. The seven gardens featured in this region extend from north of Auckland, just below Whangarei, up to the far north at Lake Ngatu, north of Awanui, cose to Ninety Mile Beach. The strip of land at the northern end of New Zealand is accessible by a sealed road right up to Cape Reinga at the very tip. This isthmus is very narrow in some portions, only four kilometres at one point where both the west and east coasts are visible simultaneously. Ninety Mile Beach borders the Tasman Sea, while the Pacific Ocean lies to the east.

The southernmost garden, Greens' Bromeliads, incudes the largest collection of bromeliads in New Zealand. This subtropical garden is just 25 kilometers south-west of Whangarei. Then we come to Harbourbank, a garden east of Whangarei on the coast, planted on a steep bank overlooking Tutukaka Harbour.

Northland's Bay of Islands was the first area settled in New Zealand, and still features buildings and trees planted in the early 19th century. The garden surrounding the 1833 Treaty House at Waitangi is being restored, with magnificent views out over the Bay of Islands.

The water's edge garden at Pompallier in Russell has also now been restored as the Edwardian garden it once was, planted in 1880 in front of the restored historic printery built in 1841. The New Zealand Historic Places Trust is gradually restoring its buildings and gardens to replicas of the originals.

Kerikeri is notable for being the site of the oldest European wooden building in New Zealand, the Mission House having been built in 1821, with the adjacent Stone Store the oldest stone building, built in 1832. On the outskirts of Kerikeri is the cottage garden Matariki, featuring many subtropicals which flourish in the warm "winterless" north. Accommodation is also available.

Butler Point is located opposite the historic township of Mangonui, 45 minutes drive from Kaitaia. The garden surrounds a restored historic house built around 1846, and features a huge old pohutukawa grove. Added attractions at Butler Point are a Maori pa site and a small whaling museum. Pohutukawa feature throughout the coastline of the far north, with their magnificent red blooms flowering at the end of the year, giving them the name "The New Zealand Christmas Tree".

The northernmost garden is at Lake Ngatu, north of Awanui, just minutes from Ninety Mile Beach which stretches up to the north tip of New Zealand. The garden at Lake Ngatu Lodge is full of frost-free subtropicals including an organic orchard featuring banana groves, citrus, stone fruit and nut trees. The Lodge also provides accommodation. The far north offers a warm climate year-round, popular over the winter months with visitors from cooler climes. Most of these gardens are open all year.

Spirits
Bay

Great Exhibition Bay

Rangaunu
Bay

Doubtless
Bay

Stephenson I
Cavalli Is

N

Awanui

Mangonui

Ahipara
Bay

Kaitaia

Kaeo

Takou
Bay

Bay of
Islands

Ahipara

Kerikeri

Okaihau

Paihia

Russell

Kaikohe

Kawakawa

Moerewa

Whangaruru Harbour

Omapere

Hokianga Harbour

TUTAMOE RANGE

Hikurangi

Kamo

Maungatapere

WHANGAREI

Maungakaramea

Marsden
Point

Dargaville

Ruakaka

Te Kopuru

Waipu

Ruawai

Wellsford

Kaipara Harbour

Warkworth

Ōrewa

Helensville

Takapuna

Kumeu

AUCKLAND

Manurewa

Scale

0   50km

Cartography by Terralink Ltd

BUTLER POINT
Mangonui

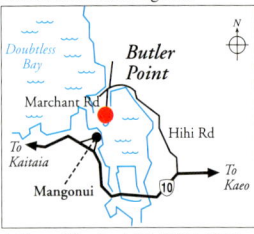

Owners:
Lindo and Laetitia Ferguson

Address: Marchant Rd, R D 1, Hihi, Mangonui
Directions: 27km north of Kaeo turn off SH 10 at Hihi Rd. Travel 6km to Marchant Rd leading to Butler Point.
Phone: 0-9-406 0006
Fax: 0-9-406 0006
Email: butler.point@xtra.co.nz
Website: friars.co.nz/gardens/pages/butlerpoint.html
Open: All year, daily, by appointment
Fee: $5 per adult; $7.50 includes Butler House & whaling museum
Size: Large – 4ha (10 acres) including smaller (1 acre) house garden
Terrain: Garden flat, grounds hilly
Nursery: Pohutukawa, *Elingamita johnsonii*, & *Dracaena draco*
Historic house: Open by appointment; small whaling museum adjacent
Attraction: Maori pa site nearby

self-serve

Butler Point takes its name from whaler Captain William Butler, who built his home on its shores in the 1840s and is now buried in an attractive cemetery among mature pohutukawa. This historic pohutukawa grove incudes a 700-year-old giant, recorded in *Great Trees of New Zealand* as having a trunk girth of 10.5 metres. Another feature of Captain Butler's legacy is a superb *Magnolia grandiflora* which guards the old house and is underplanted with ferns and clivia. The secluded gardens provide year-round interest. A traditional cottage garden surrounds Butler House and expands into more exotic tropical species such as palms, agaves, tibouchina and dombeyas. A water garden is surrounded by huge gunneras and a variety of irises and daylilies. Many natives include cordylines, arthropodiums and *Elingamita johnsonii* from the Three Kings Islands. The orchards feature citrus, cherimoya, figs and olives, while the picturesque picnic shelter looks on to a blaze of hibiscus. The gardens and orchard are flanked by park-like grounds with a harbour backdrop. A substantial macadamia plantation supplies processed nuts for sale. Red geranium and blue agapanthus brighten the impressive ponga fence which separates Butler House from Mangonui Harbour. Adjacent is a Whaling Museum reflecting Mangonui's history. A notable Maori pa site nearby is easily accessible.

LAKE NGATU LODGE
Waipapakauri

Lake Ngatu

Owners:
Graeme and Diane Jay

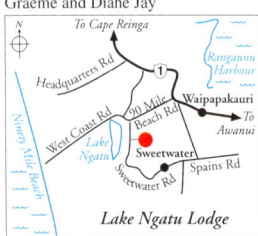

Lake Ngatu Lodge

Address: Sweetwater Rd, R D 1, Awanui, Northland
Directions: Take SH 1 north through Awanui to Waipapakauri. Turn left into Ninety Mile Beach Rd. Travel 2km into Sweetwater Rd. Garden is 3rd driveway on left – signposted.
Phone: 0-9-406 7300
Fax: 0-9-406 7300
Email: lakengatulodge@hotmail.com
Website: www.homestead.com/ lakengatulodge/ngatu2.html
Open: All year, by appointment only
Fee: $4 per adult, children free
Size: Medium – 0.4ha (1 acre)
Terrain: Flat to rolling
Nursery: Plants from garden for sale
Accommodation: In Lodge by request
Shop: avocado, macadamia nuts, almonds, feijoa & Maori potatoes

 by arrangement

Overlooking Lake Ngatu, this garden of almost half a hectare (one acre) has been established since 1987 on a four-hectare lifestyle block, just minutes from Ninety Mile Beach. The subtropical climate enables frost-tender species to flourish all year and the rate of growth is consequently very rapid. The dry garden area has developed well, predominantly with plants that enjoy light soil such as succulents, aloes, agaves, yukkas and grasses. The organic orchard includes banana groves, citrus, stone fruit, nuts and a variety of other fruit. Maori potatoes are also grown and sold. The Lodge is sited at the top of a driveway lined with natives and mature pine trees through which Lake Ngatu can be seen. The expansive front lawn is edged with colourful perennial borders. A pergola clad in wisteria and pandorea leads to the hothouse and home potager. Exotics include michelia, idesia, jacaranda, liquidambar, ginkgo, melia, frangipani, albizzia and calliandra trees, providing colour through the seasons. The swimming pool is one of Diane's favourite areas, surrounded with climbers such as the native *Tecomanthe speciosa*, white mandevilla, Painted trumpet, Cat's claw and Flame vines. A number of palms also feature in the pool area, with *Strelitzia nicolai*, hibiscus and native puka and ponga. Visitors can complement their garden tour with a stroll round the perimeter of the adjacent lake.

MATARIKI
Kerikeri

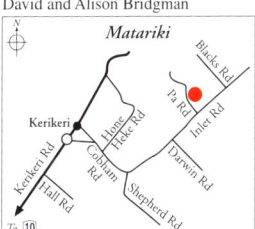

Matariki

Owners:
David and Alison Bridgman

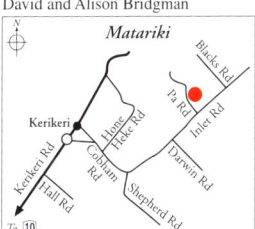

Address: Pa Rd, Kerikeri, Northland
Directions: Turn off SH 10 towards
Kerikeri. At roundabout, turn right
into Hobson Ave. Veer right into
Cobham Rd, then left into Inlet Rd.
Take 1st left into Pa Rd. Garden is
4th on right. (3km from town centre.)
Phone: 0-9-407 7577
Fax: 0-9-407 7593
Mobile: 025 278 2423
Open: November to April, by
appointment only
Fee: $4
Size: Medium – 0.4ha (1 acre)
Terrain: Flat
For sale: Fruit in season
Devonshire teas: $3.50 by request
Accommodation: B&B available

 by arrangement

Begun in the 1950s, this cottage garden has been extended over the years into three separate areas including subtropical plantings. The older established area features abelia hedges surrounding an original jacaranda tree. A theme of 12 *Thuja occidentalis* 'Pyramidalis', grouped in threes, unifies the garden. Prominent are three weeping pears, two robinia 'mop tops', a weeping elm and weeping copper beech. Other exotics include a floss silk tree, Brazilian tree-fern, Illawarra flame tree and bauhinias. Roses climb up the trees and box hedging provides some formality. Raised garden beds add structure and pergolas lead into garden rooms. The colours are grouped into blues and yellows in one area and reds and greys in another. The warm climate allows vireya rhododendrons to flourish throughout the garden, along with bromeliads, succulents, agaves, palms, tamarillos and mandarins. Spring features include blue and white wisteria, magnolias, rhododendrons and roses. The roses continue through the summer with hemerocallis, alstromeria, amaryllis, bougainvillea and hydrangeas. Then autumn brings the salvias into flower, along with ripening feijoas, tamarillos and mandarins. Native plantings include arthropodiums in spring, hebes and the climbing *Tecomanthe speciosa*. Matariki is only four minutes by car from the Kerikeri township and provides views over orchards and farmland to the horizon.

TREATY HOUSE GARDEN
Paihia

Owner:
Waitangi National Trust (Private Estate)
CEO: Johnny Edmonds

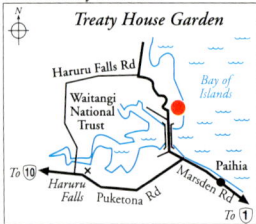
Treaty House Garden

Address: 1 Te Henare Drive, Paihia
Postal: P O Box 48, Paihia
Directions: From Paihia, travel north, crossing bridge over Waitangi River to Waitangi National Trust Visitor Centre.
Phone: 0-9-402 7437
Fax: 0-9-402 8303
Email: waitangiestate@xtra.co.nz
Website: www.waitangi.net.nz
Open: Daily, from 9am
Closed: Christmas Day only
Fee: $8 per adult, children free; includes access to Treaty House, Maori War Canoe, Carved Meeting House, grounds
Size: Large – 506ha (1,265 acres) estate
Terrain: Mostly flat
Nursery: Perennials, salvia, fuchsia, impatiens, heliotropium, pohutukawa
Shop: High-quality souvenirs
Café: On site
Kiwi Reserve: Open

The garden surrounding the Waitangi Treaty House is set in an extensive estate, gifted to the nation in 1932 by Lord and Lady Bledisloe. This semi-formal cottage garden features colourful annuals summer and winter, the mild, frost-free climate allowing cineraria and impatiens to flourish during winter. Clipped hedges of *Buxus sempervirens* 'Suffruticosa' separate beds of old English plants, with perennials and annuals complemented by native ferns. A surviving cutting from reputedly the first rose planted in New Zealand grows along the fence behind the historic Treaty House, built in 1833. Red 'Dublin Bay' roses climb a picket fence beyond the back courtyard herb garden, where fragrant *Heliotropium arborescens*, rosemary and other herbs feature within a brick-edged square, with pelargoniums and foxgloves in an adjacent bed. Daphne, fuchsia and bougainvillea are among favourites with visitors. Curved beds border the expansive lawn, with panoramic views of the Bay of Islands towards Russell. An oak and Norfolk Island pine, planted in 1836, grow beside indigenous species, including cabbage trees and pohutukawa with their spectacular red blossoms in summer. A large pale pink camellia, planted by the Busby family in the 19th century, grows alongside the native bush track to the Treaty House. A boardwalk leads through mangrove forest to Haruru Falls.

POMPALLIER
Russell

Owner:
New Zealand Historic Places Trust

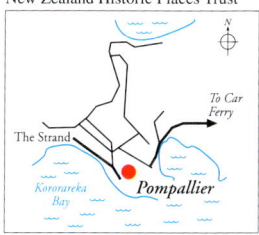

Address: The Strand, Russell
Directions: Take car ferry to Russell
or passenger ferry from Paihia.
Pompallier at south end of the beach.
Phone: 0-9-403 9015
Fax: 0-9-403 8588
Email: pompallier@historic.org.nz
Open: All year, daily; summer &
school holidays: 10am–5pm;
winter: tours at set times
Closed: Christmas Day
Fee: $5 per adult, $2 per student, NZ
Historic Places Trust members &
children free
Size: Medium – 1ha (2½ acres)
Terrain: Flat & hilly
Tours: Guides available at all times,
pre-booking recommended

to flat areas

The heritage colonial gardens at Pompallier surround the only surviving building of the Catholic Mission to Western Oceania. The Mission operated from 1839 to the 1850s, but the garden was started much later. Both are open to visit. Around 1879 the Greenway family converted the derelict Mission factory into a home, and the garden replaced other buildings. Eleagnus and tecoma hedges, flower borders and an orchard were planted in the locations that survive today. In 1905 the Stephenson family moved in and transformed the Greenway vegetable garden into a lawn tennis court. A flagpole, shell paths, box hedges and brick edging added formality. The Stephensons converted the home paddock into a hillside parkland, with a winding pathway and spectacular views. Today the building is carefully restored to its original Mission function, while the gardens are kept at their Edwardian peak. The property provides a variety of vistas from easily walked pathways in their historic setting. The beds hold a profusion of old-fashioned flowers. Many are descended from the first plants grown in the garden, such as the Poor Knights lily, the heritage roses, snowball trees, palms, camellias and old bulbs. Nineteenth-century cultivars have been re-established in the orchard. Visitors enjoy wandering through the hillside wilderness and orchard, picnicking and even playing croquet on the lawn.

HARBOURBANK
Tutukaka

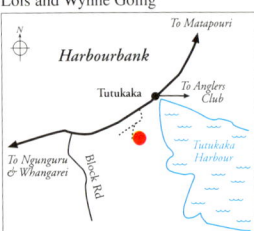

Owners:
Lois and Wynne Going

Harbourbank

Tutukaka

To Matapouri

To Anglers Club

To Ngunguru & Whangarei

Block Rd

Tutukaka Harbour

Address: Tutukaka Rd, Tutukaka
Postal: R D 3, Whangarei
Directions: Take SH 1 to Whangarei. Travel north-east to Tikipunga. At roundabout take Tutukaka Coast Rd. Continue through Ngunguru, up over hills. On Tutukaka side, just before bottom of hill, turn right up steep drive. Harbourbank is 2nd house on left, down short drive.
Phone: 0-9-434 3705
Open: All year, by appointment
Groups: By appointment, as above
Fee: $3 per adult
Size: Medium – 0.8ha (2 acres)
Terrain: Hillside bank; non-slip footwear advisable
Refreshments: Café & hotel nearby

 nearby, opposite Anglers Club

Harbourbank is a steep coastal garden on the banks of Tutukaka Harbour. The bold colours in the garden are enhanced by sea views, the house overlooking the Tutukaka Marina. Because of the steep terrain, most of the bank is planted, with very little lawn area, steps and winding paths connecting one area to the next. There is a small natural spring in the garden and several small ponds. The top garden around the house has been established since the late 'seventies, following a disastrous landslide. The lower garden was planted in pine trees until Lois began developing it in 1993. She plants whatever grows – the predominant species including Australian and South African species, perennials with grey foliage, and grasses. She is planting more succulents and bromeliads in difficult places and developing small feature areas with pots and sculpture. Harbourbank peaks in the spring, when it is a blaze of colour with masses of daisies complementing the prunus and magnolia. These are joined by vireyas, daylilies and lots of cannas creating a subtropical look. Roses and agapanthus are the main summer features followed by autumn-flowering shrubs and perennials. In late winter camellias and Taiwan cherries blossom. Native hebes, astelia, flaxes and carex all thrive at Harbourbank. The soil is not suitable for annuals, although Lois uses some for fillers around shrubs.

GREENS' BROMELIADS
Whangarei

Owners:
Keith and Maureen Green

Address: 4 Tangihua Rd,
Maungakaramea
Postal: P.D.C., Maungakaramea,
Whangarei 0250
Directions: 25km south of
Whangarei, turn west from SH 1 into
Maungakaramea Rd. Travel 10km to
Memorial Hall. Greens' Bromeliads
garden on right, opposite.
Phone: 0-9-432 3759
Fax: 0-9-432 3759
Email: kjgreen@xtra.co.nz
Open: All year, 9.30am to 5.30pm, by
appointment
Groups: By appointment
Fee: $3 refunded if plants purchased
Size: Medium – 0.6ha (1½ acres)
Terrain: Mostly flat
Nursery: Large range of bromeliads
& succulents including agaves &
aloes; mail order catalogue $3

    partly

This subtropical garden was established in 1992 with 90 trailers full of rocks, soil, puriri stumps and the largest collection of bromeliads in New Zealand. Maureen hybridises bromeliads and is registering one with tessellated (mosaic-like) maroon foliage, which will be for sale. The gardens are studded with bromeliads complemented by rare subtropicals from Australia, South Africa, South America and the Pacific region. The Greens specialise in the unusual, the garden featuring many rare shrubs and plants such as the *Matenoa* Hawaian tree daisy, the *Ombu* tree from South Africa, with roots that grow up on stilts, *Ficus damanopsis* with its huge corrugated leaves from New Guinea, the Brazilian *Chorisia* tree with thorns on its trunk, and the *Tabebuia* national tree of Venezuela with its bright yellow trumpet-shaped flowers followed by bean-like pods. The bromeliads grow throughout the garden, with some on native tree-ferns or ponga, others on the puriri stumps. Bromeliads come in all different sizes, with various coloured foilage, many variegated or tessellated. The flowers of some bromeliads last for six months. The Greens import seed and experiment with their own, the warm climate enabling them to grow subtropicals outdoors all year round – some in large pots. Vireyas, proteas, cycads, heliconia and palms, including bananas, flourish in this environment. Rockeries and ponds add structure.

AUCKLAND

South of the City of Whangarei is Auckland with its 22 featured gardens, and Mike's Garden Tours. The gardens are spread from the Whangaparaoa Peninsula in the north-east and Helensville in the north-west down to Mercer in the south. Auckland boasts the largest population in New Zealand, enjoying a warm, consistent climate, which favours the growth of subtropical plants. Summers are sunny and warm with light rain. Winters are mild, with twice as much rain as in summer, but little frost. Being sited on an isthmus, Auckland's climate is influenced by the maritime conditions, resulting in changeable weather. Much of Auckland is built on volcanic soil with a lot of clay in parts.

Northernmost, just half an hour north of the Harbour Bridge on Whangaparaoa Peninsula, is Mel's Vision, a terraced garden with views over Manly Beach. Located in Helensville is Greenlaw, planted in garden rooms with a sunken garden as focal point, followed at the end of the north-western motorway by the Kumeu garden, at Cuzzy Casuals, designed for relaxing on the flat lawn. Sonoma County is a new garden in Henderson Valley, with walkways through native plantings and beside the stream that traverses the property, and West Lynn Gardens feature a walk-in butterfly house. The North Shore City Council has two gardens: The Maze at Ngataringa Park incorporates a Celtic labyrinth and native plantings, and Fernglen Native Plant Gardens, originally established in 1888, include rare plants from the offshore islands. Tenbury House and Gardens in Devonport date back to 1904, with borders framing a historic fountain on the lawn. Two City Council gardens in Central Auckland are: the Domain with its Winter Garden and Museum, and the Dove-Myer Robinson Park incorporating the Parnell Rose Gardens and the Nancy Steen Garden with its old roses. In Epsom is the Eden Garden, established in an abandoned quarry, with camellias predominating. A Historic Places Trust garden in Auckland is Highwic in Epsom, planted round the 1862 Gothic Revival house. Tupari Mara is a cliff-edge garden over-looking Cockle Bay. At Whitford is Quails Croft, also on a clifftop, providing harbour views, and featuring roses and perennials. By way of contrast, a garden at Mangere East, Quarter Acre Paradise, is designed to be an inspiration to all backyard New Zealand gardeners, with masses of colour and a huge conservatory.

Down the Southern Motorway at Manurewa are the Auckland Regional Botanic Gardens, and at Papakura, Atarangi features roses and natives. Rose Cottage at Clevedon is an artist's garden where art students can learn to paint. Towards Waiuku are Wrights Watergardens with 30 waterlily ponds and four lotus ponds. Then at Waiuku is Ngodevwa with its various gardens flowing from one to another, including a pinetum featuring unusual pines. Southernmost is Flashmans' Folly at Onewhero, with ponds surrounded by planted slopes.

Plants flower for much longer periods in Auckland than farther south because of the mild conditions, with spring beginning early and autumn extending into winter. The area is well known for its grapes and citrus. Other public gardens worth visiting in Auckland include Albert Park and Old Government House by the University above the city, and Cornwall Park, an extensive rural park set in the heart of Auckland surrounding One Tree Hill. The Waitakere Ranges, to the west of Auckland, offer many walking tracks through native bush, and the Hunua Ranges east of Auckland provide bush walks for experienced trampers. Wenderholm, north of Auckland, is an attractive scenic reserve.

Sandspit

Warkworth

Snells Beach

Scale
0   20km
Cartography by Terralink Ltd

Kawau I

Mahurangi

Motuora I

Waiwera

Orewa

Red
Beach

Silverdale

8

Whangaparaoa

Parakai

Helensville

9

Albany

Rangitoto I

WAIHEKE I

Waimauku

Takapuna

Onetangi

Kumeu

18

14

12

Muriwai
Beach

10

Waitemata

13

Harbour

16

St Heliers

Bucklands
Beach

Maraetai

Swanson

11

17

Bethells

Mt
Eden

19

Howick

21

Henderson

24

18

22

Oratia

15

Piha

Mangere

20

Whitford

Manukau
Harbour

23

Clevedon

26

Manurewa

Ardmore

25

Awhitu

Takanini

Papakura

Clarks
Beach

Drury

Hunua

22

Ararimu

Ramarama

N

Bombay

Glenbrook

27

Pukekohe

Waiuku

28

Tuakau

Pokeno

Mercer

29

Meremere

Waikato River

1

Port Waikato

© Friars' Guide to New Zealand Gardens Open to Visit

19

MEL'S VISION
Whangaparaoa

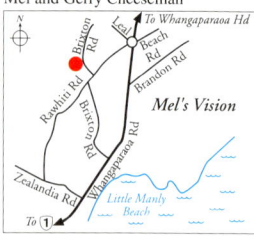

Owners:
Mel and Gerry Cheeseman

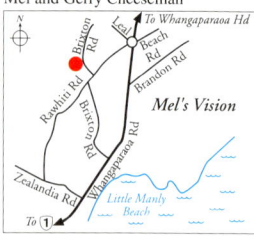

Mel's Vision

Address: 34 Brixton Rd, Manly, Whangaparaoa
Directions: (30 mins north of Harbour Bridge.) Take SH 1 from Auckland towards Orewa. After Silverdale turn-off, turn right at Whangaparaoa lights into Whangaparaoa Rd. Turn left into Brixton Rd, then right into Rawhiti Rd & immediately left into Brixton Rd again. Garden 3rd on left.
Phone: 0-9-424 3128
Open: All year; by appointment
Fee: By donation
Size: Small – 0.12ha (almost ⅓ acre)
Terrain: Terraced

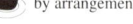 by arrangement

 hot water available

Mel had a vision of how her sloping grassed section could be transformed into a terraced garden with drifts of colour leading the eye out over Manly Beach. That was in 1989. Now Mel's Vision is a reality. Architectural features add structure, including the retaining wall, ponga archways, rose arbour and wisteria-clad pergola. Ponga-edged pathways lead down the bank to the shady area where Mel's favourite ferns and ponga flourish. Other native plantings in this area include pohutukawa, totara, cabbage trees, flax and pittosporums. Mel also loves her mixture of annuals which add to the summer colour. Mel mass plants colour, tone on tone, to create the drift effect in her herbaceous border. In spring, the blue and white wisterias are complemented by the cherry blossom, *Malus floribunda,* magnolias, paulownia, acers, azaleas and rhododendrons including vireyas. Two large Australian native crêpe myrtles, one pink and the other cerise, set the scene for summer, with roses and dahlias continuing into autumn. The maples colour up then too, while the evergreens – conifers and natives – are the mainstay in winter, when the garden layout is more apparent. Water features include a reticulated waterfall and a little pool beneath. Mel's Vision has won first prize four times now in the Hibiscus Coast garden competitions, just half an hour north of the Harbour Bridge.

GREENLAW
Helensville

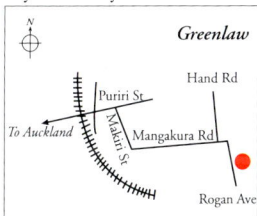

Owners:
Raywin and Wayne Cruickshank

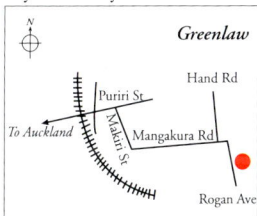

Greenlaw map — To Auckland, Puriri St, Hand Rd, Makiri St, Mangakura Rd, Rogan Ave

Address: 29 Rogan Ave, Helensville
Directions: From Auckland, take NW Motorway (SH 16) to Helensville. Cross overhead railway bridge & turn right into Puriri St. Take 1st right into Makiri St & continue into Mangakura Rd for 1km, 300m on metal/gravel. Turn right into Rogan Ave, cross railway line to garden, 2nd drive on left.
Phone: 0-9-420 8951
Fax: 0-9-420 8839
Email: greenlaw@internet.co.nz
Mobile: 025 943 877 or 025 275 7633
Open: October to May; by appointment
Fee: $3 per adult
Size: Medium – 0.4ha (1 acre)
Terrain: Flat
Nursery: Perennials from garden & hand-crafted wooden seats for sale

   by arrangement

Greenlaw is surrounded by countryside, the cattle pastureland creating a peaceful rural atmosphere. Beginning just with lawn round the house, Raywin sat down and designed the garden areas she has developed since 1991. It is planned in garden rooms, softened with self-seeding flowering plants. A new sunken garden provides a semi-formal air, planted with cream roses and lavender. Raywin's favourites are the perennials and roses such as 'Souvenir de Malmaison' and 'Albertine' that adorn the verandah. From there the sunken garden edged with brick and featuring a sun-dial can be seen across the resited driveway, hidden from view by a haha. Raywin's terracotta pots harmonise with the brickwork and unify the garden, a specialty being the urn sculpted by Christchurch potter, Peter Burelli. A yellow and blue garden follows a long curving path dominated by a nine-metre pergola covered in yellow roses and blue wisteria. Blue echiums also add height. Spring is a time of cherry blossom, bulbs, magnolias, lots of lavenders and forget-me-nots. The perennials, roses and daisies take over in summer, then the silver birches and gleditsias feature in autumn while roses continue along with the tall blue salvias and perennial lobelias. Natives include pittosporums, flaxes and hebes, but Raywin can't wait for the exotic and evergreen trees to mature.

CUZZY CASUALS & GARDEN
Kumeu

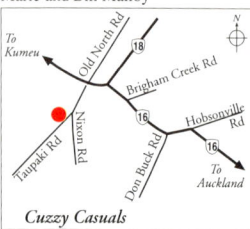

Owners:
Marie and Bill Malloy

Cuzzy Casuals

Address: 312 Taupaki Rd, Kumeu
Postal: 312 Taupaki Rd, R D 2,
Henderson
Directions: 20–25 minutes from
Auckland City. Take North-western
Motorway (SH 16) from Auckland to
northern end. Turn left towards
Kumeu. Turn left into Taupaki Rd.
Travel 1.5km to garden on right.
Phone: 0-9-412 8103
Fax: 0-9-412 8138
Open: Daily, by appointment
Fee: $2 per adult
Size: Medium – 0.05ha (⅛ acre)
Terrain: Flat
For sale: NZ-made children's wear;
wool handknits; dolls' clothes
Display: dolls & prams from 1919 to
today – pedigree, Barbie & English

Marie planted her small rural garden in 1998, aiming for lots of colour and areas where people could sit and enjoy themselves. She has retained a spacious lawn area with views over the adjacent fields. The flat terrain is broken up with beds edged in native ponga trunks. The ponga tree ferns are also used for the backdrop to the fish pond and small waterfall. The water feature is one of Marie's special areas, but with hindsight she would have made it bigger. The only problems she has encountered are the westerly winds. Structures include the pergola covered with cream wisteria over the driveway, and the new wishing well. Statuary adds interest. Marie has mixed plantings of colourful flowers most seasons, with spring bulbs followed by cottage flowers and dahlias. In the summer she enjoys sitting beneath the large fig tree and admiring the colourful range of flowers, which changes each year. Marie's favourites include the wisteria in springtime and the dahlias in summer. Autumn features the colourful foliage of the large trees, then in winter there is still the pond area and the indoor doll display. Marie has an extensive collection of dolls and prams dating from 1919 to the present day. These include pedigree dolls, Barbies and English dolls. She also sells dolls' clothes, New Zealand manufactured children's wear, and wool handknits.

SONOMA COUNTY
Henderson Valley

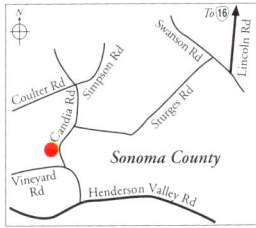

Sonoma

Owners:
Cushla and Ian Foster

Address: 101-103 Candia Rd,
Henderson Valley, West Auckland
Directions: From Auckland City, take
north-western motorway (SH 16) to
Lincoln Rd exit. Take Lincon Rd to
"T" junction & turn right into Swanson
Rd. Turn left into Sturges Rd & at
"T" junction turn left into Candia Rd.
Travel 100m to garden on right.
Phone: 0-9-836 7699
Mobile: 021 410 014
Open: Labour weekend (end October)
to Easter, daily, 10am to 4pm, by
appointment
Fee: $? per adult
Size: Medium – 1.6ha (4 acres)
Terrain: Flat to undulating
Nursery: Seasonal plants from garden
For sale: Arts, crafts & collectables

Established in 1995 on the site of the historic Western Vineyards Estate in Henderson Valley, the garden at Sonoma County still retains some wild grape vines. The 200-metre-long winding driveway leads to the north-facing homestead and garden with all-day sun. The house is surrounded by terracotta paving stones bordered with container planting. A mature phoenix palm overlooks the driveway which is fenced with white railings and a row of pruned pines. A myriad of flat wide pathways are grassed to blend in with the surrounding green slopes and provide garden walks of varying times from five to 20 minutes. A 30-metre foot-bridge crosses the stream that runs through the length of the garden, linking the vine trails to the homestead. A riverstone brook powers a windmill and a waterfall drops into a creek lined with weeping willows and with grass pathways terraced along the creek bed. This opens into a pond where a path leads past the jetty with its old boat to the fisherman's hut. Future developments include installing a large water wheel from a pump house. The predominant species at Sonoma County are the extensive native plantings which include mature tree-ferns or ponga. These are complemented by a large variety of perennials and shrubs, as well as a row of red maples and a backdrop of numerous tall gum trees. A big American-style barn is planned, for selling crafts and collectables.

NGATARINGA MAZE
Devonport

![maze photograph]

Owner:
North Shore City Council

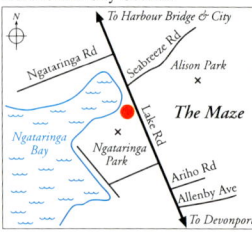

Address: Lake Rd, Devonport
Postal: Private Bag 93500, Takapuna, North Shore City
Directions: From City, take Northern Motorway (SH 1) & cross Harbour Bridge. Travel 1.5km & take Devonport exit. Travel towards Devonport on Lake Rd. Ngataringa Park & The Maze on right.
Phone: 0-9-486 8400
Fax: 0-9-486 8510
Email: cooks@nthshore.govt.nz
Open: All year, daily
Fee: No charge
Size: Small – 0.21ha (½ acre); set in Ngataringa Park – 8ha (20 acres)
Terrain: Flat

 mostly

The Maze at Ngataringa Park was designed by landscape architect Heather-Ann McConachy in 1993. The concept involves the interweaving of Celtic and Maori cultural histories into this archetypal form of labyrinth known as a Cretan seven-ring maze. The project was given approval by local Maori iwi (or tribes) and nearby residents each brought a rock to build into the central cairn. Most of the trees were planted by school children. The plants within The Maze provide a visual chronology of significant planting patterns throughout New Zealand's history. This extends from early Maori gardening practices, through to the plants introduced by the colonists, to the 19th century cottage gardening style, and today's indigenous flora. The structure of The Maze includes rocks arranged into cave-like spaces, and hedges bordering the pathways that wind and curve to form the design of the labyrinth. The hedges at the Ngataringa Maze are predominantly taupata (*Coprosma repens*) and box (*Buxus sp.*) and will be kept clipped at 1.8 metres high. The traditional processional pattern of the walkways is planned to encourage contemplation and calmness, with the choice of planting and sculptural artworks designed to inspire the imagination. The Maze is located in Nataringa Park, adjacent to the estuary which is bounded by a walkway, with views over the mangroves.

TENBURY HOUSE AND GARDENS
Devonport

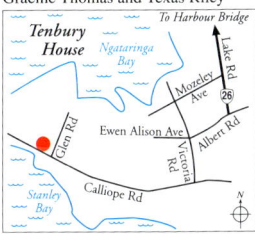

Owners:
Graeme Thomas and Texas Riley

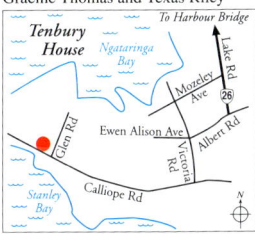

Address: 152 Calliope Rd, Devonport, Auckland
Directions: From City, cross Harbour Bridge & take Devonport exit. Travel to end of Lake Rd & turn right into Albert Rd. Turn left into Victoria Rd, & right into Calliope Rd. Travel 1km to Tenbury House & Gardens on right.
Phone: 0-9-445 3670
Fax: 0-9-445 3670
Open: October to March, 10am–4pm, by appointment only
Closed: April to September
Fee: $5 per person
Size: Small – 0.1ha (¼ acre)
Terrain: Flat
Teas: $5 per person, by arrangment
House tour: By arrangement
Weddings: By arrangement

 by arrangement only

Tenbury House was built in 1904 and is still surrounded by some of the original trees in the garden, such as the native puriri. Other trees include a weeping ash which together with colourful borders of perennials and annuals create an English feel to the garden. The borders contain hollyhocks, foxgloves, lavenders, snapdragons, Granny's bonnets, verbenas and scabiosa, framing the lawn with its centrepiece, a large fountain erected prior to 1930. Spring features include the camellias, colourful bulbs and wisteria over the driveway. In summer, the roses, dahlias, hemerocallis and gladioli are favourites. The gazebo's roof is canopied with creepers, and vireya rhododendrons hang in baskets from the archway to the house. The ground floor reception rooms of Tenbury House are open to visit by appointment. Built by the three Fendall sisters as a girls' finishing school, Tenbury was sold 16 years later and had a chequered history as a boarding house until bought and restored in 1984. The garden changes from season to season and each year the colour scheme varies with the use of annuals, such as the petunias which splash the borders with creams, reds and purples. This small urban garden provides a step back in time for visitors from October to March, with morning and afternoon teas available by arrangement. It is also a popular setting for marriages and wedding photography.

FERNGLEN NATIVE PLANT GARDENS
Birkenhead

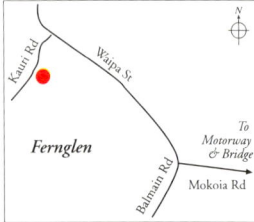

Owner:
North Shore City Council

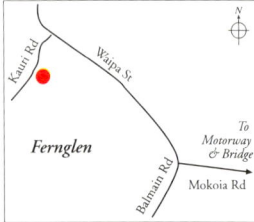

Fernglen

Address: 36 Kauri Rd, Birkenhead
Postal: Private Bag 93 500, Takapuna
Directions: Take Northern Motorway
(SH 1) out of City. Cross Harbour
Bridge & take Northcote exit. Travel
to end of Onewa Rd, then continue
round Highbury Bypass into Mokoia
Rd. Continue into Waipa St. Turn left
into Kauri Rd. Fernglen is in the
extension of Kauri Rd, on left.
Phone: 0-9-486 8400
Fax: 0-9-486 8500
Open: All year, daily, 9am–4pm
Groups: As above
Fee: No charge
Size: Large – 3ha (7½ acres)
Terrain: Flat & hilly
Brochure: Available from Parks &
Environment Dept, NSCC, as above

Fernglen Native Plant Gardens were established in 1888 by the Fisher family. The native bush on the property was added to in the early 1920s, by plantings of rimu, kahikatea and pohutukawa, which are mature specimens today. Since then, the gardens have been used for research and education, based on native species. Fernglen has a significant collection of New Zealand alpines (as well as subalpine grasses, sedges and hebes), indigenous ferns, *Drachophyllum* (grass trees), and rare plants from the off-shore islands. In 1989 the gardens were bought by the City Council, including the gazebo which was built in memory of Dr Lucy Moore and gifted by the late Dr Lucy Cranwell. Water features include the small pool surrounded by the rockery which displays the offshore islands collection, such as *Elingamita johnsonii*, a member of the cabbage tree family *Cordyline kasper*, the Poor Knights Island lily *Xeronema callistemon*, and *Geranium traversii*. A 1950s specimen of the now popular *Tecomanthe speciosa* features beside the house, flowering profusely in early winter. A bush walk leads down a ridge of kauri to a small stream from where a historic rimu covered in epiphytes can be seen, probably over 200 years old. Another track leads through an area of cabbage trees, astelias, nikau palms and ground ferns to the Fern House where species such as the Prince of Wales feathers and kidney ferns can be found.

WEST LYNN GARDENS
New Lynn

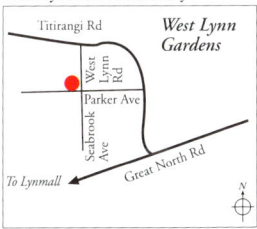

Owner:
West Lynn Gardens Society

West Lynn Gardens were established by Jack Clark, founder of Eden Gardens, with a continuous band of hard-working volunteer helpers, and opened to the public in 1983. The predominant species are camellias, magnolias, conifers and New Zealand conifers attracting plenty of birdlife which feed on the Taiwan cherry and other favourite flowers. Special features of the garden include a native area with unusual plants, a tropical area with bananas, bromeliads and palms, and a huge walk-in butterfly house. Monarchs and some native butterflies feature from December until April when they are released. The building has recently been professionally rebuilt and now houses hundreds of monarch butterflies. Other special areas include a gazebo with many garden seats in the centre of the garden, small ponds, a dry stream bed and a developing cacti garden. West Lynn is an all-seasons garden displaying bulbs and blossoms during spring, perennials over summer, vireyas and autumn foliage, then conifers and camellias in winter. The gardens are popular for garden weddings and photography. Visitors can join an endowment scheme, by selecting a tree in memory of a loved one for $350. The West Lynn Gardens Society was formed in 1992, annual family membership is $15; or life membership is $100.

Address: 73 Parker Ave, New Lynn
Directions: Take Great North Rd towards New Lynn. Turn into Titirangi Rd. Turn left into Parker Ave. West Lynn Gardens on right.
Phone: 0-9-827 7045
Open: All year, daily except Christmas Day; 10am– 4pm
Groups: By appointment
Fee: $2 per adult; $1 per child
Size: Large – nearly 2ha (4½ acres)
Terrain: Flat and sloping
Nursery: Plants & camellias $3–$5
Attractions: Butterfly House open December to April
Functions: Available for garden weddings & photography

 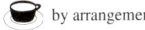 by arrangement

AUCKLAND DOMAIN
Grafton

Owner:
Auckland City Council

Address: Park Rd, Grafton, Auckland
Postal: Private Bag 92 516, Wellesley St, Auckland
Directions: From City, take Grafton Bridge to Park Rd. Domain on left past hospital. Car access also from Parnell Rd, & Stanley, Titoki & George Sts.
Phone: 0-9-379 2020
Fax: 0-9-353 9560
Email: domain@cityparks.co.nz
Open: All year, daily, daylight hours; Winter Garden/Fernery: April–Oct. 9am–4.30pm; Nov.–Mar. 9am–5.30pm Mon.–Sat., 9am–7.30pm on Sundays
Groups: Guided tours 0-9-379 0794; All event bookings 0-9-379 2027
Fee: No charge
Size: Large – 136ha (340 acres)
Terrain: Flat & hilly
Refreshments: Domain Kiosk 10am–3pm; Restaurant 11.30am–2.30pm; Museum Coffee Shop 10am–3.30pm

Land for the Domain was set aside in 1841, where a Maori pa once stood on the site of an extinct volcano, its "tuff ring" still visible now. Some of the trees produced from the nursery and seen today in the formal gardens include a Norfolk Island pine, redwood, Wellingtonia and *Agathis robusta.* The Valkyrie Fountain was erected in the formal gardens in 1929 after the Museum was opened, and a reflective pool and bronze statuary were erected in 1955 on the site of one of the original ponds. Adjacent is a totara grove, the earliest native plantings recorded in 1865, adding to the predominant kanuka. The oaks by the main gates were also planted then, the gates completed in 1936. A year-round attraction at the Domain is the Winter Garden and Fernery. Its neo-Georgian design comprises two glasshouses separated by a formal courtyard. The first stage, opened in 1921, was the Cool House, now the Temperate House filled with a floral display of 25,000 annuals and perennials. The second stage, the Tropical House, was opened seven years later and is heated for the growth of palms, cycads, bromeliads, orchids and the huge Victorian waterlilies in its central pool. The disused scoria quarry behind the courtyard was converted the following year into the Fernz Fernery, which was reopened in 1994. It features some 150 native ferns, including tree ferns in both dry and wet areas, and simulated forest pools.

28

DOVE-MYER ROBINSON PARK
Parnell

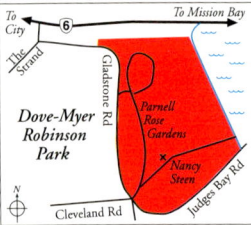

Owner:
Auckland City Council

Address: Corner Gladstone Rd &
Judges Bay Rd, Parnell, Auckland
Postal: Private Bag 92 516, Wellesley
St, Auckland
Directions: From City, take Quay St.
Turn right into The Strand, turn left
into Gladstone Rd. Gardens on right.
Phone: 0-9-379 2020
Fax: 0-9-353 9560
Email: domain@cityparks.co.nz
Open: All year, daily, daylight hours
Groups: Tours & weddings by
arrangement, phone 0-9-379 2027
Fee: No charge
Size: Large – 4ha (10 acres) parkland
& 0.4ha (1 acre) formal rose gardens
Terrain: Flat in gardens & hilly park
Restaurant: Lunches available; teas
by arrangement; functions

at restaurant by arrangement

The Parnell Rose Gardens are the main attraction at the Dove-Myer Robinson Park, renamed in 1981 after the former mayor of Auckland from 1959 (when the Harbour Bridge opened) for 18 years. Before 1981 it was called Parnell Park, from land originally comprising two estates in the 1800s. The rose gardens were established in 1932, now numbering over 5,000 roses. The Nancy Steen Garden is a special memorial garden commemorating Nancy Steen, a New Zealander who was a world authority on old-fashioned roses. It was opened in 1984, just two years before her death, and is laid out as an English cottage style garden featuring old species roses. These heritage roses are underplanted with perennials, and climbing roses cover the brick pergolas. Of special interest are the ancient roses *R. sancta, R. x alba* 'Semi-Plena', and *R. officinalis,* while the white garden is often hired for weddings. Modern roses abound in the main gardens. But the park comprises more than roses. There are a number of notable trees, including natives such as the two-century old kanuka and 150-year-old pohutukawa, the oldest on the Auckland isthmus. Sculptures also feature and two lookouts provide views over Judges Bay to Rangitoto Island. The sheltered beach at Judges Bay is popular in summer for swimming and picnicking. The Rose Garden Restaurant is available for functions.

EDEN GARDEN
Epsom

Eden Garden

Owner:
The Eden Garden Society Inc

Address: 24 Omana Ave, Epsom, Auckland
Directions: From the city, take Gillies Ave exit from Southern Motorway. Turn right into Gillies Ave, then take 2nd right up Albury Ave. Turn left into Mountain Rd, then right into Omana Ave. Eden Garden at end.
Phone: 0-9-638 8395
Fax: 0-9-638 7685
Email: eden@edengarden.co.nz
Website: friars.co.nz/gardens/pages/eden.html
Open: All year, daily, 9am–4.30pm
Café: Open 10am– 4pm
Groups: As above; refreshments by arrangement
Fee: $5 per adult; $3.50 per senior citizen/tertiary student; children free
Size: Large – 2.2ha (5½ acres)
Terrain: Flat and hilly
Wheelchair: Available

Eden Garden, once an abandoned quarry on the slopes of Mt Eden, has been transformed since 1964 into a "Garden of Eden". It has the largest and most varied collection of camellias in New Zealand. Rhododendrons, azaleas, vireyas and conifers also predominate, many of these areas underplanted with ferns, hostas and clivias, bulbs, fuchsias and hellebores. The camellias are complemented in spring by cherry blossom, magnolias, *Cedrela sinensis* and a variety of maples. Bromeliads have naturalised in a glade which features a rock surround. A large collection of New Zealand natives includes pohutukawa, ponga, nikau palms, cabbage trees and flaxes which encourage birdlife, such as the tui, waxeyes and native pigeons. Other native trees and plantings include rimu, totara, kauri, titoki and puka. Views of the harbour and Rangitoto Island can be enjoyed from the higher slopes. Eden Garden offers year-round interest with colour every season. The camellias start flowering late in March, filling the garden with colour, which continues from then until October. The subtropical vireya rhododendron collection thrives in the sheltered conditions and flowers throughout the year. The daylilies and hydrangeas provide added colour from December through to April, with the hibiscus flowering until July. There is colour and interest for all at Eden Garden.

HIGHWIC
Epsom

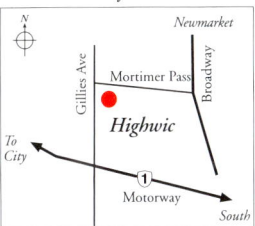

Owners:
New Zealand Historic Places Trust
and Auckland City Council

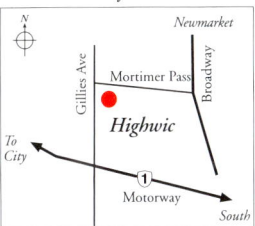

Highwic

Address: 40 Gillies Ave, Epsom, Auckland. Entrance Mortimer Pass
Directions: Opposite Southern Motorway exit. Turn left into Gillies Ave, then first right into Mortimer Pass. Entrance on right.
Phone: 0-9-524 5729
Fax: 0-9-524 5575
Email: highwic@historic.org.nz
Open: All year, Wed. –Sun; garden & house 10.30am–noon & 1pm–4.30pm
Closed: Mondays & Tuesdays; Good Friday & Christmas Day
Fee: $5 per adult, group discounts; NZ Historic Places Trust members free; $2 per unaccompanied child
Size: Medium – over 1ha (about 3 acres)
Terrain: Mainly flat
Functions: Bookings for catered functions & special events

Highwic homestead was built in Gothic Revival style in 1862, when it was surrounded by farmland. Trees around the homestead were planted at that time, including old, once fashionable, pines underplanted with clivias. The Norfolk Island pines that dominate the croquet lawn and front entrance are home to magpies. Beyond, huge mature camellias line a pathway down to the drive, with ivy and South African bulbs underneath. The original layout of the Victorian garden is still in evidence, the house and grounds having remained in the Buckland family until 1978. An old orchard borders Gillies Ave, with tall echiums above the corner of Mortimer Pass overlooking a sea of commercial buildings beyond. Some of the garden design at Highwic is quite formal, especially a hedged, circular garden with narrow, curving pathways around rosebeds. Other formally edged beds contain old-fashioned perennials and annuals. Native species include ferns, palms, a cabbage tree, and a large totara on the edge of the lawn underplanted with a silver and white border. A fern house features many further varieties of indigenous ferns. A rock walkway leads past a bank of agapanthus, once a sophisticated rockery, under ivy-clad trees, past belladonna lilies down to the driveway by the original stables.

QUARTER ACRE PARADISE
Mangere East

Dale Harvey

Owners:
Dale Harvey and John Newton

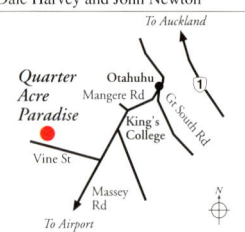

Address: 23 Vine St, Mangere East
Directions: Take Mt Wellington or
Otahuhu exits from Motorway.
Follow signs toward airport. From
Mangere/Massey Rd, take Vine St
near Hospital & King's College.
Phone: 0-9-276 4827 (office); or
0-9-276 1600 (florist shop)
Fax: 0-9-276 4025 or 0-9-276 1600
Email:
quarter.acre.paradise@4flowers.com
Website: 4flowersnz.com
Open: All year, by appointment;
Garden: 10am–4pm; Florist Shop:
Monday to Friday 8.30am–5pm
Fee: $5 per adult
Size: Small – 0.14ha (over ¼ acre)
Terrain: Flat
Nursery: Perennial & annual seed;
landscape & garden consultants

 groups only   limited
    by arrangement

Quarter Acre Paradise is designed to be an inspiration to all backyard New Zealand gardeners, to encourage the greening of our country into a garden paradise. Dale is an international garden expert and media personality who revels in colour and abundance. His specialty is annuals for all seasons. He loves the fleeting colour massed into borders and corridors, creating different displays each season. John specialises in design and artistry. His florist shop, located within the focal point of the garden – a huge 6-metre-high conservatory – provides a startling subtropical atmosphere. The conservatory opens to a woods walk, then a central lawn encircled with roses, bulbs, annuals and hardy perennials, including colourful North American specimens, with shrub borders. A cut-flower meadow supplies John's florist shop, and a pond features a cascade. A wide range of spring bulbs gives way to begonias, lilies, and masses of summer flowers. Then autumn foliage mixes with late-season colour, followed by continuing displays throughout winter in the conservatory. Exotic trees from almost every continent provide shade, with cypress and karaka windbreaks. The skyline features other natives, including totara and titoki, underplanted with shrubs and ferns. Grapevines, ornamentals, citrus and other fruit trees were planted by Dale's forebears over three generations.

34

TUPARI MARA
Howick

Owners:
Jean and Bob Willyams

Address: 109B Pah Rd, Cockle Bay,
Howick, Auckland
Directions: From Southern Motorway,
take Howick exit. Turn left into Ti
Rakau Rd, then right into Pakuranga
Highway. Travel through Howick to
Cockle Bay. Continue into Pah Rd. At
top, turn left into Little Pah Rd. Park
on road verge on right & walk down
right-of-way past 2 houses on left.
Then take left driveway past another
house to Tupari Mara garden behind.
Phone: 0-9-534 7607
Open: 1 September to 1 April, by
appointment
Fee: $3 per person
Size: Small – 0.13ha (⅓ acre)
Terrain: Three levels, steep at the top

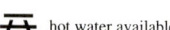 hot water available

Colour and form are the predominant features at
Tupari Mara, Maori for "cliff-edge garden", named
appropriately as the garden is planted on the clifftop site
of a historic pa. In 1969 the vegetaton was mainly gorse,
the soil solid clay, and the topography steeply sloping.
Bob cut and filled, building retaining walls, which
provided the foundation for the garden. Jean planted
strong colours against the dark bush and seascape, using
oranges, reds, intense blues and purples. Only behind the
house was a pastel garden possible, with soft pinks, mauves
and creams. Jean loves blue flowers and colours that blend
and graduate, using lots of vertical accent. Her favourites
are roses of all varieties, delphiniums and Asian lilies.
Spring features include the babiana (baboon flowers) that
line the drive, bluebells, tulips and maples. Architectural
features include the wisteria pergola, dovecote, three
small fish ponds and waterfall. The vege garden is
bissected by a path and an archway for pumpkin, beans,
tomatoes and cucumber to climb over. A *Pyrostigia
venusta* vine grows along the balcony, attracting waxeyes
and Monarch butterflies from June to October. Roses,
mostly in oranges and yellows, feature in summer, with
climbing roses up the drive in November. A narrow strip
of natives on the cliff edge frames the panoramic ocean
view, with a track leading down to the beach below.

QUAILS CROFT
Whitford

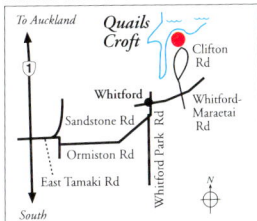

Owners:
Susanne and David Lee

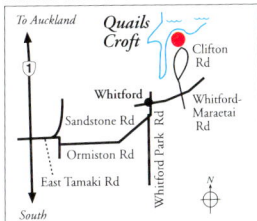

Address: 397 Clifton Rd, Whitford, Auckland
Directions: From Southern Motorway, take Otara turn-off to East Tamaki Rd, turning right into Ormiston Rd, then to end of Sandstone Rd. Turn left into Whitford Park Rd, right into Whitford-Maraetai Rd, then left into Clifton Rd. Quails Croft garden on left.
Phone: 0-9-530 8741
Fax: 0-9-530 8741
Open: October to mid December, by appointment only
Fee: $5 per adult
Size: Medium – over 1ha (about 3 acres)
Terrain: Mostly flat, with steps between levels

Quails Croft was named after the quail that roamed the garden until the mid 1980s. This old-English-style romantic garden is sited on a clifftop, providing wonderful harbour views. The impressive wrought-iron gates set the scene. At the top of the drive, a curve of piceas greets visitors, and 'Claire Jacquier' roses climb the verandah posts with prostrate junipers at their feet. The garden has been planted since 1973 on the oldest site in Whitford. It features expansive lawns with pergolas covered in old, modern and David Austin roses, over 300 altogether. A lavender border leads down to a paved area under a horizontal elm and a loggia, with views to Rangitoto Island framed through roses. Further seating in the summer house and under cherry trees provides panoramic views. Susanne loves her 80 maples, which give autumn colour and rise above perennial borders. Spring colours are mainly pinks, creams, whites and blues, featuring clematis and standard wisterias, azaleas, rhododendrons and magnolias. A yellow and white garden surrounds a fish pond with a hedge of the golden David Austin rose 'Graham Thomas'. A native bush walk, a further pond and a bog garden are in the course of formation.

AUCKLAND REGIONAL BOTANIC GARDENS
Manurewa

Owner:
Auckland Regional Council

Address: 102 Hill Rd, Manurewa
Directions: From Auckland, take SH 1 to Manurewa exit. Turn left into Hill Rd. Gardens on left. From south, take Takanini exit. Take Great South Rd towards Manurewa. Turn right into Alfriston Rd, left into Claude Rd, & right into Hill Rd. Gardens on left.
Phone: 0-9-267 1457
Fax: 0-9-266 3698
Email: botanicgardens@arc.govt.nz
Open: All year, daily, 9am to dusk
Groups: Phone bookings required for guided tours – $50
Entrance Fee: No charge
Size: Large – 64ha (160 acres)
Terrain: Varied; good access
Visitor Centre: Open daily
Reference Library: Mon, Wed, Sat

groups by arrangement
(phone 0-9-267 0773)

The Auckland Regional Botanic Gardens were opened to the public in 1982, after nine years' development of the original farmsite. The gardens include extensive native plant collections, rare and endangered plants as well as 10 hectares of native bush. The natives are complemented by many exotic plant collections, providing year round interest in the Gardens. Spring is welcomed by a display of flowering camellias, magnolias, daffodils, cherry blossoms and kowhai. The Rose Display Trial gardens are a popular summer attraction, complemented by colourful perennials, pohutukawa, hebes, the Herb Garden, annuals, hanging baskets and containers. *Camellia sasanqua* come out in bloom for autumn, then winter is brightened by the abundant proteas, leucadendrons and succulents of the Southern Africa Collection, as well as the Rock Garden. Each plant collection is labelled, and signage helps visitors discover and explore the world of plants. There are also a wide range of Advisory Leaflets available which provide more information of specific plants and gardening topics. The Visitor Centre is open from 9am to 4pm on weekdays and from 10am to 4pm on weekends. The Friends Horticultural Reference Library is open Monday, Wednesday and Saturday from 11am to 3pm.

MIKE'S GARDEN AND SCENIC TOURS
Auckland

Operator:
Mike Maran
Address: 3 Edith St, Pt Chevalier
Directions: Mike's Mini Coach will
collect you from your Auckland
accommodation.
Phone: 0-9-846 5350
Mobile: 025 784 779
Fax: 0-9-846 5315
Email: m.maran@clear.net.nz
Website: friars.co.nz/gardens/pages/
mikestours.html
Open: Depart daily at 9am or 1.30pm
Groups: Licensed for up to 9 people;
minimum of 2 people
Fee: $55–$95 per person for ½ day or
day tours; entry fees to gardens are
included in tour price
Size: Various
Terrain: Varies
Tours: 6 different tours available
1 Auckland City Highlights
   (9am–12.30pm) $55 per person
2 Waitakere Ranges Tour
   (1.30pm–5pm) $55 per person
3 Auckland's Botanical Treasures
   (9am–5pm day tour) $95 per
   person excluding lunch cost
4 Regional Botanical Gardens
   (3.5 hrs) $55 per person
5 Private City Gardens Tour
   (3.5 hrs) $69 per person
6 Country Gardens Tour
   (3.5 hrs) $69 per person

🍲 included in fee

With his extensive horticultural background, Mike is the ideal garden guide. He escorts garden tours around Auckland, personally providing a commentary on the gardens visited. Mike collects you from your accommodation either morning or afternoon, in his air-conditioned mini coach, then takes you around private and public gardens, showing you the sights of Auckland. Tours last three to four hours, or a full day tour can be arranged to combine the city and country tours or take in the Waitakere Gardens Tour. Mike's Tours operate in all weather, with umbrellas supplied and all paths are asphalt. Each of the two or three private gardens visited has its own character, whether terraced, bush, English style, country estate, Spanish, Japanese, bonsai, or small city garden. Mike also visits Auckland's public gardens as part of the City Tour itinerary. These include the Parnell Rose Gardens, the Savage Memorial Gardens overlooking the Waitemata harbour, Cornwall Park studded with plantations of native trees leading up to One Tree Hill, the Domain and Wintergardens with rare native ferns and tropical flowers, or the Regional Botanical Gardens. The Waitakere Ranges garden tour features New Zealand native forest with its mature kauri trees and panoramic views of Auckland.

ATARANGI
Papakura

Owners:
Wendy and Neville Guy

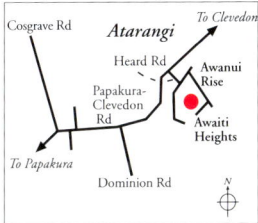

Address: 85 Awanui Rise, R D 2, Papakura
Directions: From Clevedon Rd, turn right into Heard Rd, left into Ohiwa Rd, right into Awanui Rise, then right into private road, Awaiti Heights.
Phone: 0-9-298 3238
Mobile: 025 758 977
Fax: 0-9-296 7206
Email: nevillegmitsubishi@xtra.co.nz
Open: All year, daily, by appointment; weekends & public holidays 10am–7pm during daylight saving; 10am–4pm autumn & winter
Fee: $4 per adult
Size: Medium – 0.8ha (2 acres)
Terrain: Flat and steep
Nursery: Miniature rose 'Atarangi', climbing roses from local breeder Doug Grant; selection of perennials

partial   by arrangement

Developed since 1986, an extensive rose garden looking over Manukau Harbour at Atarangi now features over 600 old and new roses. Beyond is a native area with two kauri, 10 different pohutukawa, ferns, hebes and massed arthropodiums. Indigenous trees attracting tui and native pigeons are underplanted with rhododendrons, kalmias and hostas. Below is a pond developed from swamp, with flaxes and ducks. A rock garden in the gully above incudes a waterfall and stream. A collection of over 30 vireyas forms a walk, with maturing ponga bordered by mollis azaleas. An extensive perennial garden with a thyme walkway emphasises collections of salvias, penstemons and aquilegias, planted among camellias, magnolias and shade trees. A pink terrace features azaleas and camellias in varying shades of pink, and *Camellia sasanqua* line the boundary. A wilderness area is home to quail, pheasants and eastern rosella. Above the house, a U-shaped grove of specimen trees, with a border of shrubs and perennials, has been developed for alfresco dining. An orchard grows along the fenceline, and a conifer garden with companion plants separates the property from the driveway. Future plans include the establishment of a walled garden above the roses and a sunken garden beside it. Atarangi, meaning "new beginning", is living up to its name.

ROSE COTTAGE
Clevedon

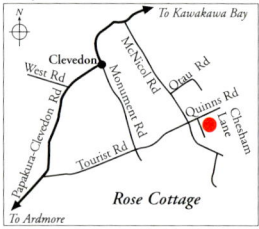

Owner:
Robyn Harrison

Rose Cottage

Address: Chesham Lane, Clevedon
Directions: Take Takanini exit from
SH 1. At Clevedon turn right into
Kawakawa Bay Rd, right into McNicol
Rd & left into Quinns Rd. Turn right
into Chesham Lane. Garden on left.
Phone: 0-9-292 8759
Open: 1 October to 1 April,
10am–4pm, by appointment
Groups: By appointment
Fee: $5 per adult
Size: Medium – 1.2ha (3 acres)
Terrain: Flat & bushwalk
Studio: Paintings for sale
Painting classes: Art tuition privately
or in groups; beginners to advanced;
water colours, oils, acrylics, pastels;
still-life, landscapes

  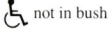 not in bush

Robyn has designed the garden at Rose Cottage as an artist's haven – to share with her pupils and provide different "rooms" where they can sit and paint and enjoy the peace of the valley. Robyn also wants to inspire other older women to achieve beautiful gardens too, simply through growing cuttings. By repetitive plantings of agapanthus, geranium, ageratum and daisies interspersed among her 300 roses, Robyn has created saturations of colour. Self-seeding flowers produce drifts of blues and lavender to complement the pinks. White and silver are also used liberally for moonlight wanders, and yellow and orange provide the occasional contrast, as does the foliage, such as *Robinia frisia* against the prunus. A two-metre high sea of salvias edges the perimeter of the garden in blue, which is very tranquil for Robyn, complementing the green of the grass. She has been planting densely since 1992 to prevent weeds from appearing. She specialises in painting her favourite old roses. A potager was inspired by a trip to France and a grape cloister at one end shows an Italian influence, as does the olive grove, where 15 varieties of olives are grouped around a spring-fed pond. Robyn loves to bring the rural views beyond into the garden. A stream runs through the adjacent stand of native bush, predominantly kahikatea, which features a bush walk for visitors.

WRIGHTS WATERGARDENS
Patumahoe

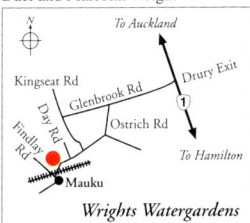

Owners:
Dael and Malcolm Wright

Wrights Watergardens

Address: 128 Mauku Rd, Patumahoe
Postal: R D 3, Pukekohe
Directions: From SH 1, take Drury exit
into SH 22. Take Glenbrook Rd & turn
left into Ostrich Rd. From Patumahoe
travel 1.5km on Mauku Rd to gardens.
Phone: 0-9-236 3642; Shop:
0-9-236 3211; Café: 0-9-236 3036
Mobile: 021 623 636
Fax: 0-9-236 3007
Email: wriwatgdn@xtra.co.nz
Website: www.wrightswatergardens.co.nz
Open: Mid-Sept. to mid-Oct.,10am–
4.30pm; other times by appointment
Fee: $5 per adult
Size: Large – over 2ha (6 acres)
Terrain: Easy walking on 3 levels
Nursery: Aquatic & garden plants
Café: Quality home-made teas & lunches
Shop: Cut flowers, dried lotus pods, pots,
crafts &
souvenirs. by arrangement
 mostly

Wrights Watergardens and Waterfall Café are set beside the 10-metre Mauku Waterfall and Stream. These tranquil gardens offer a great diversity of plantings. The watergardens, developed within an abandoned quarry, feature over 30 ponds covered with massed lotus flowers and waterlilies in season, creating a kaleidoscope of colour. The Wrights specialise in tropical waterlilies with long stems, in colours including purples and blues. Many of the waterlilies are scented, as are the spectacular lotus flowers, their petals falling to leave the seedpod exposed. Cactus and succulent gardens provide marked contrast. Perennial gardens, as well as aquatic plantings, irises and ferns provide a range of interest on three different levels, designed to surprise visitors at every turn. The Watergardens Nursery sells a full range of aquatic plants including the waterlily and lotus, as well as garden plants. The Watergardens shop also stocks cut waterlily flowers, dried lotus pods, water-gardening requirements, pots, souvenirs and crafts. The Waterfall Café is fully licensed and offers a good selection of home-made cuisine, quality teas and coffee. The Watergardens and Waterfall Café is a peaceful location to celebrate special occasions, such as birthdays, anniversaries and family reunions. Weddings can be fully catered for from the ceremony to photographs and the wedding breakfast.

NGODEVWA
Waiuku

![garden photograph]

Owners:
Anthea and David Adams

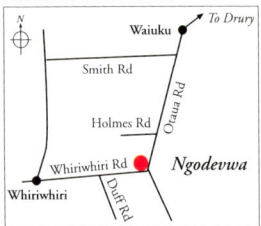

Address: 8 Whiriwhiri Rd, R D 2, Waiuku
Directions: From SH 1, take Drury/ Pukekohe exit. Turn right & travel 26km to Waiuku township. Turn left into Queen St & continue into Otaua Rd. Travel 3km & turn right into Whiriwhiri Rd. Garden on right corner.
Phone: 0-9-235 9812
Fax: 0-9-235 9812
Website: friars.co.nz/gardens/pages/ ngodevwa.html
Open: Sept.–April, by appointment with 24 hours' notice
Fee: \$5 per adult
Size: Medium – 0.6ha (1½ acres) within 2ha (5 acres) fields & trees
Terrain: Flat to gently sloping
Nursery: Some plants from garden & rustic seats sometimes available

    pending
by arrangement

Meaning "flowers of the angels" in Tibetan, Ngodevwa is filled with flowers in colour blends from blue, gold and cream through to crimson, white, pink and lavender, with other areas in apricot to the wine spectrum, complementing silvery plantings. The garden has been carefully developed since 1972 into a series of flowing areas, incorporating two ponds and a stream with adjacent pinetum and woodland area including some rare pines. Surrounded by two hectares of park-like fields planted with ornamental trees, Ngodevwa is a peaceful all-seasons country garden where stone steps and pathways lead from one area to another, past rustic seats, and over a boardwalk through an iris water garden. Other special areas include the gnarled orchard, paved courtyard featuring colourful pots, and the hexagonal conservatory. Hellebores, spring bulbs and magnolia blossom are followed by the rhododendrons and deciduous azaleas. After these begin to fade from the scene, the favourite heritage roses take centre stage, complemented by various wisterias and clematis, then summer perennials, irises and lilies. Autumn colouring includes the maples, oaks and parrotias accompanied by chrysanthemums, hollyhocks, salvias, rudbeckias, sunflowers and autumn crocuses and clematis. Added attractions are the small Arabian horse stud and the rare restored 1932 Sunbeam vintage car.

FLASHMANS' FOLLY
Tuakau

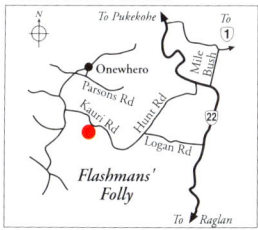

Owners:
Ken and Helen Flashman

Address: 168 Kauri Road, Onewhero,
R D 2 Tuakau
Directions: From Auckland, take SH 1
Motorway south to Mercer. Take
Mercer Ferry Rd, turn left into Mile
Bush Rd & right into SH 22. Turn left
into Hunt Rd & continue into Kauri
Rd. Garden on left.
Phone: 0-9-232 8556
Fax: 0-9-232 8506
Mobile: 025 264 3381
Open: All year, by appointment only
Fee: $3
Size: Medium – 1.2ha (3 acres)
Terrain: Flat & hilly
Nursery: Native plants, grasses &
succulents
For Sale: Antiques & collectables
Accommodation: Available
Golf: Can be arranged locally

by arrangement

Named by their friends Flashmans' Folly, this garden has been established in a valley since 1998, with two large ponds and contours of the hillside above bulldozed into pathways. Bullrushes and a pine shelter were removed and a bog garden and fernery developed with rustic fencing. The biggest challenge has been a steep dry bank, too steep to bulldoze. Being hilly, the soil and conditions vary from one spot to another – some hot, others dry, damp, frosty, fertile or arid. Foliage plants predominate, the colours of flowers blending with the greens. Azaleas and rhododendrons feature in spring, along with new foliage on the deciduous trees. Then in summer, the perennials are complemented with flowering shrubs, particularly buddleias and native hebes. Other native plantings include ferns, ponga tree-ferns, cabbage trees, rimu, akeake, kawakawa, coprosma, lancewood and carex grasses. In autumn, the liquidambar, oak and other English trees colour up, then in winter ericas are the mainstay. Water is a major feature with a stream feeding the waterlily ponds and a fountain. Other plantings include irises and gunnera in the bog garden, flowering gums, lavenders and succulents. Walking tracks are planned through the adjacent native bush and a log cabin "folly" is being constructed. There is plenty of seating around the ponds with easy walking paths for visitors.

THE COROMANDEL PENINSULA
AND THE BAY OF PLENTY

We feature 12 gardens from the Coromandel and Bay of Plenty region, south of Auckland as far as Rotorua. The Coromandel Peninsula has a warm climate with greater-than-average rainfall, favouring moisture-loving plants. North of Thames township are the well-kown Rapaura Watergardens with 14 waterlily ponds, three streams and a cascading waterfall. In Coromandel itself is Waitati, a florist's garden including native areas. The Coromandel Peninsula gardens are surrounded by the rugged indigenous forest that has largely regenerated to cover the effects of early gold mining and kauri logging. South of the Coromandel Peninsula on the east coast is the Bay of Plenty, with its abundant sunshine and popular beaches.

The Bay of Plenty gardens stretch from the coast, which is drier, to inland areas, both experiencing warm summers and cool winters with frosts, and only very occasionally some snow. Two Tauranga gardens are Siesta Orchard at Te Puna, a cottage garden with raised beds, and Lorien, a terraced garden of different layers, with hill vistas. At Te Puke there are two more gardens: Windrest Cottage where a colonial tearoom overlooks a valley of cottage plants and trees, and Rose Villa which is becoming as popular for its delphiniums as its roses. Further along the coast at Whakatane is Stuckey's Garden, developed from a rose display garden for the nursery, with long axes and focal points.

In the Rotorua region are five gardens, spread out surrounding Lake Rotorua. Proceeding clockwise around the lake, we come first to Tikitere Gardens out past the airport, where there is space for their 12 hectares of parkland. Then within the Lake Okataina Scenic Reserve is Glade House, with spectacular views down over the lake. North of the city, at Kawaha Point is the Goodwins' garden with colonial-style structures, archways, rose pergolas and gazebo. Then at Mamaku is Brackenhill, the high altitude and rainfall favouring its rhododendrons and bog gardens. Finally, south of Rotorua in the Waikite Valley is Puaiti, with panoramic rural views and features including a formal rose garden.

Rotorua City also features Government Gardens around the historic Bath House, and Tauranga has Robbins Park, as well as The Strand gardens. The Rotorua area is volcanic, with underground thermal activity causing spectacular geysers, steaming mineral pools and boiling mud pools. Many attractive lakes incorporate surrounding scenic reserves, including Lakes Okataina, Tarawera, Okareka, Rotomahana, Rotoiti, and Rotorua itself and the Blue and Green Lakes. Walkways provide access to these natural beautiful areas, as well as to the exotic Whakarewarewa Forest with its magnificent Redwood Memorial Grove.

Cuvier I

Port Charles

Great Mercury I

Red Mercury I

Colville

Kennedy Bay

[31]

Matarangi Beach Kuaotunu

Coromandel

Whitianga

Mercury Bay

Cooks Beach

Hahei

Hot Water Beach

Whenuakite

Coroglen

The Aldermen Is

[5]

Tapu [30]

Tairua

Pauanui

Waiomu

Te Puru

Thornton Bay

Hikuai

Slipper I

Thames [25A]

Opoutere

Kopu

Whangamata

Ngatea

Mayor I

Kerepehi

[26]

Paeroa [25]

Waikino

Waihi

[27]

Waihi Beach

Athenree

Te Aroha

MATAKANA I

Karewa I

Waihou

Katikati

Waitoa

[2]

Morrinsville

Pahoia

Mt Maunganui

Te Puna

Motiti I

[32]

Bethlehem

TAURANGA

Papamoa Beach

[33]

Matamata

[29]

Te Puke

Maketu

[34]

[35]

Paengaroa

Motuhora I

[24]

Karapiro

Matata

Lake Karapiro

[28]

Tirau

[33]

Edgecumbe

Whakatane

[5]

Arapuni

Putaruru

[36]

Lake Arapuni

[38]

Lake Rotorua

L Rotoiti

[30]

L Rotoehu

Taneatua

Mamaku

[37]

[39]

L Okataina

Kawerau

ROTORUA

[40]

Tokoroa

[41]

L Tarawera

L Rotomahana

[32]

[30]

Rotomahana

L Rerewhakaaitu

IKAWHENUA RANGE

Mangakino

Waiotapu

[5]

[38]

Atiamuri

Reporoa

Whakamaru

Lake Ohakuri

Scale

0 _____ 50km

Cartography by Terralink Ltd

N

Piako River

Waikato R

RAPAURA WATERGARDENS
Tapu

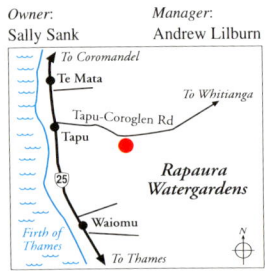

Owner: *Manager*:
Sally Sank   Andrew Lilburn

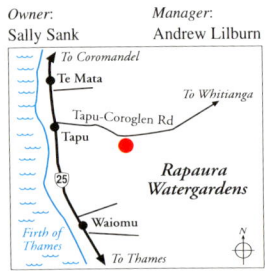

Address: 586 Tapu-Coroglen Rd,
Tapu, Coromandel Peninsula
Postal: R D 5, Thames
Directions: From SH 1, take Thames
exit & travel on SH 25 for 30 mins.
Turn right into Tapu-Coroglen Rd &
travel 6.5km to gardens on right. From
Coromandel, travel south for 45 mins.
Phone: 0-7-868 4821
Fax: 0-7-868 4821
Email: lilburn@wave.co.nz
Website: friars.co.nz/gardens/pages/
rapaura.html
Open: All year, daily, 10am–5pm;
tearoom & craftshop: Sept.– June
Groups: By appointment; 10+ discount
Fee: $7 per adult, $2 per child
Size: Large – over 2ha (5–6 acres)
Terrain: Sloping & steeper bush walk
Shop: Trellis Tearoom & Craft Shop

limited

groups by arrangement

Rapaura, a Maori word meaning "running spring water", is a woodland watergarden in a native bush setting. Developed in the late 'sixties by the Loennigs from a derelict farm, Rapaura was extended by the Lowes and is being further expanded by Sally and the manager, Andrew. Sally is dedicated to the philosophy that "The best garden is a well-kept wilderness", one of the sayings on the Poet's Walk which meanders through the garden past the 14 waterlily ponds. Three streams and a cascading waterfall are also incorporated into Rapaura, reached by a bush walk through the native forest park that surrounds the watergardens. Many native species are further used in the garden, including kauri, rimu, rewarewa, cabbage trees, toothed lancewoods, and hebes. More predominant are varieties of native ponga tree fern and kanuka. These are interplanted with exotic species such as the ginkgo, taxodium, oaks, maples and weeping elm that provide autumn colour. The waterlilies flower from November, after the spring features of the gardens such as camellias, rhododendrons, azaleas, and orchids. Spring pondside plantings include primulas, irises, and calthas, followed by pontederia and hostas in summer. These are accompanied by hanging baskets of annuals. In winter the hellebores and plectranthus come to the fore, with the garden sculpture and mountain views year-round features.

WAITATI
Coromandel

Waitati

Owners:
Kate and Graeme Jacobsen

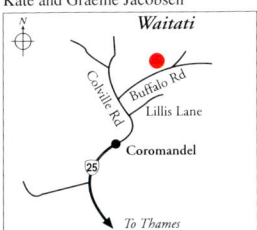

Waitati

N

Colville Rd

Buffalo Rd

Lillis Lane

Coromandel

25

To Thames

Address: Buffalo Rd, Coromandel
Postal: P O Box 83, Coromandel
Directions: From Coromandel
township, take Colville Rd north for
2km. Turn right into Buffalo Rd.
Garden on left. Parking opposite at
stamper battery or at house.
Phone: 0-7-866 8659
Mobile: 025 841 736
Fax: 0-7-866 8659
Email: waitatigardens@xtra.co.nz
Website: friars.co.nz/gardens/pages/
waitati.html
Open: All year
Fee: $5 per adult
Size: Medium – 0.7ha (1¼ acres)
Terrain: Varied
Nursery: Perennials & natives from
garden
Nearby: Historic battery & gold trails

by arrangement for groups

Waitati, named after the North Otago town where Kate's family settled in 1856, is primarily a florist's picking garden. Created since 1994 from a cow paddock, Waitati has been landscaped to take advantage of the slopes and contours. Graeme has incorporated native trees and indigenous orchids into the garden, and more recently the vireyas which are his passion. Kate on the other hand uses the garden for her florist classes and plant identification, her favourites being campanulas, delphiniums and the species bulbs. She has planted a wide variety of flowers, colour grouping them both for visual effect and for picking. A blue and green area featuring delphiniums and a scented garden, with a seat in it for relaxing and enjoying the perfumes, includes daphnes and a lot of old scented varieties, which are popular with groups of older visitors. Two ponds on different levels run into each other, planted with rocky alpines below, including meconopsis. Spring bulbs and blossom include the magnolias up the driveway. Then the roses emerge, climbing over structures, underplanted with phlox, romneyas, aquilegias, foxgloves and other perennials. Annuals such as zinnias are popular for picking. There is lots of autumn colour when the leucadendrons, proteas and isopogons flower, followed by the camellias and winter-flowering clematis.

SIESTA ORCHARD
Tauranga

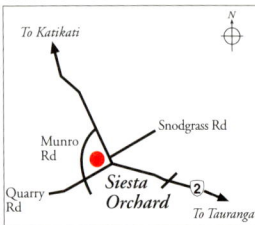

Owners:
Colleen and Stewart Thwaites

Address: 6 Quarry Rd, Te Puna,
R D 6, Tauranga
Directions: Off SH 2, 12km north of
Tauranga or 23km south of Katikati.
Turn west into Quarry Rd. Garden
immediately on right.
Phone: 0-7-552 5888
Open: All year, Wednesday to Sunday
Groups: By appointment
Fee: $2 per adult
Size: Medium – 0.4ha (1 acre)
Terrain: Sloping
Shop: Studio – dried flowers &
arrangements for sale

  limited

A cottage garden developed since 1986 on bare land is now a series of pretty beds under established trees. The lower part was planted first, and the upper slopes have been developed since 1990. Colleen works with raised beds for convenience, using ponga, rocks, and half-rounds for edging, perennials spilling over the sides, with mown grass between beds. Annuals such as helichrysum are grown for use as dried flowers, which Colleen arranges in her studio. A shadehouse contains an orchid collection, and some flourish outside too. Colleen uses lots of white between hotter colours, planting phlox in the borders, with alyssum, daisies, and hostas. In spring the softer colours emerge, with foxgloves, azaleas and cottage garden flowers such as pansies under the *Magnolia campbellii* and three kowhai. Then the hot colours come out in summer, with dahlias, roses and summer-flowering perennials under the shade trees, while tuberous begonias blaze in the summer house. Autumn bulbs are complemented with deciduous foliage, including the lovely male idesia. Then camellias take over in winter. There is a sprinkling of natives throughout the garden, such as groups of ferns. Walks through the adjoining Siesta Orchards can be arranged. These are mainly citrus and kiwifruit. The family enterprise was named from a combination of family initials.

LORIEN
Tauranga

Owner:
Dinah Warren

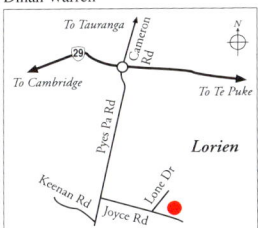

Address: 445 Joyce Rd, R D 3, Tauranga
Directions: From Tauranga, take Cameron Rd to Barkers Corner. Take Pyes Pa Rd towards Rotorua for 2.2km. Turn left into Joyce Rd. Travel 4.5km to Lorien on left.
Phone: 0-7-543 3037
Fax: 0-7-543 3037
Email: dwarren@clear.net.nz
Open: October to March, by appointment
Fee: $3.50 per adult, $2 per child or senior citizen, groups by arrangement
Size: Medium – 1.2ha (3 acres)
Terrain: Terraced
Accommodation: Double $140, single $100 per night; dinner $30 per person
Courses: From gardening to design

🐕 🏃 👪 ⛩ ♿ limited
🛏 🍲 🍽 by arrangement

Created since 1992 from a hillside of gorse and blackberry, Lorien is now a layered garden of many rooms, each with its own colour scheme and view over the rural hills and native bushland, to Tauranga Harbour and the ocean beyond. Lorien means peace and tranquillity, as evidenced by the peaceful setting with pathways zigzagging down to the river below. The terracing forms strong lines with ponga archways and gates leading into the various garden rooms on each layer. Ponds and waterfalls feature with lawns on different levels, making this garden ideal for outdoor entertaining for up to 100 guests. Trees, shrubs, roses, lilies and a profusion of other plants provide seasonal colour and variation. Large mature walnut trees offer shade and a nearby bank of agapanthus is stunning in summer. Red maples flank the walkway on one level and dovecotes add to the birdlife. The home was architecturally designed by John Little with entertaining in mind, lunches often served alfresco on the wisteria-clad balcony overlooking the garden, which is set in almost six hectares (14 acres) of ponga tree ferns and native bush. A variety of courses are held at Lorien, throughout the year, ranging from gardening to interior decor. Two double ensuite bedrooms are available for accommodation at Lorien and dinner can also be provided for guests.

WINDREST COTTAGE
Te Puke

Windrest

Owner:
Chris Leadley

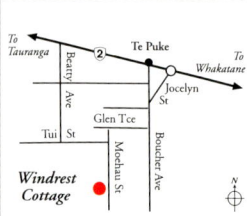

Address: 15 Moehau St, Te Puke
Directions: At Te Puke main round-about, turn into Jocelyn St. Turn right into Glen Tce, then left into Moehau St. Garden on right. Well signposted.
Phone: 0-7-573 9418
Fax: 0-7-573 9418
Open: September to April; Tuesday to Sunday; 10am–4pm
Groups: By appointment
Fee: Garden walk: $4 per adult, $1 per child
Size: Medium – 1.2ha (3 acres)
Terrain: Undulating valley
Nursery: Roses & other plants
Tearoom: Open as above; 10am–4pm; silver service Devon teas & light lunches available
Functions: Weddings & groups

  limited

Created from a derelict apple orchard in 1983, Windrest Cottage has been transformed from a wilderness into a secluded country cottage garden. Perennials, bulbs and annuals have been carefully planted to harmonise with camellias, rhododendrons, azaleas, old-fashioned roses and specimen trees in an undulating valley. Meandering paths lead to surprises round each bend. Coast redwoods (*Sequoia sempervirens*) and an old bead tree (*Melia azedarach*) tower over the tranquil gardens. A spring feature is the beautiful wedding cake tree (*Cornus controversa*), its tiered branches topped with clusters of small, white "icing" flowers. Cherry blossom and roses cover the summer house, and dogwoods, maples and persimmons add colour. The atmosphere of yesteryear is recreated with cottage perennials, wildflowers and hundreds of roses throughout the garden, with old roses entwined about branches of trees. A small stream flows through the bottom of the garden, providing a spot for hostas and other bog plants. Yellow candelabra primulas encircle the fountain in a shady area. A sun-dial features among beds of roses backed by climbers. The combination of birdlife, butterflies and fragrance enhances the peaceful setting. Silver service Devon teas and light lunches are available in the colonial tearoom and outdoor treehouse, or under umbrellas in the garden, popular for weddings.

ROSE VILLA
Te Puke

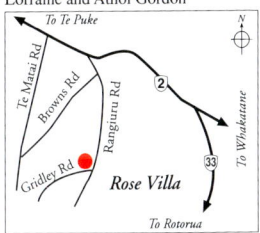

Owners:
Lorraine and Athol Gordon

Address: 264 Rangiuru Rd, R D 8,
Te Puke
Directions: From Te Puke, take
SH 2 towards Rotorua turn-off &
Whakatane. Turn right into Rangiuru
Rd & travel 2.64km to Rose Villa on
right, on corner of Gridley Rd.
Phone: 0-7-573 8685
Fax: 0-7-573 8685
Open: Mid October to mid March,
daily, 10am–4pm; other times by
appointment
Groups: By appointment
Fee: $4 per adult, groups $3 per head
Size: Medium – 1ha (2½ acres)
Terrain: Flat
Nursery: Plants from garden
Accommodation: B&B available

  by arrangement

This large country style garden of one hectare has been developed in stages since 1980. Lorraine loves open spaces in her garden and avoids confined areas, resulting in expansive lawns and vistas to the surrounding country-side. As the name suggests the predominant species are roses, about 600 of all varieties providing summer colour and fragrance. Lorraine coordinates her colours, grouping bright colours together in threes, with the cooler ones on the other side of the garden. She loves the effect of reds, yellows and hot colours blazing together, then the pinks and mauves and whites separately, with wine red climbers for contrast. She finds that whites, silvers and blues mix well, such as the plantings of delphinums among the massed roses and perennial beds. Structures include the rose arbour surrounded by a formal shamrock-shaped rose garden, rose pergola featuring modern and old-fashioned roses, and large gazebo. There is a double waterlily pond on two levels with waterfall and fountain, near an arbour clad in wisteria and wongawonga. A rockery has been established since 1996 and a woodland area is developing with acers, rhododendrons and native species to complement the mature deciduous trees. Lorraine also has an area of David Austin roses. Her champion winners include golden orange 'Playboy', the brightly coloured 'Disco Dancer', and blood red 'Invincible'. Accommodation is available.

STUCKEY'S GARDEN
Whakatane

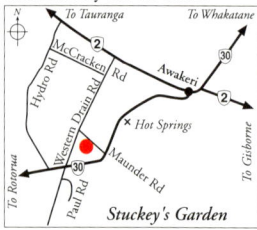

Owners:
James Stuckey and Val Collier

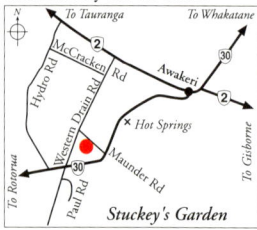

Address: Maunder Road, R D 2
Whakatane
Directions: From Te Puke, take SH 2
towards Whakatane. Turn right into
SH 30. After Awakeri Hot Springs,
turn right into Maunder Rd. Stuckey's
Garden on left.
Phone: 0-7-304 8352
Fax: 0-7-304 8352
Open: All year, 9.30am to 5pm
Closed: Christmas Day, Boxing Day,
New Year's Day & 2nd January
Fee: No charge
Size: Medium – 0.6ha (1½ acres)
Terrain: Flat
Nursery: Roses, irises, daylilies,
perennials & annuals
For Sale: White fantail pigeons

by arrangement

Stuckey's Garden was originally developed in 1996 as a display garden for their rose nursery. The gardening "bug" took hold and James and Val began to garden in earnest. Their garden today is the result. The flat terrain lent itself to a formal design for easy walking and wheelchairs. The roses still predominate, planted in rows with vistas leading the eye to focal points. Then cross axes provide intersecting squares of, for instance, chamomile. White roses climbing the fences complement a white statue surrounded by lavender. This in turn continues along the axis to the red "Birthday Present" roses beyond. Other vistas end at the focal point of a garden seat, while cross-axes takes the eye to the iris garden or a water feature. Mixed plantings of perennials and annuals edge the garden, backed by mature trees. The hills and rural landscape of Awakeri form a backdrop beyond. The irises flower in spring, followed by the early roses in October. Summer brings the daylilies into bloom, and the roses continue into the autumn, with rosehips providing colour before they are pruned. Special features include the fish and the white fantail pigeons which are also for sale. The large nursery specialises in roses of all varieties, as well as irises, daylilies, perennials and annuals as seen in the garden. Stuckey's Garden is open to visit any month of the year, free of charge.

BRACKENHILL
Mamaku

Owners:
Joan and Geoff Bracken

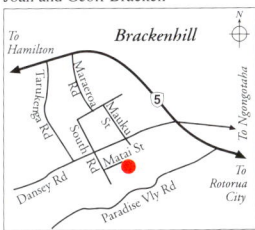

Address: 32 Matai Street, Mamaku
Directions: From SH 5, turn west into
Dansey Rd. Travel 8km to Mamaku
School. Turn left into South Rd.
Travel 50m & turn left into Matai St.
Brackenhill garden on right.
Phone: 0-7-332 5745
Fax: 0-7-332 5945
Mobile: 025 262 7717
Open: Late October to April, by
appointment only
Closed: May to early October
Fee: $3 per adult
Size: Medium – 0.4ha (1 acre)
Terrain: Flat to hilly
Nursery: Mostly hostas, Chatham
Island forget-me-nots &
cardiocrinums
Shop: Terracotta pottery

by arrangement

Brackenhill was planted in May 1990 so that it would be ready for Joan and Geoff's garden wedding in November the same year! There was only one tree on the property, but the undulating contours lent themselves to meandering paths and garden rooms. After being inspired by Pukeiti, Joan mowed the shape of the paths to be edged in ponga. She sometimes had to change her plans when the soil was too rocky to plant trees, as Mamaku is sited on a volcanic plateau. Another restriction is the high altitude and the rainfall. But such wet conditions favour the bog gardens and pond areas where Joan grows ligularias, rodgersias, hostas, Japanese irises, candelabra primulas and Chatham Island forget-me-nots. Geoff constructed the architectural features of the garden, such as the rustic teatree seats, the rose stoops, the new wisteria house, and the gazebo which is decorated for weddings. Camellias and rhododendrons enjoy the altitude and are underplanted with bluebells and hostas. Clematis climbs through the trees and some of the 350 roses that flourish in Brackenhill's environment. Cardiocrinums complement the autumn colours of the liquidambars, acers and oak trees. Joan loves Monet blues, which abound in the garden. Other features include the magnolias, her sundial garden, the daffodil hill, and the new potager established with companion planting.

GOODWINS
Kawaha Point

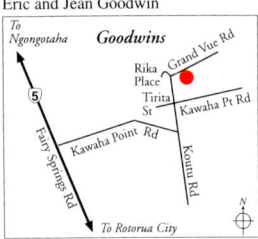

Owners:
Eric and Jean Goodwin

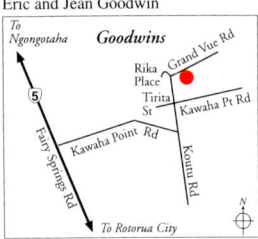

Address: 82 Grand Vue Rd, Kawaha
Point, Rotorua
Directions: From Rotorua City, take
road north towards Ngongotaha.
Turn right into Kawaha Pt Rd, then
left into Koutu Rd. Turn right into
Grand Vue Rd. Garden on right.
Phone: 0-7-347 6888
Open: All year, by appointment only
Groups: By appointment, as above
Fee: $3 per adult; $2 pp for groups
over 10 persons
Size: Small – 0.15ha (⅓ acre)
Terrain: Flat

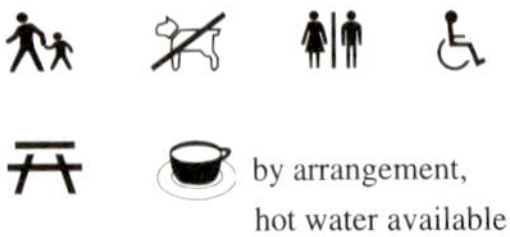

  by arrangement,
hot water available

Although the Goodwins are both octogenarians, they are actively involved in their award-winning garden, which Eric developed from a bare paddock in 1981. Jean and Eric enjoy meeting enthusiastic fellow gardeners and Eric is Patron of the annual Rotorua Festival of Gardens. Goodwins is an urban shrub garden with open spaces, many hybrid and reticulata camellias featuring in spring, with rhododendrons, wisteria, clematis, weeping cherries and echiums for height. Colonial-style structures and statuary harmonise with the house architecture, including rose archways and pergolas, a gazebo covered in 'Dublin Bay' and 'Wedding Day' and a pond and fountain area planted with aquatics. A cool area features fuchsias, hostas, ferns, gunneras, irises, lilies and astilbes. With his background as a florist, Eric likes to make a picture with plants, grouping together whites and pinks, with reds and yellows together in other areas. Eric uses pots extensively, with freesias and tulips in spring, then lilies and annuals in summer, followed by potted chrysanthemums in autumn. Eric also grows many irises – Japanese, water and beardeds. Over 200 begonias flower in February accompanied by raised beds of perennials and Eric's favourite roses and delphiniums. In autumn hanging baskets provide colour, adding to the dahlias and potted chrysanthemums. The garden is planted for a continuity of colour through the seasons.

GLADE HOUSE
Rotorua

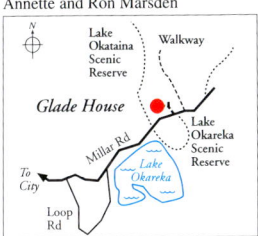

Owners:
Annette and Ron Marsden

Address: 313 Millar Rd, Lake
Okareka, R D 5, Rotorua
Directions: Travel 3km from Rotorua.
Turn right into Tarawera Rd, continue
into Loop Rd, veer left into Millar
Rd, continuing for 3km into Reserve.
Phone: 0-7-362 8542
Fax: 0-7-362 8542
Email: gladehse@clear.net.nz
Open: All year, by appointment
Groups: By appointment, as above
Fee: $3 per adult
Size: Small – about 0.3ha (less than
1 acre), plus 2ha (5 acres) bush walks
Terrain: Steep drive, but flat garden
Nursery: Some plants from garden
Accommodation: B&B available at
Glade House Lodge

 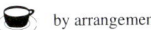 by arrangement

Glade House is a Lockwood home set in the middle
of a glade surrounded by native bush, on a plateau
within Lake Okataina Scenic Reserve. A sweeping
croquet lawn is bordered by raised beds full of bulbs,
annuals and perennials, edged with ponga walls. Since
1990 the Marsdens have introduced cherries, maples,
camellias and old-fashioned roses into the garden.
Annette likes to colour-block the planting, providing
patches of warmth against the impressive green backdrop.
The indigenous bush, including titoki, rewarewa, kowhai,
kawakawa, red kaka-beak, and mamaku tree ferns, attracts
native birds, such as pigeons, bellbirds and tui. The clifftop view down to Lake Okareka is a special feature from
the Lodge behind the house, 105 metres above the lake or
510 metres above sea level. The high altitude means that
spring comes late, with camellias, bulbs, cherries, and
clematis followed by azaleas and rhododendrons. Summer
brings more bulbs, a variety of perennials, and roses
including 'Iceberg' and 'Ispahan', with climbers such as
'Wedding Day' scrambling up trees after the clematis.
Close planting helps to conserve moisture as the tank
supply is insufficient for garden needs. Walks through the
native bush provide access to pools and views of the fern
and tree canopy overhead. Bed and breakfast is available
at the adjoining Glade House Lodge.

TIKITERE GARDENS
Rotorua

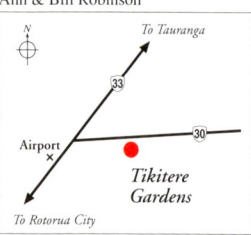

Owners:
Ann & Bill Robinson

Address: SH 30, Te Ngae Junction,
Rotorua
Postal: P O Box 819, Rotorua
Directions: Travel east out of Rotorua
along SH 33. Past the airport turn
right into SH 30. Travel 1km to
Tikitere Gardens on right; 13km from
Rotorua.
Phone: 0-7-345 5036
Fax: 0-7-345 5036
Email: tikitere.gardens@xtra.co.nz
Open: Daily, 8am–5pm
Groups: As above
Fee: $5 per adult
Size: Large – 12ha (30 acres)
Terrain: Flat to rolling
Nursery: Rhododendrons, hostas,
azaleas, maples, *Hemerocallis*, iris,
camellias, perennials
Shop: Craft shop & tearooms pending

These extensive gardens, developed since 1987 from a boysenberry farm, incorporate a natural stream and established trees. Tikitere means "precious waters", referring to the dominant feature, the Waiohena Stream, walled in stone by local craftsmen. Bog plants including hostas and primulas are planted along the stream, with hellebores under a silver birch plantation featuring in winter. Bridges cross the stream, which is lined by maples, with cherry trees in the more established areas. Azaleas, both mollis and evergreen, and rhododendrons cover the slopes beyond the stream banks, with gums, laburnums and other woodland trees behind, surrounded by farmland. A waterfall is a focal point, with lavenders and azaleas edging the banks. A driveway winds throughout the garden, following the contours of the stream. The predominant colour is yellow, with Japanese and many other varieties of iris, *Hemerocallis* (daylilies) and astilbes flowering in summer in a bog area under the canopy of trees. Oaks and liquidambars add to the autumn foliage, complemented by natives including kauri and totara. Magnolias, camellias and prunus blossom in spring, followed by tree peonies and dogwoods. *Fothergilla* shrubs also flower in spring, the foliage a brilliant red in autumn. Imported and rare plants are displayed, and many are sold in the adjacent nursery.

PUAITI
Waikite Valley

Owners:
Barb and Philip Hawken

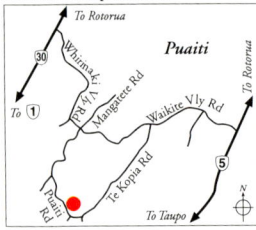

Address: 471 Puaiti Road, Waikite Valley
Postal: 471 Puaiti Road, R D 1, Rotorua
Directions: From Rotorua, take SH 5 south & turn right into SH 30. Travel 13km & turn left into Whirinaki Valley Rd. Travel 15km & turn right into Mangatete Rd. Travel 0.5km & turn left into Puaiti Rd. Travel 4.5km to Puaiti garden on left.
Phone: 0-7-333 1540
Fax: 0-7-333 1501
Mobile: 025 854 258
Open: November to May, 10am–5pm, by appointment only
Fee: $5 per adult
Size: Medium – 0.8ha (2 acres)
Terrain: Sloping & terraced
Teas: $5 pp includes muffin/cake

by arrangement

Puaiti is Maori for "little flower", referring to the native flowering manuka or teatree that originally covered the countryside. But by the time Barb and Philip decided to establish a garden in 1982, they had a paddock of thistles to contend with! Shelter was planted to break the strong winds on the elevated site, and with the help of a designer, the garden began to take shape. Borrowed views of the surrounding panorama of farmland have been incorporated into the garden as a backdrop, with a new lawn area planned to take in a different perspective. Rock walls were built to contain the garden and natives planted. This initial indigenous planting has now developed sufficiently for young kauri trees to be added. Special features at Puaiti include the formal rose garden enclosed with trellis and low box hedging, the long perennial border and the vege garden. Spring brings the bulbs, rhododendrons, azaleas and tree peonies into flower, to complement the new spring growth on the deciduous trees. These include liriodendrons, magnolias, cornus, maples and oaks. In summer, the old-fashioned roses in the formal garden bloom, accompanied by delphiniums, cardiocrinums and numerous perennials. Then autumn foliage provides colour through May. Pastel colourings in the front garden do not distract from the view to the hills, while oranges and other brighter colours are behind the house.

THE WAIKATO AND KING COUNTRY

A total of 22 gardens are featured from the Waikato and King Country regions. The Waikato is one of the most fertile areas in the country, being renowned for its dairy pasture. The volcanically rich soil and abundant rainfall contribute to its fertility. Hamilton, the only city in the Waikato, is about an hour and a half's drive south of Auckland on State Highway 1.

The Waikato gardens featured stretch from Waitakaruru in the Hauraki Plains to Tirau in the east and Te Awamutu in the west. Located in the Hauraki Plains is Elrose, where a colourful road frontage leads to a woodland garden. Parnassus at Huntly offers a holistic concept where visitors can relax and enjoy refreshments in the garden or even choose to be accommodated on site. Riverview is a semiformal urban garden in Morrinsville with views over the Piako River and countryside. Two gardens are located north of Hamilton at Gordonton: Willow Glen, with extensive indoor gardens and new function room for garden weddings, and, nearby, Wairere Nursery specialising in roses.

In Hamilton City itself are the Hamilton Gardens, on the banks of the Waikato River. This expansive public garden complex includes individual gardens such as the extensive rose gardens, a Chinese Garden, Japanese Garden, old-fashioned English flower garden, herb garden, and huge kitchen garden. The City Council also owns Taitua Arboretum, with its glorious autumn colour, situated just north of Hamilton.

Just south of Hamilton is Gails of Tamahere, which features dried flowers hung in historic churches, and The Poplars at Matangi incorporating a large lake and thousands of daffodils with an exhibition nursery. Then further south at Cambridge is Earth and Clay, an enterprising rammed earth home built in an old quarry, transformed into a garden. A small rural garden north of Waharoa is Garden of Joy, featuring three water gardens among immaculate flower beds, while south of Matamata is the farming district of Tirau with three more gardens. Oraka Wapiti Deer Park is a working farm offering deer tours, a shop, refreshments and a self-contained cottage for accommodation, as well as garden visits. The Cottage is set in a woodland cottage garden, the historic cottage now a garden café for fine food and catering. The focal point at Purdys' Place is the 100-metre water feature overlooking the lush Waikato countryside. Further south of Hamilton is Te Awamutu, where the final Waikato garden is found. Amberlea is a rambling woodland country garden set in a farmscape.

South of Waikato is the King Country, a hilly, rugged region, with increasingly cooler temperatures closer to National Park and the Central Plateau. The seven King Country gardens stretch from Otorohanga, taking in the Waitomo Caves area, down past Te Kuiti to Taumarunui. This area has a high rainfall, being a higher-altitude climate. The first garden is Parkwood at Otorohanga, with features including two bog gardens and a formal rose garden. Atawhai is sited on a Rewarewa farm where trees are abundant. At Waitomo is Altura Gardens and Wildlife Park incorporating a wide range of hand-reared animals. Aramatai, south of Te Kuiti, has roses and a large rockery, and Tapuwae grows many rhododendrons. Then 30 kilometres west of Taumarunui is Wicky's Garden, an extensive 40-hectare woodland garden featuring lakes, trees and whole hillsides of rhododendrons. Finally, just north of Taumarunui is the McKenzies' garden, a floral artist's domain, with roses and other suitable flowering plants and trees.

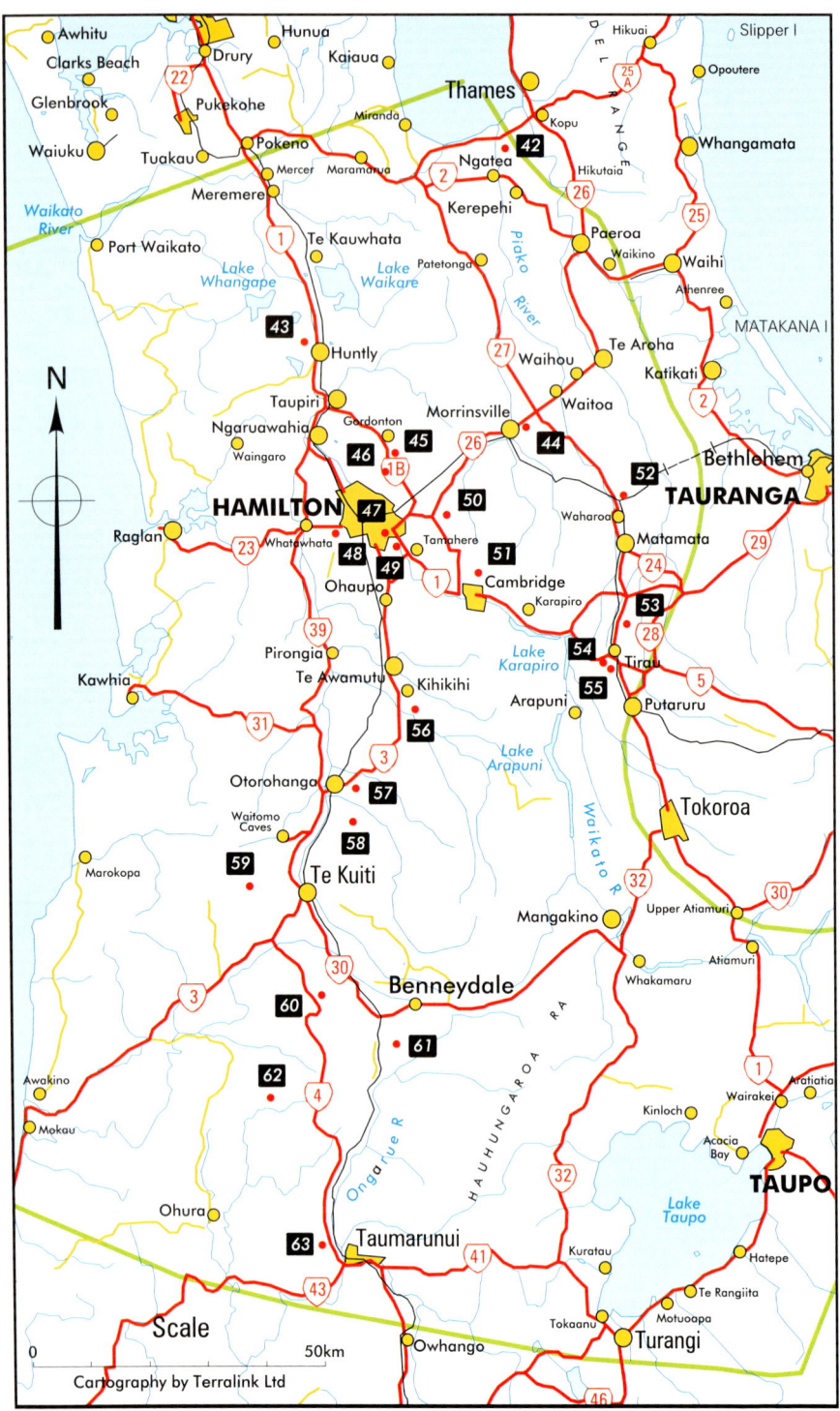

Scale

0   50km

Cartography by Terralink Ltd

ELROSE
Waitakaruru

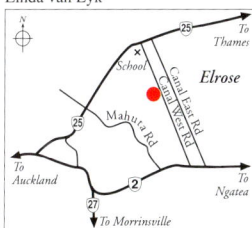

Owner:
Linda van Eyk

Address: 90 Canal West Road,
Waitakaruru, Hauraki Plains
Postal: 90 Canal West Road, R D 6,
Thames
Directions: Take SH 25 towards
Thames. At Waitakaruru School, turn
right into Canal West Rd. Travel 1km
to Elrose garden on right.
Phone: 0-7-867 3237
Mobile: 025 669 2578
Open: 1 September to 30 November,
9am–5pm, by appointment only
Closed: 1 December to 31 August
Groups: Welcome by appointment
Fee: $3 per adult
Size: Medium – 1ha (2½ acres)
Terrain: Flat

Elrose has won "Best Country Garden" twice and "Best Road Frontage" in the Hauraki Plains. Linda planted the roadside after clearing blackberry and weeds from the open country drains. Now they are a mass of colour in summer attracting passing motorists to the garden. The house garden was established in 1980, but after winning $500 worth of plants 12 years later, Linda decided to extend her garden. She was inspired by ideas from a garden ramble she had just been on, so began laying out curving pathways and creating diverse garden rooms. Today Elrose is full of spring blossom and colour. A woodland walk alongside the driveway was established after Linda cut down all the casuarina trees along the drain. Instead of mowing the grass, she created the woodland with honesty, forget-me-nots and other plantings beneath the trees. Over 90 camellias and daffodils flower there in the early spring, followed by a paddock of irises in November. Then over 300 different roses, which are the predominant species at Elrose, bloom. Linda loves the heritage roses and climbers, and a weeping specimen rose that flowers at Christmas time. She does all the heavy physical work herself, including the fencing, felling, digging, planting and weeding. Linda dug out the fishpond herself too! Another feature in the garden is the dovecote which is home to free-range pigeons.

PARNASSUS
Huntly

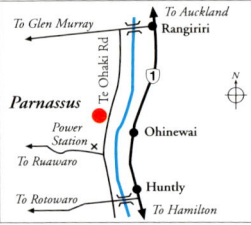

Owners:
Sharon and David Payne

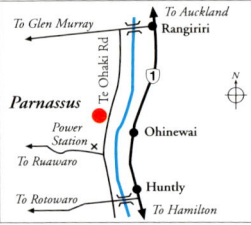

Address: 191 Te Ohaki Rd, R D 1, Huntly
Directions: From north, turn right off
SH 1 across Rangiriri Bridge towards
Glen Murray. Turn left into Te Ohaki
Rd. Garden 12km on right. From south,
turn left off SH 1 across Tainui Bridge.
Turn right to power station. Take Te
Ohaki Rd for 2km to garden on left.
Phone: 0-7-828 8781
Mobile: 021 458 2284
Fax: 0-7-828 8781
Email: parnassus@xtra.co.nz
Open: 1st weekend Oct.–26 April;
9.30am–4.30pm, daily
Groups: All year, by appointment
Fee: $4 per adult; $6 with Devonshire
tea, $10–$15 includes lunch
Size: Medium – 1.2ha (3 acres)
Terrain: Flat
Accommodation: Available & dinner

 & to toilet

& groups by request

Parnassus is a dairy farm of 100 hectares with over a
hectare in garden. Named after Mt Parnassus, the sacred
home of the deities in Greek mythology, the garden has
developed since the farm orchard was planted in 1972,
with the woodland area established in 1987 and the two
ponds two years later. A trip to France in 1983 was the
inspiration for the garden concept as a place to relax with
refreshments and a range of accommodation available.
The teas, lunches and dinners are prepared with produce
from the kitchen gardens and fruit from the orchard and
berryfruit courtyard. The house gardens feature roses
complemented by spring shrubs. Beyond, a horseshoe of
camellias, magnolias, dogwoods and malus providing
spring blossom encircles the formal rose bowl which is
a blaze of fiery colours in summer. This is flanked by the
ponds, the top pond garden planted with hebes, camellias,
magnolias, maples, and further roses. The lower pond
garden features mainly perennials including native
arthropodiums. A shady garden room contrasts with an
adjoining hot spot and an adjacent enclosed area provides
a quiet garden. Beyond the woodland area is a tilia avenue
leading to further planting on the boundary which forms
the farm walk. After the spring and summer colours,
dahlias, chrysanthemums, and autumn foliage feature, but
green on green is also cleverly used throughout the garden.

RIVERVIEW GARDEN
Morrinsville

Owners:
Toni and Peter Spooner

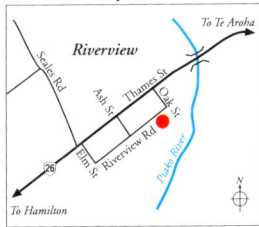

Address: 64 Riverview Rd,
Morrinsville
Directions: Take SH 26 to
Morrinsville. From Thames St, turn
south-east into Oak St, Ash St or Elm
St. At end of street, turn into
Riverview Rd to garden.
Phone: 0-7-889 5383
Mobile: 025 923 866
Fax: 0-7-889 5383
Website: friars.co.nz/gardens/pages/
riverview.html
Open: September to May, 9am–4.30pm
daily, by appointment only
Closed: June, July & August
Fee: $3 per adult
Size: Small – 0.13ha (⅓ acre)
Terrain: Slightly sloping southwards
Nursery: Perennials & annuals from
garden

 by arrangement

Riverview is an award-winning garden in the township of Morrinsville, but with rural views over the Piako River. Begun in 1990 this semi-formal garden now contains a number of exotic trees such as a weeping elm that Toni keeps trimmed on the roadside, a ginkgo, albizia and mature pepper tree. She loves the maples which feature in the spring and again in the autumn. A serpentine block wall forms the front boundary and the rose-lined driveway leads to 'Dublin Bay' roses climbing the railings of the balcony. Another red rose 'Josephine Bruce' flourishes at a side boundary, underplanted with nasturtiums to obviate spraying. 'Wedding Day' is one of Toni's favourite roses, many of which are underplanted with purple pansies.

A secluded fountain in a front corner of the garden is set among trees carpeted in ajuga. A Mexican water feature is the focal point of a subtropical garden where a variety of fruit ripen. Architectural structures include pergolas, seating, paving stones, statuary, a patio with hanging baskets and terracotta pots. As well as the roses, other climbers in spring are the clematis and wisterias in pale pink, white and purples. These complement the camellias, rhododendrons and weeping cherry tree. After the irises, the summer brings the fuchsias, daylilies and daisies into flower. Toni hopes to extend the back terracing, with its box and lavender hedging, to a gazebo in the paddock below.

WILLOW GLEN GARDENS
Gordonton

Owners:
Cindy and Del Henley

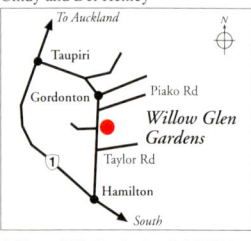

Address: 934 Gordonton Rd, R D 1, Hamilton
Directions: From Hamilton, take SH 1 north for 11.6km. Turn right into Gordonton Rd. Garden on right. Or from Huntly, take SH 1 south. At Taupiri, turn left into Gordonton Rd. Travel 14.7km to garden on left.
Phone: 0-7-824-3691
Fax: 0-7-824 3691
Email: del_and_cindy@hotmail.com
Open: All year, Mon to Fri, by appointment
Groups: By appointment
Fee: $5 per adult
Size: Medium – 0.9ha (2½ acres)
Terrain: Flat & hilly
Functions: Weddings & receptions

    mostly

  by arrangement, for groups only

These unique botanical gardens and tropical houses were developed from 1978 to 1995 by New Zealand gardening "guru" Eion Scarrow and his family, as educational gardens. Present owners, Cindy and Del, have tended and further developed the gardens, adding a rustic function room seating 76 guests, pétanque terrains, toilets, and parking areas for cars and buses. This has made Willow Glen a popular venue for weddings and receptions. Garden lovers continue to enjoy Willow Glen, with its mature trees and garden "rooms" of specialist plantings including a conifer garden with rare weeping picea, fuchsia glade, rhododendron garden, camellia collection, stone-edged water garden, and rose garden. Indoor display houses are a special feature. An octagonal Mist House, known locally as "The Guru's Temple", contains a 10-metre-high "Bromeliad Tree", with orchids and other aerial plants clinging to beams and ponga walls. Ferns, native orchids and cymbidiums thrive in the cool of an adjoining shade house. A 33-metre-long tropical house displays an impressive cacti collection, succulents, hoyas, and an array of exotic plants and tropical creepers. Group talks and tours are a speciality. Teas and lunches are available to groups only, by arrangement. Visitors are advised to phone first to avoid disappointment.

66

WAIRERE NURSERY
Gordonton

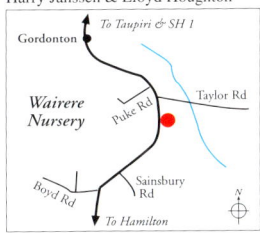

Owners:
Harry Janssen & Lloyd Houghton

Address: 826 Gordonton Rd, R D 1, Hamilton
Directions: 10km north of Hamilton, via Tramway Rd. Take bypass on Gordonton Rd. Garden on right. Or from north, turn left off SH 1 at Taupiri. Travel 18km on Gordonton Rd to Wairere Nursery on left.
Phone: 0-7-824 3430
Fax: 0-7-824 3468
Email: wainur@ihug.co.nz
Open: All year, daily, 9am–5pm
Groups: Any time
Fee: Garden: $3 per adult; Nursery: no charge for entrance
Size: Small – 0.3ha (¼ acre)
Terrain: Bank overlooking pond
Nursery: Rose specialist – all types, very extensive, catalogue available; plants not readily available elsewhere; mail order all stock

    partly

Roses are the predominant species at Wairere, the nursery specialising in roses of all varieties and the garden featuring roses from spring through into autumn. The roses are underplanted with perennials and accented with exotic trees. The garden is designed in formal lines, softened with more informal plantings that extend down the bank overlooking the large pond. Box-edged pathways intersect the hillside and lead down to the pond which features native flax, cabbage trees, and gunneras. This pond area is being further developed with formal lawns, a walkway and interesting landscaping ideas. Standardised santolinas and lavenders border the paths on the slope, with standard wisteria as the focal point. A seat beneath flowering cherries provides a spot for contemplation, complemented by adjacent native astelias. Above the bank is a persimmon tree in the centre of a circular bed. Spring features include the wisteria tree, cherry blossom, medlars, michelias, dogwoods and plum-coloured foliage of *Gleditsia triacanthos* 'Rubylace', accompanied by early old-fashioned roses and perennials. These are followed by different species and hybrid roses which peak in summer and flower into the autumn, when the deciduous foliage colours up. The garden design and tree shapes can be clearly seen in the winter, which is the season when many of the roses are dispatched throughout New Zealand.

HAMILTON GARDENS
Hamilton

Owner:
Hamilton City Council

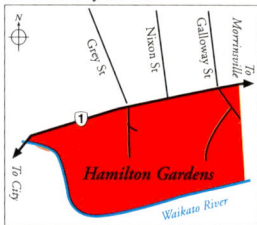

Address: Cobham Drive, Hamilton
Postal: Private Bag 3010, Hamilton
Directions: Take SH 23 west of
Hamilton. From city, take SH 1
towards Cambridge. Cross Cobham
Bridge. Hamilton Gardens on right.
Phone: 0-7-856 3200 or 0-7-838 6897
Fax: 0-7-856 2132
Email: hamilton_gardens@hcc.govt.nz
Open: All year, sunrise until sunset;
Pavilion & Café open 10.30am
Groups: Tours booked
Fee: $2.50 per head for tour, $2 each
if over 15 tour members
Size: Large – 54ha (135 acres)
Terrain: Varies – mainly flat
Café: Turtle Lake Garden Café &
Restaurant on site;
book for groups & functions

   mostly

Hamilton Gardens, although one of the newest public gardens in the country, is full of interest and diversity. Established on the original city rubbish tip in the 1960s, the gardens began traditionally with the Victorian Flower Garden of formal beds, specimen trees and display houses. It now features Greenhouses and Music Conservatory. The Rogers Rose Garden was then designed for the inaugural World Rose Convention in 1971. But recent development, since the 1980s, broke with tradition. A number of gardens were planned, telling the story of gardening. The Paradise Gardens include The Chinese Scholar's Garden with its Court of Frozen Clouds and contrasting elements of surprise depicting a miniature seascape; The English Flower Garden divided geometrically into garden rooms by walls and yew hedges; The Japanese Garden of Contemplation using the symbolism of water, asymmetrical placement of rocks, raked gravel and plants; The American Modernist Garden, recently completed, and The Italian Renaissance Garden due for completion in 2002. Another theme is The Productive Garden Collection, with its Kitchen and Herb Gardens. Native trees feature in the New Zealand Cultivar Collection and the Valley Walk. Waikato River walks are being extended westward to the City Centre and eastward past the Magnolia Garden.

TAITUA ARBORETUM
Hamilton

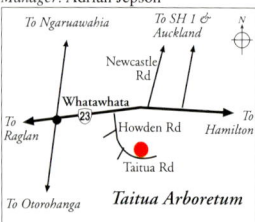

John Mortimer

Owner:
Hamilton City Council
Manager: Adrian Jepson

Address: Taitua Rd, R D 9, Hamilton
Postal: Private Bag 3010, Hamilton
Directions: From Hamilton take SH 23
west. Continue 4km past Dinsdale.
Turn left into Howden Rd. Taitua Rd
veers left again. Garden on left.
Phone: 0-7-847 5847
Fax: 0-7-847 5847
Email:
parks.and.gardens@hcc.govt.nz
Open: All year, by appointment with
the Manager, Adrian Jepson
Groups: As above
Fee: $5 per adult
Size: Large – 20ha (50 acres)
Terrain: Hilly in places
Farm walk: An additional optional
1-hour "Tall Trees" farm walk is
available

Taitua Arboretum focuses on trees and foliage, with over 1,000 different exotic and native species, some with magnificent autumn colour. The Arboretum, which is continually being developed, was originally designed and planted by John and Bunny Mortimer from 1970. Paths lead through a China-inspired moon gate overhung with Chinese quinces and persimmons, down through the Rainbow Garden to tree collections and specimens, some very rare. Alders, pines, dogwoods, oaks, Australian and North American sections feature, with spring bulbs under magnolias. Over 250 different Chinese species include mulberries and the rare *Glyptostrobus*. New Zealand native coprosma and kowhai line a pathway past a grassed stone circle. Three of the five ponds, all bird sanctuaries, contain islands for nesting sites, one edged with "knees" of swamp cypress. Swan Lake is home to black swans, Canada geese and ducks, with cabbage trees and other hardy natives as shelter. Boardwalks lead over swampy areas and a rustic seat is strategically placed looking down an avenue of elegant 'Tasman' poplars. Paths lead through a circle of redwoods, with a slope of maples behind. Arthropodium-edged pathways wind through a woodland garden to a door into a fernery. Through another native area, the one-hour walk ends with a stunning view from the Jacaranda Lawn.

GAILS OF TAMAHERE
Hamilton

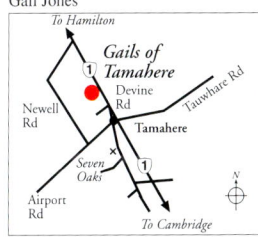

Owner:
Gail Jones

Address: Main Rd, R D 3, Hamilton
Postal: Shop 1, Centreplace, Victoria St, Hamilton
Directions: North of Devine Rd, Tamahere, on SH 1, the main road from Hamilton to Cambridge.
Phone: 0-7-856 6609
Fax: 0-7-856 6610
Email: gailjones@gails.co.nz
Open: All year, daily, 10am–4pm
Groups: By appointment
Fee: No charge
Size: Medium – 1.5ha (3–4 acres)
Terrain: Flat
Nursery: Plants
Shop: Dried flowers, fungi, seed pods, berries, dried arrangements, pot-pourri, etc

 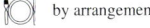 by arrangement

Gail is a professional florist, winner of many awards and teacher of design seminars. She uses two historical churches as ideal buildings for displaying her dried flower products. The oldest church was the first built in Coromandel in 1867, transported to Tamahere and restored by Gail. The gardens are planned and filled with flowers appropriate for use as fresh cut flowers and for dried flowers. Gail displays dried arrangements, posies, wall hangers, pot-pourri, essential oils, candles set in miniature roses, spice balls, dyed statice, stems of camella berries, pink sponges, budlah nuts, green fungi, red ting tingh, gypsophila, stems of delphiniums, mini roses, and bunches of statice hanging from the arched ceilings. Flower beds outside the churches are laid out attractively, with grass walkways throughout. A sea of English lavender and long beds of roses are broken with lupins, watsonias and agapanthus for height. An ivy-covered fence curves round masses of *Stachys lanata*, white lychnis, pyrethrum daisies and stoechas lavender, with a weeping red standard rose in a rock-edged bed. Yellow conifers contrast with green foliage, and silver birches border the lawn beside a large pool and fountain. Twenty-five metres was cut from Gail's garden for roadway, resulting in an entire revamping of her garden frontage. The changes include an Italian-style garden.

THE POPLARS AT MATANGI
Hamilton

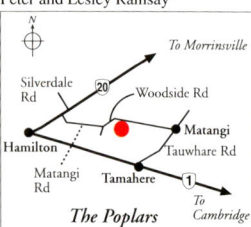

Owners:
Peter and Lesley Ramsay

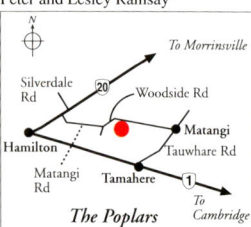

The Poplars

Address: 402 Matangi Rd, Matangi
Postal: 402 Matangi Rd, R D 4,
Hamilton
Directions: From Hamilton, take
SH 26 towards Morrinsville. Turn
right into Matangi Rd. Travel 4.02km
to garden on right. From south, exit
SH 1 at roundabout. Turn right into
Tauwhare Rd, then left into Matangi
Rd. Garden about 2km on left.
Phone: 0-7-829 5551
Email: ramsay@waikato.ac.nz
Open: 1 August to 15 December,
daily, by appointment
Fee: $5 per adult
Size: Medium – 1.2ha (3 acres)
Terrain: Flat & easy walking in gully
Nursery: Range of plants for sale.
Orders taken for daffodil bulbs

    partial
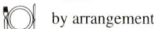 by arrangement 

This country garden has been developed since 1987 by the Ramsays, although it was landscaped by the original owners 16 years earlier, when the stand of huge poplars (*Populus cotinus*) lining the driveway was planted. Peter has incorporated a commercial exhibition nursery of named daffodils into the property and thousands of daffodils have naturalised under the trees. Over 80 varieties of camellias emerge in September and blossom trees are complemented by over 80 different rhododendrons in October. Lesley has planted more than 800 roses of all types as the mainstay in summer, adding to the colour of spring and summer annuals and perennials. A formal sunken garden is symmetrically planted in pinks, purples and white, with windows in the trellis looking down to the garden below. Paths through the gully area, a boardwalk and bridge lead across the stream to the large lake where further daffodils cover the banks in spring. A waterfall tumbles gently down a slope to the bog garden which features primulas, hostas, ligularias, lobelias, astilbes and irises. Weeping blossom trees form a walkway to the woodland area. Elsewhere a conifer collection is interplanted with natives and exotics. Many of the daffodil bulbs for sale are exclusive to The Poplars.

EARTH AND CLAY
Cambridge

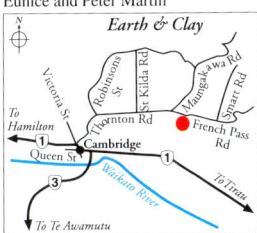

Owners:
Eunice and Peter Martin

Earth & Clay

Address: 44 French Pass, R D 4, Cambridge
Directions: From Cambridge, take Victoria St north. Turn right into Thornton Rd. Travel 4 minutes to "Y" & veer right into French Pass Rd. Earth & Clay garden on right.
Phone: 0-7-827 5427
Open: All year, Thursday to Monday, 9am to 4pm, by appointment only
Groups: By appointment, as above
Fee: $4 per adult
Size: Medium – 1.2ha (3 acres)
Terrain: Various flat levels

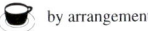 by arrangement

Eunice and Peter shocked their friends in 1994 when they bought the French Pass quarry and proceeded to "retire" there. They built their rammed earth home and began clearing the noxious weeds that covered the old quarry site and deep gully. They worked on a shoe-string budget without any heavy equipment, using grey water to irrigate the dry gardens and recycled materials wherever feasible. The north-facing long sand and clay bank has been cleared in sections, then trees planted. A year later the trees are interplanted with natives and flaxes. As a cooler microclimate develops, other plantings will be possible. In the meantime, pittosporums round the top hold the bank up, and any hardy natives that can survive the hot easterlies are planted. In contrast, the south bank features sugar maples which provide rich autumn colour. A circle of flowering shade trees on the lawn area includes melias, American yellow-woods and strawberry trees, as well as the acers. Eunice and Peter have chosen many trees to attract birdlife and provide them with fruit and nuts in years to come, such as pears, persimmons, almonds, apricots, citrus, apples, plums, feijoas, and cherries including the almond-flavoured Capulin cherry that the birds love. They have also planted an olive grove with 100 trees of eight different varieties. A dovecote is home to fantail pigeons and a gazebo covers the water tank.

GARDEN OF JOY
Waharoa

Owners:
Joy and Ken Booker

Address: 106 Wardville Rd, R D,
Waharoa
Directions: Travel north from
Waharoa on SH 27. Turn right into
Wardville Rd, past asparagus growers
to second driveway on right. NZ
Dairy Co. number 7244, or Fire
Number 106.
Phone: 0-7-888 8237
Fax: 0-7-888 8230
Website: friars.co.nz/gardens/pages/
gardenofjoy.html
Open: September to May, daily,
by appointment
Groups: By appointment, as above
Fee: $3 per adult
Size: Small – 0.26ha (⅔ acre)
Terrain: Flat
Hot water: On request
Nursery: A few plants from garden

Garden of Joy has been a labour of love for Joy Booker since 1976, as she has gradually extended her garden into the surrounding paddocks. Large native and exotic trees provide a framework, with water gardens, cottage plants and over 120 mainly old roses predominating, which she chooses not to spray. She enjoys colour but is aware of form and texture too. Joy avoids mono-colour, using whites such as mignonettes and lychnis to separate the colours. She finds silver artemisias provide contrasting foliage all year, as do variegated plants and conifers. She likes yellow to give the garden a lift, especially on wet days. Joy loves perennials such as fluffy astilbes and thalictrum, with penstemons, campanulas, and Siberian irises among her favourites. She is growing more wisterias, and a huge white one climbs over her ponga pergola. A gazebo is adorned with pink miniature roses including 'Fairy', with an old plough languishing nearby. A stone bridge crosses a figure-eight waterlily pond, teeming with goldfish. A huge pepper-tree provides dappled shade over another little pond planted with hostas. Clematis grows up through trees in a native corner, where a third pool has a waterfall splashing into it through a hollow log. This immaculate garden, with its attention to detail, won the local rural garden competition in 1993. Then in 1997 it featured on national television in *Maggie's Garden Show*.

ORAKA WAPITI DEER PARK
Tirau

Owner:
Linda and Ian Scott

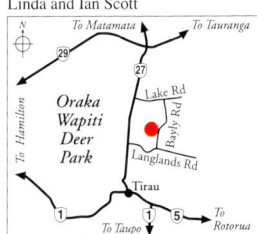

Address: 71 Bayly Rd, R D 1, Tirau
Directions: From Hamilton take SH 1
or from Rotorua take SH 5 to Tirau.
Take SH 27 north for 3km. Turn right
into Langlands Rd. Travel 2km &
turn left into Bayly Rd. Travel 710m
to Oraka Wapiti Deer Park on left.
Phone: 0-7-883 1382
Freephone: 0800 835 838
Mobile: 025 732 657
Fax: 0-7-883 1384
Email: oraka@voyager.co.nz
Open: All year, by appointment only
Fee: $6 pp for groups over 10
Size: Medium – 1.2ha (3 acres)
Terrain: Flat – easy access
Shop: Interesting garden products
Tours: Deer tour by arrangement
Accommodation: Quality cottage

 by arrangement

Just five kilometres out of Tirau is Oraka Wapiti Deer Park. This 56-hectare farm includes 48 hectares for the wapiti deer and just over a hectare of landscaped garden. Although the garden has only been developed since 1995, some of the trees were planted around 1930. These huge trees are Linda's favourites, providing structure for the underplanting. Walks have been established in the garden, through the eight-hectare pine forest and beside Oraka Stream that borders the farm. Spring features include the bulbs lining the driveway, daffodils followed by forget-me-nots, magnolias, azaleas, rhododendrons and camellias. Then in summer the old-fashioned roses flower, along with penstemons and delphiniums. The maples turn lovely colours in autumn, and the bark of the trees and structure of the garden are of interest in winter, with the tranquil views of the surrounding countryside. The garden is predominantly mauves and pinks, with yellows and brighter colours by the restaurant and shop. Ian is also developing a native area, with rimu and kauri trees planted in the 1960s. English trees include weeping willows, scarlet oaks and copper beeches. The wapiti provide year-round interest for visitors, from the growth of deer velvet in spring to the birth of fawns in summer and bottle feeding pet fawns, then the noisy mating roar of the stags in autumn. A self-contained cottage is available.

THE COTTAGE
Tirau

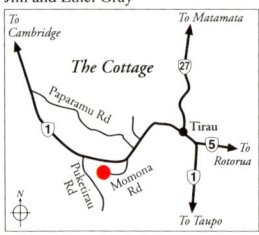

Owners:
Jim and Ethel Gray

Address: 60 Momona Road, R D 1, Tirau

Directions: From Tirau, travel north on SH 1 for 3km. Turn left into Momona Rd. Garden at end. From Cambridge, take SH 1 south to SH 29. Continue on SH 1 to 3rd road on right. Turn right into Momona Rd to garden.

Phone: 0-7-883 1300

Fax: 0-7-883 1300

Website: friars.co.nz/gardens/pages/thecottage.html

Open: All year, daily, by appointment

Fee: $3 per adult, or no charge if dining at The Cottage

Size: Medium – 1.2ha (3 acres)

Terrain: Hilly

Café: Teas, lunches & dinners for groups, by arrangement only

by arrangement

A century-old macrocarpa tree dominates this woodland cottage garden, with views to the hills beyond. Ethel's father lived in the 1896 cottage for 22 years before the Grays took it over in 1967. They moved their farmhouse on to the property 16 years later and began developing the rest of the garden. They transformed the historic cottage into a garden café for fine food and catering, and extended the planting round it into the surrounding sheep paddocks. Two areas of native bush are still being developed, with kauri, rimu, beeches and nikau palms. These are complemented with maples, conifers, deciduous English trees and a weeping pagoda tree. Cherry blossoms in spring are accompanied by rhododendrons, camellias, vireyas, clematis and wisteria. Then the roses begin. There is always colour in the cottage garden – perennials providing a kaliedoscope during the summer months. Meandering grassy paths lead visitors through the mature trees and into different areas. The micro-climate is almost frost-free, allowing Ethel and Jim to grow avocados, tamarillos, and even bananas at times! Jim plans to plant more vireya rhododendrons which also thrive in the garden. The Cottage café offers lunches, dinner parties, and Christmas dinner for groups by arrangement. A finger food lunch is $7.50 per person, Ploughman's lunch is $12, and a full lunch is $15.

PURDYS' PLACE
Tirau

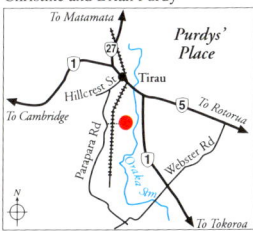

Owners:
Christine and Brian Purdy

Address: 169 Parapara Road, Tirau
Directions: From Cambridge, take
SH 1 to Tirau. At hotel at top of hill,
turn right into Hillcrest St. Travel
100m & turn left into Parapara Rd.
Continue 1.69km to Purdys' Place on
left. Cross railway line carefully &
travel up driveway to garden. From
south, travel under railway bridge &
up hill to hotel. Turn left into Hillcrest
St, then as above.
Phone: 0-7-883 1482
Mobile: 025 271 3432
Open: All year, by appointment
Groups: By appointment, as above
Fee: $4 per adult
Size: Medium – 0.8ha (2 acres)
Terrain: Flat to sloping
Weddings: Welcome by arrangement

This park-like country garden has been expanded since the original house garden was planted in 1981. At that time silk trees were planted at either end of the swimming pool, with climbing roses to disguise the fences and erigeron edging. Bromeliads enjoy the moist conditions, contrasting with cacti near the spa pool. In 1996 the rose garden was established. This comprises a 20-metre rose pergola covered in mostly scented roses, including many English varieties. The most recent extension is the elaborate watergardens, created in 1998. These are based on the 100-metre water feature, from the belvedere by the spring at the top, to the waterfalls, ponds and rocky stream falling into the lake below. A stone bridge over the creek is a popular spot for garden weddings. The bog garden at the end of the lake is planted with irises and native astelias, while ponga tree-ferns, hebes and indigenous grasses grow among the stones on the hillside. There are further native plantings at Purdys' Place such as nikau palms and kowhai that flower in the spring, attracting the birds. Spring features also include cherry blossoms, camellias, rhododendrons, azaleas, clematis and freesias. Summer is filled with colourful flowers set off by the spacious green lawns that blend in with the 360-degree vistas over the lush Waikato farmland. Rustic farm machinery provides added focal points, with bikes and wheelbarrows too.

AMBERLEA
Te Awamutu

![Amberlea garden photograph]

Amberlea

Owners:
Jan and Roger Sutherland

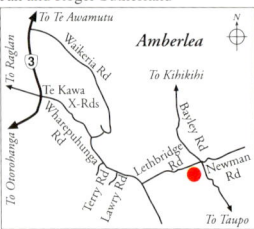

Address: 342 Lethbridge Road,
R D 3, Karakonui, Te Awamutu
Directions: From Kihikihi, take SH 3
south to Te Kawa crossroads. Turn
left into Wharepuhunga Rd. Turn left
again into Lethbridge Rd & travel
6km to Amberlea garden on right.
Phone: 0-7-872 2766
Mobile: 025 226 1001
Fax: 0-7-872 2767
Email: jankorakonui@hotmail.com
Website: friars.co.nz/gardens/pages/
amberlea.html
Open: October to June, 10am–5pm,
by appointment only
Closed: July, August & September
Fee: $5 per adult
Size: Medium – 0.8ha (2 acres)
Terrain: Flat to gently rolling
Shop: Weaving for sale

by arrangement

Jan has developed her garden at Amberlea since 1970, when she married and moved to the farm, beginning with a bulldozed clay site. She wanted a woodland rambling country garden surrounding a tennis court, but was able to establish it only little by little. She would have positioned the big trees further from the house had she been able to plant them there from the beginning. The lack of water, apart from the large waterlily pond, and heavy frosts did not daunt Jan who is now planning to plant the rest of the paddock as woodland. Special features include the cherry blossom walk which peaks in spring, followed by the yellow laburnum walk. Crab apples blossom and dogwoods are covered in their "floating" bracts in spring too, before adding to the autumn colour along with maples, elms, copper beeches and the liquidambars after which the garden is named. Jan also has a dog called Amber! Her favourites are the English David Austin roses which predominate in the summer, covering archways intertwined with Morning Glory. Wisteria and clematis climb through the trees and daisies, nepeta, Himalayan poppies and bluebells are spread throughout the garden. A new area focuses on hostas and Chatham Island forget-me-nots which continue Jan's favourite colour combination of greens with soft blues, white and pinks. She plans to have plants for sale in 2001.

PARKWOOD
Otorohanga

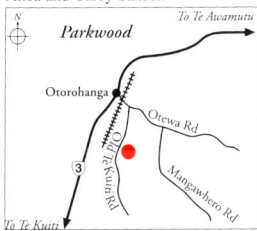

Owners:
Ailsa and Carey Sanson

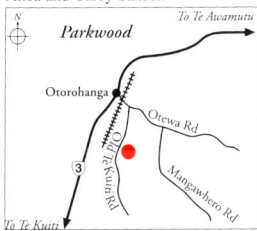

Address: 107 Old Te Kuiti Rd, R D 6, Otorohanga
Directions: From Otorohanga, continue south on SH 3 over Waipa River. Turn left into Otewa Rd. Travel under railway bridge & turn right into Old Te Kuiti Rd. Travel 1km to Parkwood garden on left.
Phone: 0-7-873 8831
Fax: 0-7-873 8831
Open: All year, by appointment only
Fee: $5 per adult
Size: Medium – 1.2ha (3 acres)
Terrain: Flat & sloping on different levels
Nursery: A few perennials from garden for sale

  by arrangement

A native bush area at the bottom of the garden was planted in 1993, two years before the house was built and the garden at Parkwood established. The earth from the house excavations was landscaped into a hill to provide an overview of the garden and the rural vistas. Different plants are used in separate areas of the garden, according to various themes. For instance two bog gardens feature different plants, the top garden with Louisiana irises and primulas, and the lower one with other bog plants. A rock garden is adjacent to a three-level waterfall which drops into the goldfish pond planted with waterlilies and bordered by water-loving plants such as black taro and *Elegea capensis*. A formal enclosed English-style garden features David Austin roses, clematis and perennials edged with lavender and box hedging. Roses are Ailsa's favourites, with climbers covering rustic pergolas, archways and old gates, as well as providing hips in winter. A border of 20 single white 'Sally Holmes' roses edged with *Nepeta* 'Superba' is a special feature. The grassy Bridal Walk leads under an archway of pink clematis and roses, to 'Wedding Day' cascading at one end and golden banksia roses at the other. The woodland garden is full of deciduous trees underplanted with rhododendrons, azaleas and camellias. There is also a Hot Bank, Rainbow Garden, Mediterranean Garden, and the new Gate of Memories garden.

ATAWHAI
Otorohanga

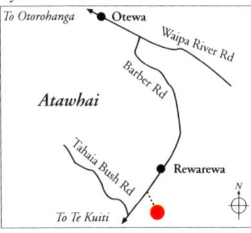

Owners:
Lyndon and Keith Wilson

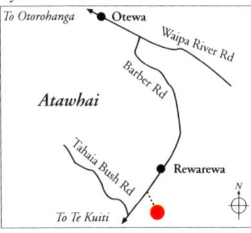

Address: 773 Barber Rd, Rewarewa, R D 5, Otorohanga
Directions: 20km from Otorohanga. From north, turn left off SH 3 under rail subway into Otewa Rd. After Otewa School, take 2nd right into Barber Rd. Travel 7.73km to garden on left. From south, turn right off SH 3 at Te Kuiti into Rangitoto Rd. Then take Barber Rd to garden on right.
Phone: 0-7-873 0883
Open: All year, by appointment
Groups: As above
Fee: $4 per adult
Size: Medium – over 1ha (about 3 acres)
Terrain: Undulating, easy walking
Nursery: Julie Jackson's perennials for sale to large groups only

 & lunchroom   ♿ mostly

Trees became the absorbing interest for Lyn and Keith on their sheep farm, after they discovered how trees prevent erosion, provide shelter and beauty, and are a valuable source of timber. So successful was the planting programme, that Atawhai won the Waikato Farm Environment Award in 1994. The arboretum provides a wonderful backdrop to the garden, developed since 1950 on a bare hillside. When the new house was built 18 years later, the plantings were extended. The driveway sweeps through native trees to the house garden. A rhodohypoxis-edged path leads to a waterlily pond planted in pinks, blues and creams on the lawn, with taller shade trees framing the view of pastureland planted with trees and native bush beyond. The garden beside the lunchroom is planted in reds, yellows and oranges, behind a fence covered in red 'Dublin Bay' roses. A woodland walk winds through ponga tree ferns to a small goldfish pond edged with native ferns, beneath bird boxes on the tree trunks. The woodland unexpectedly opens into a clearing of pinks and creams, the pathway lined with hostas and bergenias leading to a white Judas tree, *Cercis siliquastrum alba,* encircled with soft pink cranesbill *Geranium macrorrhizum,* and a rose archway beyond covered in a 'Nancy Steen' seedling. Conifers are underplanted with silvery-leafed plectranthus, and hebes border the path back to the house garden.

ALTURA GARDENS AND WILDLIFE PARK
Te Kuiti

Owners:
Ross and Leigh Balemi

Address: 477 Fullerton Rd, Waitomo
Postal: 477 Fullerton Rd, R D 1, Te Kuiti
Directions: From SH 3, take Waitomo Rd west towards Waitomo Caves for 7.5km. About 200m before the caves, turn left into Fullerton Rd. Travel 4km to Altura Garden on right.
Phone: 0-7-878 5278
Fax: 0-7-878 5278
Open: 25 September to 31 May, daily, 10am to 4pm
Closed: 1 June to 24 September
Fee: $7 per adult, $4 per child
Size: Large – 2ha (5 acres)
Terrain: Flat to rolling
Snack & refreshment shop: Open as above

 mostly

The two hectares (five acres) of park-like garden at Altura are complemented by four hectares of wildlife park, featuring a large range of hand-reared animals. Originally planted in the 1960s, the garden was redeveloped in 1995 to include a wide range of unusual trees and shrubs. Spring is announced with extensive drifts of jonquils, daffodils and bluebells, followed by many varieties of cherry trees, magnolias, michelias and maples. The summer borders range from the common to the unusual. Autumn is coloured with the foliage of a large selection of English and uncommon deciduous trees. There are also groups of native plantings and the garden is edged by native bush, with views extending northwards to Mount Pirongia and Otorohanga. Large limestone rocks feature throughout the garden and pergolas add structure. Free-flight aviaries house parrots, finches, budgies and canaries. There are up to 15 varieties of birds at Altura, such as pheasants, quail, partridges and Polish hens. Animals include llama, Tibetan yaks, exotic cattle such as Scottish highland cattle, red and fallow deer, emus, miniature horses, donkeys, sheep, goats, rabbits, and Italian guard dogs. Three ponds are home to various breeds of water fowl and swans. A natural stream feeds the waterlily ponds and two waterfalls. Altura Gardens and Wildlife Park opened in January 2000.

ARAMATAI
Te Kuiti

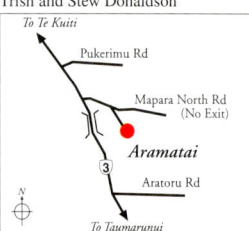

Owners:
Trish and Stew Donaldson

Address: Mapara North Rd, Te Kuiti
Postal: P O Box 13, Te Kuiti
Directions: 55km north of
Taumarunui, or 26km south of Te
Kuiti, turn off SH 4 into Mapara
North Rd. Aramatai up private drive
on right, over cattle-stop.
Phone: 0-7-878 8071
Mobile: 025 954 289
Fax: 0-7-878 8071
Open: All year, by appointment
Groups: As above
Fee: $3 per adult
Size: Medium – 1ha (2½ acres)
Terrain: Hilly
Nursery: Perennials, shrubs,
seedlings, trees
Shop: Dried flowers

  mostly

  by arrangement

Aramatai (meaning "Matai Path") is the name of the valley, represented by the big matai stump in the garden encircled by a pathway. The Donaldsons began planting in 1992, attracted by the lie of the land, the availability of rhyolite rocks and a magnificent weeping willow over two natural ponds, now connected by a cascading waterfall. Waterlilies add colour to the ponds, edged with irises. Hostas are massed nearby under the willows next to primulas. A bridge leads to a huge hillside rockery which is the prominent feature of the garden. Rocks gradually moved into place from around the farm are now surrounded with rock plants and groundcovers. Rhododendrons, camellias, spring bulbs and magnolias complement the lilies, including Trish's favourite *Cardiocrinum giganteum* and Easter lilies. Trish loves old roses rambling over ponga pergolas and through trees, such as 'New Dawn', 'Westerland' and 'Graham Thomas'. Summer perennials and annuals accompany the roses. Other features include Trish's herb garden, hydrangeas, and the predominantly hazelnut orchard. Stew has planted conifers and young exotics, particularly weeping varieties and rare specimens. Brilliant autumn colours feature acers, malus, ginkgos, dogwoods and liquidambars. Abundant natives edging the pond include ponga, cabbage trees, grasses and flaxes that attract native tui.

TAPUWAE
Te Kuiti

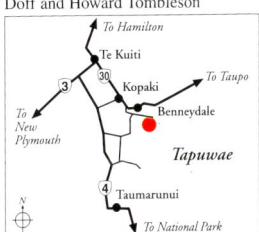

Owners:
Doff and Howard Tombleson

Address: 488 Tapuwae Rd, R D 7, Te Kuiti
Directions: North of Taumarunui, travel through Ongarue and Waimiha. Turn right into Tapuwae Rd & follow for 5km. Or south from Te Kuiti, take SH 30 towards Benneydale, travel through Kopaki and Mangapehi. Take first right towards Waimiha, then first left into Tapuwae Rd. Travel 5km to garden at end of road.
Phone: 0-7-878 4837
Fax: 0-7-878 4837
Open: September to winter, any time
Groups: By appointment
Fee: $5 per adult
Size: Large – 3.2ha (8 acres)
Terrain: Undulating
Hot water: Available

   by arrangement

Tapuwae, a Maori name meaning "sacred footstep", is sited at more than 500 metres above sea level. In the 1960s it was just a small house garden. Trees were planted from 1968 and the garden extended since 1982, to ramble over three hectares now. The high altitude means spring bulbs bloom late, with blossom trees and azaleas providing colour against the new maple foliage. Clematis climbs through trees and rhododendrons display their varied hues. In summer, innumerable perennials flower, with bog plants around large ponds and streams. Sited in pockets created by the undulating landscape, each area has its own special appeal. Everywhere views of the surrounding countryside rest the eye, especially in the colourful rhododendron season. The trees are now well established, and natives are interplanted with conifers, magnolias, dogwoods, cercis and camellias. These are underplanted with drifts of forget-me-nots, scillas and ajuga groundcover, and in bog areas with hostas, gunneras, ligularias, rheums and primulas. Old logs and rocks, collected from all over the farm, edge paths and form rustic seats. In the Long Acre, a separate garden to one side of the driveway, cherries and rhododendrons flower on the slope below a huge ancient log, from a tree felled in 1929. Ducks and peacocks are a special feature at Tapuwae.

WICKY'S GARDEN
Matiere

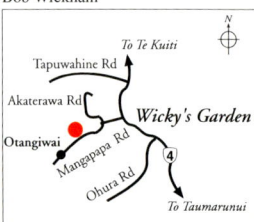

Owner:
Bob Wickham

Address: Mangapapa Rd, Otangiwai,
R D, Matiere, King Country
Postal: P O Box 14 062, Hamilton
Directions: 56km south of Te Kuiti or
30km west of Taumarunui. Turn south
into Mangapapa-Otangiwai Rd &
travel 7km to garden on right.
Phone: 0-7-855 0368
Fax: 0-7-855 0369
Email: wickham.house@clear.net.nz
Open: By appointment
Fee: $5 per adult
Size: Large – 40ha (almost 100 acres)
woodland; plus 1ha (2½ acres) house
& rose garden
Terrain: Flat around house, plus hilly
woodland

   partly

  by arrangement

A hillside of white 'Everest' rhododendrons welcomes the visitor to Wicky's Garden. Bob began his garden in 1985 as a colour concept, transforming whole hillsides into single colour masses of rhododendrons. Now Wicky's colour theme is developing into a woodland garden, with truckloads of trees introduced, then under-planted to continue the colour throughout the year. Bob is introducing more red which contrasts well against the greenery. An extensive collection of flowering cherries, magnolias and cornuses begin the display from mid August, extending to mid November with the massed rhododendrons and azaleas. The Blue Garden features four levels of blue flowers, from the paulownias above, to the ceanothus, rhododendrons, then bluebells beneath. The roses in the house garden take over in summer, the woodland blooms and water features come into their own. Waterlilies adorn the many stream-fed lakes which are home to Bob's duck families. The deciduous trees, especially the maples, provide a mass of autumn colour, contrasting with the natives. The late Sydney Harpley's sculpture is a special feature in the garden. Gumboots are recommended, as the grass is long in many places while the trees grow up. Although Wicky's Garden is large, pathways are formed for wandering and picnicking. Arrangements can be made to drive elderly people around.

McKENZIES' GARDEN
Taumarunui

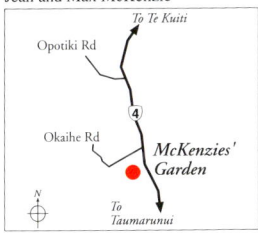

Owners:
Jean and Max McKenzie

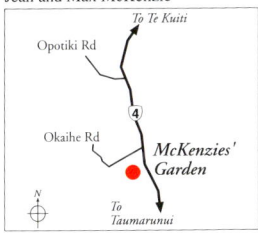

Address: SH 4, Taumarunui
Postal: P O Box 88, Taumarunui
Directions: On SH 4, 3km north of
Taumarunui. Garden on left.
Phone: 0-7-895 7475
Fax: 0-7-895 5166
Email: maxmck@xtra.co.nz
Website: friars.co.nz/gardens/pages/
mckenzies.html
Open: End September to mid
December, & February to March; by
appointment
Groups: Turning space for buses,
plenty of parking space beyond house
Fee: $4 per adult
Size: Medium – 0.8ha (2 acres)
Terrain: Sloping front section, with
plateau above

to top garden only

From the main highway just north of Taumarunui the more recent addition to this garden can be seen – colourful terraces behind a huge retaining wall, with cherries, cannas and *Hemerocallis* (daylilies) planted right along the fenceline. Up behind is a rhododendron dell, established since 1966 and underplanted with woodland perennials including trilliums, hostas and drifts of purple honesty. This dell looks like fairyland when the rhododendron petals drop and cherry blossoms fall like giant snowflakes carpeting the slopes in colour. Spring also ushers in camellias and magnolias, with standard wisteria and clematis like lace curtains. Peonies thrive on the plateau, as do delphiniums and bush roses behind the perennial beds. 'Fairy' roses cascade from standards. Jean's love for roses can be seen in large beds of hybrid teas especially established for her floral work. She also grows flowering shrubs such as azaleas for this purpose. Max has built a gazebo for Jean's climbing hybrid clematis. And a new gazebo adjacent to the swimming pool is set among hostas, cardiocrinum, heuchera and irises. Rockery plants, their colours interweaving like a tapestry, feature in a sunken rockery, with ericas mirroring the lichen-covered rock shapes. Jean blends her colours as they change with the seasons, always with the King Country hills as a backdrop to the garden.

EASTLAND AND HAWKE'S BAY

The 14 gardens featured from these two coastal areas extend south from the Bay of Plenty, enjoying the same warm sunshine and temperate climate. The Eastland gardens are situated from the City of Gisborne to Whangara on the coast north of Gisborne and Tiniroto, on the inland route south to Lake Waikaremoana. Being located on the east coast, Gisborne has a low rainfall, and as the sunniest region in the North Island, the Poverty Bay beaches are popular. These sunny conditions, along with the fertile alluvial plains, have resulted in Gisborne being well known for its orchards and vineyards.

In Gisborne City itself are the Gisborne Botanical Gardens on the banks of the Taruheru River. The bridges across the river are lit by a changing coloured light display at night. One of the central themes of the Gardens is "Sharing and fostering friendship ties" with sister cities around the world. On the coast north of Gisborne are two Whangara gardens: Glenroy is a garden of contrasts, from an exposed dry top area to a sheltered moist dell, while Wensleydale features colour waves of roses and a shrubbery, as well as orchids. North of Whangara the road winds up round the picturesque East Cape, lined with pohutukawa, past Te Araroa, reputed to be the first point of land in the world to greet the touch of the first dawn of the new millennium. To the west of the City is Encore Grove at Patutahi, named after the Encore mandarins grown there. Formal rose gardens are also part of the attractions.The two most westerly gardens, Eastwoodhill and Hackfalls, are both extensive arboretums. To the north-west of Hackfalls Arboretum lies the beautiful Lake Waikaremoana at an altitude of nearly 600 metres, set in the midst of Te Urewera National Park. Walking tracks through lush native forest abound.

Hawke's Bay is adjacent to Poverty Bay, sharing a similar climate with warm, mild weather. The northernmost coastal garden is Bremdale at Nuhaka, set amid orchards and featuring a rustic gazebo in a pond area, with roses for much of the year. North of Napier are two gardens, firstly Cotswold, a high altitude garden on the Taupo-Napier Highway where a large pond is the central feature. The other inland garden is Trelinnoe, a parklike garden, featuring rhododendrons and trees. Napier City itself includes two public gardens featured in this book. The first is the Napier Botanical Gardens planted around a central stream, and the other is the Kennedy Park Rose Gardens featuring over 4,000 roses. Along the Taihape Road from Hastings is a Swedish tree garden called Trädgård, with over 4,000 trees, as well as ponds featuring imported waterfowl. In Hastings is Cornwall Park, the public garden with a lake and Chinese garden. Finally, just south of Havelock North is the Ormonds' dry no-water garden, but features neither cacti nor many succulents.

Hawke's Bay is well known for its orchards, wineries and sunny, dry climate. Summers are hot and dry, winters are dry and crisp. Napier, the Art Deco city rebuilt after the disastrous 1931 earthquake, is well endowed with public gardens, which also include the Sunken Garden on Marine Parade, and the quarry garden with waterfall. Its sister city, Hastings, with village of Havelock North, features a springtime Blossom Festival each September.

Motiti I

White I

BAY OF PLENTY

Mt Maunganui
TAURANGA
Te Puke

Motuhora I

Te Araroa

Paengaroa

Whakatane
Ohope Opotiki

Ruatoria

RAUKUMARA RANGE

Edgecumbe
Lake Rotorua
L. Rotoiti
L. Rotoehu
L. Rotoma
Kawerau

33
30

ROTORUA
L. Tarawera

I KAWHENUA RANGE

Murupara

Tolaga Bay
35

30
5
38

HUIARAU RANGE

Ngatapa
68
67
65
66
Patutahi
64
GISBORNE
Poverty Bay

TAUPO

Lake Waikareiti

Lake Waikaremoana

69
Tuai
Tiniroto

5

Mohaka River

38
Frasertown
Nuhaka
70
Wairoa

71
Puketiri
Te Pohue
72

HAWKE BAY

Portland I

5
2

Rissington

75
74
73
NAPIER

Sherenden

Fernhill
76
HASTINGS
Havelock North

50
2
77

Otane
Bare I

Takapau
Waipawa

2
Norsewood
Waipukurau

Porangahau

N

Scale
0   50km

Cartography by Terralink Ltd

GISBORNE BOTANICAL GARDENS
Gisborne

Owner:
Gisborne District Council

Address: Aberdeen Rd, between
Roebuck Rd & Carnarvon St, Gisborne
Postal: P O Box 747, Gisborne
Directions: Take SH 35 to Gisborne.
From Gladstone Rd, turn left into
Roebuck Rd or Disraeli or Carnarvon
Sts. Travel to Aberdeen Rd. Gisborne
Gardens on riverside of road.
Phone: 0-6-867 2049
Mobile: 025 546 656
Fax: 0-6-867 2049
Email: aaron@gdc.govt.nz
Open: All year;
Gardens: daily, 7am to 8pm;
Glasshouse: weekdays, 9am to 4pm
Fee: No charge
Weddings: $25 donation
Size: Large – 5.1ha (over 12½ acres)
Terrain: Flat
Children: Playground available

The Taruheru River runs beside Gisborne Botanical
Gardens, originally established as a recreational reserve
outside the City boundaries in 1874, but now quite central.
Many trees planted in 1890 still remain to provide shade
and beauty throughout the Gardens, including poplars,
chestnuts, oaks, maples and tall phoenix palms. A row of
mature fan palms borders the Aberdeen Road frontage and
native flaxes and cabbage trees line the river. An area of
native bush was planted bewteen 1915 and 1920 and
amenities erected. Then in the 1960s the site was managed
as a park, only reverting to botanic gardens in recent years.
An Australian Garden completed in 1997 is located on the
Roebuck Road boundary and features many Australian trees,
shrubs and groundcovers. The architectural brick walls are
desert red and the Rain Catcher sculpture was donated by
the sister city Gisborne in the state of Victoria, Australia.
A Japanese watergarden has been established comprising
a waterlily lake which is well populated by ducks and
edged with Japanese flora. A landscaped Japanese-style
island is in the centre of the lake and a Japanese lantern
was donated by the sister city Nonoichi in Japan. An
American-style desert garden features a rock sculpture
from the sister city in Palm Desert. Other attractions
include seasonal colour, the annual beds, free-flight aviary,
and large cacti house. Paved pathways meander throughout.

GLENROY
Whangara

Owners:
Jenny and Pip Barker

Address: Glenroy Rd, Pouawa
Postal: Glenroy Rd, Whangara,
R D 3, Gisborne
Directions: From Gisborne take SH 35
towards Whangara. Turn left up Glenroy
Rd. Travel 5km to Glenroy on right.
Phone: 0-6-862 2636
Fax: 0-6-862 2036
Website: friars.co.nz/gardens/pages/
glenroy.html
Open: All year, by appointment
Groups: Large buses – ask re parking
Fee: $3 per adult, refundable on
purchase from craft shop
Size: Medium – nearly 1ha (2⅓ acres)
Terrain: Quite steep in parts
Nursery: A few perennials
Shop: Craft shop selling Pip's wood
turning; old English crafts & tools;
gardening things; moon calendars

  to flat areas

by arrangement

Situated atop a hill, reached by a breathtaking driveway, Glenroy is a garden of contrasts, from the exposed hilltop where proteas and leucadendrons thrive, down to the sheltered dell where bog plants flourish beside a waterlily pond. In 1985 it was just a bare hillside with two poplars growing. South African and Australian plants were all that survived until shelter was established by planting banksias as windbreaks. Then the whole fence was close-battened, which enabled roses to be established. The short slab fences have now disappeared into the undergrowth as a micro-climate has developed, allowing other plants, including rhododendrons, to grow. Jenny loves vireyas, which she grows in a shade house with *Primula obconica*, and hanging baskets galore. Pip has built a chalet-style barn with a well nearby, where Jenny groups her yellows, oranges and apricot colours, nasturtiums contrasting with blue echiums, love-in-a-mist and lavender. Jenny finds that blues are great for lifting yellows. She keeps her flower garden 40 per cent white, with pinks and blues accented by stronger colours. Several *Clematis montana* climb through trees in spring and large hybrid clematis cling to fences. Massed daisies and roses abound, especially old varieties and Austin roses, which grow over Pip's arches and gazebo. Grevilleas feature in the frost-free winter. Peak times to visit are spring and autumn.

WENSLEYDALE
Whangara

Owners:
Nick and Pat Seymour

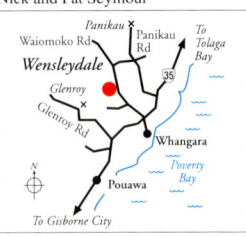

Address: 901 Waiomoko Rd,
Whangara, Gisborne
Postal Address: R D 3, Whangara,
Gisborne
Directions: 38km from Gisborne, via
SH 35, towards Tolaga Bay. Travel
28km to Whangara, then turn left into
Waiomoko Rd. Travel 10km over 5
cattle stops to Wensleydale on left.
Phone: 0-6-862 2697
Mobile: 025 725 997
Fax: 0-6-862 2703
Open: October to January,
by appointment only
Groups: Bus tours a specialty
Fee: $3 per adult; includes tea/coffee
Size: Medium – almost 1ha (2 acres)
Terrain: Flat lawns & sloping banks
Nursery: Plants available seasonally,
eg violets, hostas, fuchsias, selected
perennials

by arrangement

Wensleydale is named after the Yorkshire dales, the
original home of the first settlers. The garden has
been developed in stages from a bare site since 1966.
Early plantings included prunus, silver birch, liquidambar
and Japanese umbrella pine (*Sciadopitys verticillata*). The
shrubbery and rose gardens are planted in colour waves,
a white and pink bed set in paving stones with delphiniums,
catmint, statice, and love-in-a-mist complementing pink
roses, white daisies and alyssum. Another bed features
deep blue lobelia with matching pansies under mixed
roses. A row of gold roses edges the lawn and driveway,
underplanted with yellow pansies and white daisies. Behind
the house is a *Magnolia* 'Iolanthe', with white and pink
roses and white daisies. The garden bordering the roadside
is pink, white and blue, with a sweeping lawn edged with
deep pink lavatera, dark blue delphiniums, white daisies
and creamy sisyrinchiums. The lower driveway is lined
with hostas, hydrangeas, pink and white watsonias, honesty,
and pale blue agapanthus. A waterfall trickles into a lily
pond. Spring bulbs accompany camellias, azalea mollis,
an extensive hosta collection and prunus and malus blossom.
Summer features Pat's orchids, old and modern roses,
with large collections of perennials and heat-loving annuals
such as petunias and zinnias. The Whangara gardens make
a pleasant day trip.

ENCORE GROVE
Patutahi, Gisborne

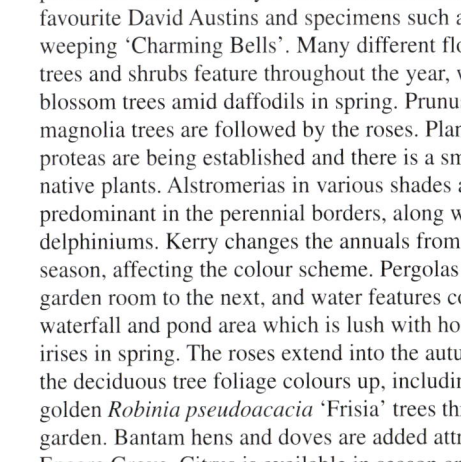

Owners:
Kerry and Paul Smith

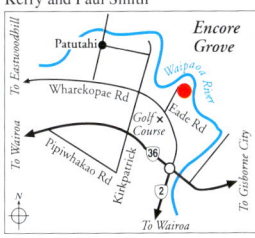

Address: 20 Eade Road, Patutahi,
R D 2, Gisborne
Directions: From Gisborne City,
travel south to Waipaoa Bridge
roundabout. Turn right into
Wharekopae Rd towards
Eastwoodhill. Take 1st right into
Eade Rd. Garden on right.
Phone: 0-6-862 7830
Mobile: 025 495 098
Fax: 0-6-862 7890
Email: encore.grove@clear.net.nz
Open: All year, by appointment only
Fee: $3 per adult
Size: Medium – 0.75ha (almost 2 acres)
Terrain: Flat
For Sale: Citrus in season
Teas: Devonshire tea $4 pp by
arrangement

by arrangement

Named after the Encore mandarins that the Smiths market commercially, Encore Grove was established in 1989 after the stopbank was moved as a result of Cyclone Bola. The flood catchment covered their original 40-year-old garden. The bare paddock they started again with is now filled with camellias, formal rose beds and perennial borders. Kerry's named roses include her favourite David Austins and specimens such as the weeping 'Charming Bells'. Many different flowering trees and shrubs feature throughout the year, with blossom trees amid daffodils in spring. Prunus and magnolia trees are followed by the roses. Plantings of proteas are being established and there is a small area of native plants. Alstromerias in various shades are predominant in the perennial borders, along with delphiniums. Kerry changes the annuals from season to season, affecting the colour scheme. Pergolas connect one garden room to the next, and water features comprise a waterfall and pond area which is lush with hostas and irises in spring. The roses extend into the autumn when the deciduous tree foliage colours up, including the golden *Robinia pseudoacacia* 'Frisia' trees throughout the garden. Bantam hens and doves are added attractions at Encore Grove. Citrus is available in season and Devonshire teas are served by prior arrangement.

EASTWOODHILL ARBORETUM
Ngatapa

Owner:
Eastwoodhill Trust Board

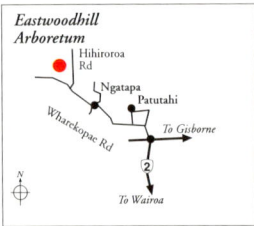

Address: 2392 Wharekopae Rd, Ngatapa
Postal: R D 2, Gisborne
Directions: 35km from Gisborne.
Travel south to Waipaoa River
roundabout, take Wharekopae Rd to
Ngatapa. Follow signposts to garden.
Phone: 0-6-863 9003
Fax: 0-6-863 9093
Email: office.eastwoodhill@xtra.co.nz
Website: www.eastwoodhill.org.nz
Open: Daily except Christmas Day &
Good Friday, 9am–5pm
Groups: Guided tours by arrangement
Fee: $8 per adult
Size: Large – 65ha (162½ acres)
Terrain: Varied
Disabled access: Trailer seating 6
disabled persons, by arrangement
Shop: Guide maps & self-guided tour
books for colour-coded walks

  & wheelchair
available
conferences only

The land for Eastwoodhill was acquired in 1910 by William Douglas Cook, who collected plant material worldwide to create a beautiful park inspired by English gardens. Today, it probably possesses the largest collection of northern hemisphere trees in the southern hemisphere. Eastwoodhill was gifted to New Zealand in 1975, its Trust Board aiming to develop the Arboretum for educational, scientific and recreational purposes. Ten years later the Friends of Eastwoodhill was formed. The Douglas Cook Centre was opened in 1992 as a venue for seminars. In spring, one hectare of daffodils bloom under the trees, with magnolias and horse chestnuts in flower. Exotic trees are dressed in spring foliage, including the lime needles of swamp cypress. Cherry and apple blossom are complemented with dogwoods, wisteria, then azaleas and rhododendrons. Almost a hectare of a more formal garden around the homestead features bulbs, perennial beds and a spring bog garden. But the most dramatic time to visit Eastwoodhill is in autumn, when over 100 different oaks, nearly as many maples, liquidambars, ashes, ginkgos, and other deciduous trees are in their full glory, contrasting with conifers and almost 300 camellias. Altogether over 3,000 introduced species are represented, and a native section has been recently established. There are colour-coded walks throughout, with maps available.

© Friars' Guide to New Zealand Gardens Open to Visit

HACKFALLS ARBORETUM
Tiniroto

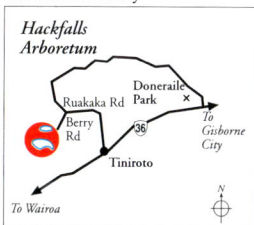

Hackfalls

Owners:
Bob and Anne Berry

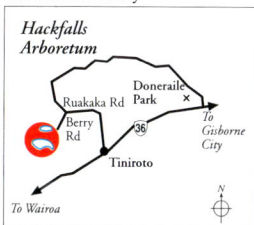

Address: Berry Rd, Tiniroto
Postal: P O Box 3, Tiniroto
Directions: Travel 61km south of
Gisborne or 44km north of Wairoa, to
Tiniroto. Then turn off SH 36 into
Ruakaka Rd. Turn left into Berry Rd.
Hackfalls at end.
Phone: 0-6-863 7091
Fax: 0-6-863 7092
Open: All year
Groups: By appointment
Fee: $5 per adult
Size: Large – 24ha (60 acres)
arboretum, plus 0.4ha (1 acre)
homestead garden
Terrain: Hilly
Lunches: 4km away at Tiniroto Tavern

  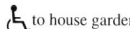 to house garden

  by arrangement

Hackfalls Station is named after a Yorkshire property with similar features. Bob has lived at Hackfalls since 1924, and from the early 'fifties has planted about 50 hectares in a unique arboretum, now a charitable trust, which with four hectares of native bush is covenanted to the QE II National Trust for Open Spaces. He has made several trips to Mexico to gather acorns, and Hackfalls has probably the biggest collection of Mexican oaks in cultivation anywhere. Many other oak specimens also feature; in all 150 different kinds spaced in rolling pastureland, allowing each to develop fully, and limbed up to enable grass to grow underneath. The oaks are complemented by over 2,000 kinds of other trees and shrubs. Two large lakes enhance the area, Kaikiore, a five-hectare wildlife sanctuary and Karangata, of 10 hectares. Anne has developed the homestead garden since 1990, including roses, climbers and many unusual alpine and herbaceous plants. She has a good knowledge of plants, evidenced by Rosemoor Garden in England, which she gifted to the Royal Horticultural Society in 1988. Hackfalls garden also features a special area for endangered New Zealand native plants, including *Muehlenbeckia astonii*, hebe species and cultivars.

BREMDALE GARDEN OF EDEN
Nuhaka

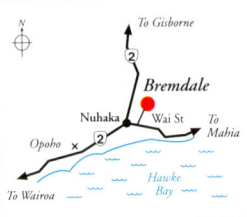

Owners:
Rose-Marie and Roger Bremner

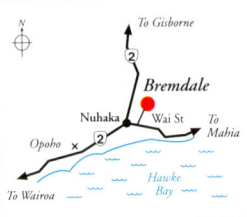

Address: Wai St, Nuhaka
Postal: P O Box 58, Nuhaka
Directions: From Wairoa, take SH 2 north for 32km to Nuhaka. Continue 0.5km to Wai St. Turn left to garden.
Phone: 0-6-837 8729
Fax: 0-6-837 8749
Email: bremdale@xtra.co.nz
Open: Sept.– Jan., 9am–5pm daily; other times & organic talks by request
Closed: Mid to 27 December
Fee: $4 per adult; groups of 10 or more $3.50 per person; $10 per family
Children: Welcome – play areas
Size: Medium – 1ha (2½ acres)
Terrain: Flat, slightly sloping
Nursery: Plants from garden
Flowerbarn & Crafts: Rustic furniture; certified organic produce; & herbal food supplements for sale

 by arrangement

Bremdale is a coastal country garden designed by Rose-Marie to create a romantic atmosphere and landscaped by Roger, featuring his manuka furniture, with stone and ponga walls. The Bremners took over Roger's parents' farm in 1978, extending the garden into a series of rooms separated by creeper-covered archways. Roses predominate, especially climbers, flowering in this mild climate for most of the year. Winter camellias are followed by drifts of daffodils and multi-coloured bearded irises. Rose-Marie bases her colour scheme on floral-art principles, each colour being enhanced by deeper shades with a touch of contrast. Soft pinks, blues, whites and lavenders with greens are the spring theme, highlighted by bolder colours. Foliage, too, is important, from broad-leafed acanthus to ajuga groundcover. There are numerous shrubs, interplanted with self-seeding annuals and perennials throughout. Fragrant plants also abound, from lilac trees to the herb garden. Birdsong from native birds is complemented by introduced birds in dovecotes and aviaries. Certified organic persimmon, kiwifruit and cash-cropping orchards adjacent to the garden provide vistas to the hills beyond. Children love the pond area with rustic gazebo set in spacious lawns, which contrasts with the densely planted areas around the house.

COTSWOLD
Napier

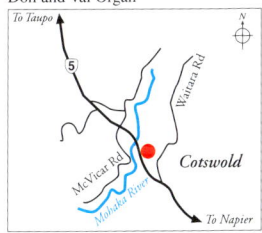

Owner:
Don and Val Organ

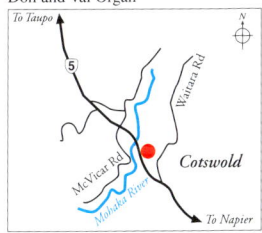

Address: Napier-Taupo Highway
Postal: Te Pohue, R D 2, Napier
Directions: From Taupo, take SH 1
south. Turn left into SH 5 & travel
86km towards Napier to garden on
left. From Napier, take SH 2 north.
Turn left into SH 5 & travel 40km
towards Taupo to garden on right.
Phone: 0-6-834 9716
Fax: 0-6-834 9716
Email: cotswoldfarm@xtra.co.nz
Open: Mid October to mid April
Closed: Mid April to mid October
Fee: $5 per adult
Size: Large – 2.4ha (over 6 acres)
Terrain: Flat to hilly
Nursery: Perennials from garden
Teas: $5 pp for groups, by arrangement
For sale: Stud sire bulls

  by arrangement

Cotswold is an English-style country garden located
on the Napier-Taupo Highway. The garden was
established when the new Tudor-style homestead was
built in 1980. Val named the garden after the part of
England she loves best. It is an informal garden of almost
two and a half hectares (more than six acres) set on a hill,
with a cherry walk leading down to the large pond and
carpark on the flat below. White swans and ducks enjoy
the pond which is crossed by a wide bridge, with a
gazebo at the opposite end surrounded by irises and arum
lilies. Doves are an added attraction. The high altitude of
450 metres (1,500 feet) above sea level means that the
garden is sometimes covered in snow in winter and spring
arrives late. But the rich autumn colour is a bonus and the
rhododendrons thrive in Cotswold's conditions. The
summer garden is very colourful with old roses, drifts of
primulas, hostas, daylilies and many other perennials,
some of which are for sale. Annuals are absent because of
the altitude, but the perennials and shrubs more than
compensate, with colour from mid October to mid April.
Morning and afternoon teas for groups only are available
by prior arrangement, and Bed and Breakfast accommodation is similarly available. Don farms a polled
Charolais stud, running the cattle in natural conditions,
and sells commercial and stud sire bulls privately.

TRELINNOE PARK
Napier

Owners:
John and Fiona Wills

Address: Old Coach Rd, R D 2, Napier
Directions: 46km from Napier on SH 5
to Taupo. Turn right into Old Coach
Rd & travel for 5.5km to garden.
Phone: 0-6-834 9703
Mobile: 025 242 8303
Fax: 0-6-834 9701
Open: Garden: all year, daily;
Café: September to end February,
daily; March to May, weekends &
public holidays by arrangement
Groups: Groups 15+ by appointment
Fee: $5 per adult, $2 per child over 12,
$12 season ticket
Size: Large – 12ha (30 acres)
Terrain: Fairly hilly
Magnolia Café: Fiona's home cooking
Nursery: Woodland trees & plants
Shop: Art & crafts
Accommodation: Tui Haven – simple
retreat at $15 per head

Trelinnoe (pronounced "Tree-linn-o") means "glade in woods". Named after the Cornwall farm where John Wills' grandfather grew up, it is appropriate for John's predominantly woodland garden, carefully landscaped since 1963, with emphasis on shape and design. The undulations of the surrounding slopes have been gradually incorporated, while retaining vistas to the hills beyond, their blues and purples mirrored within the garden. Different areas create different moods, from the expansive lawns patterned by tree shadows to the intimate walks through wooded groves, and from formal walkways edged with clipped hedging to drifts of groundcover under woodland trees. A rockery features some unusual plants, and a native arboretum with kauri grove beside Fiona's café complements the English trees planted for their autumn colour. A large collection of maples is John's favourite, and extensive use of magnolias is the highlight of spring, with dogwoods and rhododendrons followed by jacarandas, pohutukawa and hydrangeas in summer, their blues blending with the distant hills and drifts of arthropodiums like ground mist beneath. John plants in subdued tones using soft creams and whites, some parts deliberately green, with spot-colour emphasis. Plantings of perennials are increasing, especially around the five dams, which attract blue herons and other birds.

NAPIER BOTANICAL GARDENS
Napier

Owner:
Napier City Council

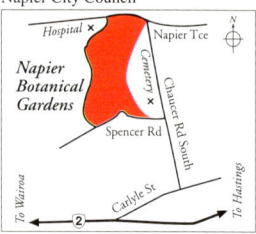

Address: Spencer Rd, Napier
Postal: Private Bag 6010, Napier
Directions: From north, take SH 2 to
Napier. Turn left into Carlyle St, then
left into Chaucer Rd Sth, & left again
into Spencer Rd to gardens on right.
From Hastings, take SH 2 to Marine
Pde. Turn left into Tennyson St, then
continue into Carlyle St. Turn right
into Chaucer Rd Sth & left into
Spencer Rd to gardens on right.
Phone: 0-6-835 7579
Fax: 0-6-835 7574
Open: All year, daily;
inner carpark closed 4pm
Fee: No charge
Size: Large – 7.2ha (18 acres)
Terrain: Hilly

 mainly

The Botanical Gardens are Napier's original park, first established in 1855. Over seven hectares (18 acres) were set aside on Barrack Reserve, now Hospital Hill, the year after the new settlement had been named Napier in commemoration of the late English general in India, Sir Charles James Napier. Many of the mature English trees date back to the arrival of the early sailing ships from Britain. The central focal point of the gardens is the stream which runs from the upper slopes down through a series of waterfalls to a pond by the main lawn. The stream bed is edged with hostas which underfurl their leaves in spring, and cinerarias which add to the colour of massed foxgloves among the arum lilies. A row of maples provides vertical accent and azaleas on the far side of the stream are a colourful spring highlight. The bedding plants, particularly along the stream, change as summer progresses, their colours set off by the sloping lawns which sweep up from either side. A perennial border lies adjacent to the main lawn and annuals create displays in both winter as well as summer. Walkways wind through the established exotic trees which bring autumn colour as the deciduous foliage turns. Other features include the developing native area, and the extensive aviary running parallel to the stream. The many varieties of birds are complemented by the flock of white doves rising like a cloud from the nearby dovecote.

KENNEDY PARK ROSE GARDENS
Napier

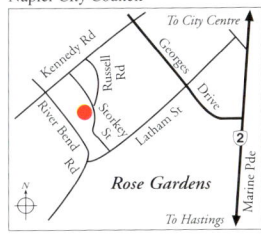

Owner:
Napier City Council

Address: Storkey St, Napier
Postal: Private Bag 6010, Napier
Directions: Take SH 2 to Napier.
From Marine Pde, turn west into
Georges Drive. Turn left into
Kennedy Rd, then left again into
Storkey St. Garden on right.
Phone: 0-6-835 7579
Fax: 0-6-835 7574
Open: All year, daily; peak display
mid November to April
Fee: No charge
Size: Medium – 0.8ha (2 acres)
Terrain: Flat

   on grass

Kennedy Park Rose Gardens were planted by the Rose Society exactly two decades after Napier's Great Earthquake of 1931, on land originally acquired by the City Council as a camping ground. The park is named after Mr C.D. Kennedy who was instrumental in the reclaiming of Napier South in the early 1900s. The design of the gardens is formal, with the rose beds arranged concentrically around a central pond and fountain which is encircled by a pergola. Climbing roses are displayed on the pergola, the inner circle interplanted with hydrangeas, adding to the summer colour. The climbers are all popular favourites such as pink 'Bantry Bay', blood-red 'Dublin Bay', the vigorous apricot 'Westerland', the creamy single 'Sally Holmes', pink 'Clair Matin', and apricot 'Compassion'. Further climbers can be seen around the perimeter of the gardens, backed by a mixed planting of mature trees including Australian eucalypts and native kowhai that bear yellow flowers in the spring. This area makes an attractive picnic spot for visitors. The main geometrical rose beds number over 180, comprising over 4,000 roses of 600 different varieties. They bloom in almost all the colours of the rainbow, from spring until autumn. In summer they are complemented by the flowering annual fibrous begonias that edge the rose beds.

TRÄDGÅRD
Pukehamoamoa, Hastings

Trädgård

Owners:
Dorothy and Robin Bell

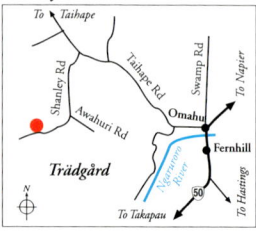

Address: Shanley Rd, Pukehamoamoa, R D 9, Hastings
Directions: 25 mins from Napier or Hastings. Take SH 50 to Fernhill. Travel north-west on Taihape Rd for 8km. Turn left into Shanley Rd. Travel 1.58km to garden on right.
Phone: 0-6-874 3708
Fax: 0-6-874 3703
Email: tradgard.garden@clear.net.nz
Open: October to April; other times by appointment
Fee: $5 per adult
Size: Large – over 6ha (16 acres)
Terrain: Flat
For sale: Small quilt projects; "Living with Quilts" can be viewed all year, by request

 by arrangement

Trädgård meaning "tree garden" is true to its Swedish name, in that half of its vast area is devoted to trees. This award-winning informal country garden covers over six hectares (16 acres). This garden was started from bare land in 1992. Half the acreage now forms the park-like grounds which feature five pergolas covered in wisteria in spring and roses in summer. Two bridges span the ponds which are home to massed waterlilies, pure-bred varieties of ducks, old-fashioned chickens and pigeons. Trees are mass-planted for effect, as are the roses, perennials and flowering shrubs. Dorothy loves roses and has planted over 500 predominantly English roses. The garden features many varieties of English trees, as well as silver birches, cherries, robinias, gleditsias and a variety of poplars, gums, and cupressus. The garden is on flat terrain, sited below the house, but guests who are not able to walk down to the garden can easily view it from the house and decks where teas are served. Or guests can drive down into the garden, as there is vehicular access provided. As well as the garden, Dorothy and Robin open their home to groups, by appointment, to view over 70 quilts, crafted by Dorothy since 1975. This "Living and Decorating with Quilts" feature is popular throughout the year, while the garden is open from October until April. Trädgård is 15 to 20 minutes west from the centre of both Napier and Hastings.

CORNWALL PARK
Hastings

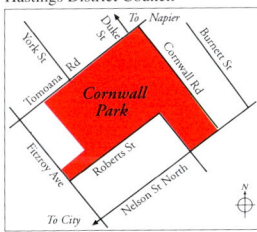

Owners:
Hastings District Council

Address: Tomoana Rd, Mahora, Hastings
Postal: Private Bag 9002, Hastings
Directions: From Hastings City, take Nelson St North to gardens on left. Main entrance on Tomoana Rd. From Napier, take Pakowhai Rd south to Hastings. Turn left into Duke St, then right into Tomoana Rd to gardens.
Phone: 0-6-878 0500
Fax: 0-6-878 0587
Open: All year, daily;
Begonia House 9am–4pm daily
Fee: No charge
Size: Large – 8.5ha (21¼ acres)
Terrain: Flat

 at Cricket Pavilion

Cornwall Park was developed in 1926 as Hastings' public garden, although the land was gifted for this purpose by Mr A.L. Williams and Mrs Lucy Warren in 1905. The mature English trees, such as the limes, elms and oaks for which the park is renowned, date back to this time. The park was laid out in traditional English style with exotic trees, spacious lawns and gardens filled with bedding displays. Special features included the roadside lake and duck pond, fountains, statuary, begonia house, and bird aviary. A stream also flows through the park. Today the concept has been extended with the addition of a native area, fernery and the recent Chinese Garden with its moon gate leading across an arched bridge to the focal point of the red pavilion. Spring attractions include the shrubberies with established camellias, Holt Begonia House, old roses in the Heritage Rose Garden, bedding displays, the azaleas that highlight the bamboo and established maples in the Chinese Garden, and the stream border of irises, cannas and massed acanthus which flower in summer. The Begonia House and bedding displays continue through summer into autumn when the mature deciduous trees colour, as do the maples and nandinas encircling the pond. Winter features include the Begonia House, and the native area which is planted in a wide range of native shrubs, groundcovers and grasses.

ORMONDS GARDEN AND NURSERY
Havelock North

Owners:
Peter and Elizabeth Ormond

Address: 189 Kahuranaki Rd, R D 14,
Havelock North
Directions: Cross river south of
Havelock North. Travel 2km to garden.
Phone: 0-6-874 7820
Fax: 0-6-874 7660
Open: 9am–5pm; 1 September to end
February, Wednesday to Sunday
except Christmas & Boxing days,
every other public holiday; March to
September every Friday to Sunday,
9am–5pm; otherwise by appointment
Fee: Group guided tours, $2 per person
Size: Medium – 1.4ha (3½ acres)
Terrain: Hilly
Nursery: Plants that grow in garden
suited to dry conditions – trees,
shrubs & perennials
Shop: Agent for Touchwood Books,
quality gifts

 limited

by arrangement

Peter Ormond has been developing the Ormond garden and nursery since 1979. It is a unique garden for hardy plants and trees that grow without watering. Only plants that survive under such conditions are grown and sold at Ormonds. Not a cactus is to be seen, despite popular misconceptions, and only a few succulents. Instead, Mediterranean and South African plants flourish, as they handle frosts as well as hot, dry conditions. Natives such as *Cordyline australis* (cabbage trees) and pittosporums grow well, as do introduced gums, oaks, magnolias and maples. Old roses survive remarkably well, although these are not Peter's favourite plants, except perhaps for the wild, rich yellow rose 'Helen Knight'. He prefers the buddleias, echiums and hardy perennials that thrive without watering, including North American *Brodiaea*, heucheras, artemisias, salvias, euphorbias, cistus, campanulas and hellebores. He grows some unusual plants, such as the butterfly or African irises of the moraea and dietes genera, as well as old-fashioned varieties including phlomis, English geraniums and eryngiums. The prevailing westerlies dry the garden, the pathways winding up the hill to superb views over the Tukituki River across pasture to the hills beyond. Peter is not expanding the garden further, but developing the detail within the boundaries already laid out.

TARANAKI

Taranaki is rich dairy land, and some of New Zealand's finest cheese is produced here. Eleven gardens are featured in the fertile Taranaki region surrounding Mt Taranaki and Egmont National Park on all sides. Many of the gardens incorporate spectacular views of the mountain, which is the focal point of Taranaki.

At Waitara is Tony and Sandy's, a suburban cottage garden of roses, cottage plants and old trees around an old cottage framed with roses. Three of the gardens are located in and around the City of New Plymouth, including Cedar Lodge Conifers, catering to the specialist conifer market.

In the centre of New Plymouth is the renowned Pukekura Park and adjacent Brooklands, featuring remnant native forest including a two thousand-year-old puriri tree, an underground fernery, rhododendron dell, lakes with rowboats, illuminated fountain and waterfall floodlit by night. On summer evenings the annual Festival of Lights is not to be missed in the Park.

Pukeiti, well-known for its rhododendrons, is located a little further out, on the foothills of Mt Taranaki. One of the two historic Queen Elizabeth II Trust gardens is also in New Plymouth – Tupare, originally planted by Sir Russell and Lady Matthews in 1932. The other is Hollard Gardens, south of the mountain, first planted by Bernard and Rose Hollard in 1929.

Early each November Taranaki holds its Rhododendron Festival, with 100 gardens taking part. A high rainfall and the alpine climate created by Mt Taranaki particularly favour the growth of rhododendrons and azaleas. To the south-west of New Plymouth on the ocean side of the mountain are two gardens: Ngamamaku, with rose garden and streamside dell, at Oakura, and the large park-like gardens of Hikurangi surrounding its lake at Okato.

West of Stratford, on the southern flank of Mt Taranaki, are the historic Hollard Gardens at Kaponga featuring mature rhododendrons and a newer garden with sweeping lawns and vistas of the nearby mountain.

South Taranaki stretches from below Stratford down the west coast towards Wanganui. In Eltham is Bridger Park set in a stream valley, making it a lovely spot for a picnic. Further south at Hawera is King Edward Park enclosed by tall hedges with its mature English trees and gardens surrounding the focal point of the lake. South Taranaki has a temperate climate and includes the fertile strip of land along the coastline down to Wanganui. Westerlies blowing off the Tasman Sea make it essential for these coastal gardens to grow shelter belts before gardening.

Scale

0   50km

Cartography by Terralink Ltd

TONY AND SANDY'S
Waitara

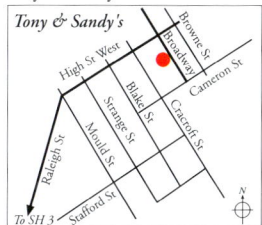

Owners:
Tony and Sandy Eva

Address: 67 Broadway, Waitara
Directions: Take SH 3 to Waitara. At Brixton, turn north into Raleigh St. At end veer right into High St West. Turn right into Broadway. Garden on right.
Phone: 0-6-754 8664
Open: October to May, by appointment only
Closed: June to September
Fee: No charge
Size: Medium – 0.2ha (½ acre)
Terrain: Flat
Nursery: Perennials & roses

 by arrangement only

Tony and Sandy's is a suburban cottage garden of roses, cottage plants and a number of old trees surrounding a very old rose framed cottage. More roses, perennials and some ornamental trees were added after 1995, when Tony and Sandy doubled their residential quarter-acre section by buying the neighbouring property. Roses are now the predominant species in the garden, including the old roses which bloom in late October and November. Hybrid musks soften the fenceline along the driveway, and more roses climb the pergolas and archways. Roses, such as the David Austin apricot rose 'Sweet Juliet', are obviously Sandy's favourites, along with the clematis, rhododendrons and maples. Special features in this garden include the mature trees, hedges, ponga-edged walkways and trellis fencing. Sandy's colour scheme is mainly in pinks, creams and lavenders. These colours predominate in the spring when the cornus and magnolias blossom, followed by the roses, delphiniums and other perennials in the full borders in summer. Maples are the main attraction in autumn. There is a dovecote and millstone in the garden, and Sandy plans to add a water feature. Roses and perennials from the garden are for sale, and morning or afternoon tea can be served by arrangement. Visitors are welcome to wander the grassy pathways and picnic under the shade trees.

CEDAR LODGE CONIFERS
New Plymouth

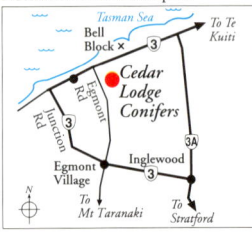

Owners:
Noeline and David Sampson

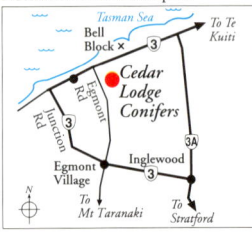

Address: 63 Egmont Rd, Bell Block,
R D 2, New Plymouth
Directions: Take SH 3 north of New
Plymouth. Travel towards Bell Block.
Turn right into Egmont Road, Conifer
Lodge 1km from SH 3 on left.
Phone: 0-6-755 0369
Fax: 0-6-755 0319
Email: sampson@conifers.co.nz
Website: www.conifers.co.nz
Open: All year, Monday to Saturday,
8am–5pm; Sunday 10am–4pm
Groups: As above
Fee: No charge
Size: Large – 2ha (5 acres) plus
nursery
Terrain: Flat & pathed hillside
Nursery: Conifers – largest NZ range
and extensive range worldwide;
catalogue & mail order available

  mostly

This display garden demonstrates the tremendous range of conifers available. The slope behind the nursery was planted in 1978, and has an ideal climate for conifers: wet enough for a wide variety from Siberian to tropical. Conifers vary in growth rates, size, shape, form, and colour. The Sampsons mass-plant in colours which change through the seasons, deepening in the winter from greens to mauves, and from yellows to bronzes. Then the new, soft, pale green spring growth of firs and spruces lightens up and freshens the landscape. Favourites include the pale blue *Picea pungens glauca* and yellow-tipped creamy *Cryptomeria japonica* 'Sekkan Sugi'. Sizes range from low prostrate forms to bun-shaped, globose, weeping and tall columnar shapes. These show a diversity of textures, from dainty to pendulous. The miniatures are special, such as *Chamaecyparis obtusa* 'Densa' or the delicate ground cover *Cedrus deodara* 'Prostrata'; the smallest conifer in the world is our dwarf rimu. Many other New Zealand natives fall into the conifer category, including totara, kauri, miro and rimu. Exotics include both the coast and Sierra redwoods – the largest and the tallest trees in the world – as well as spruces, abies and pines. There are 800 different conifers available at Cedar Lodge, with topiary variations. David and Noeline import seed and grow all conifers possible in our climate.

TUPARE
New Plymouth

Manager:
Greg Rine, QE II National Trust

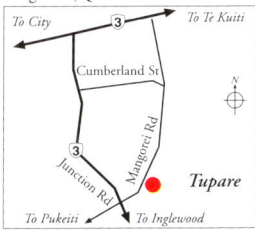

Address: 487 Mangorei Rd, New Plymouth
Postal: P O Box 40, Kaponga
Directions: From New Plymouth, travel south on SH 3. Turn left at cross-roads into Mangorei Rd. Garden 400m on right.
Phone: 0-6-758 5893 or 0-7-758 6480
Fax: 0-6-758 5893 or 0-7-758 6353
Email: hollardg@clear.net.nz
Open: All year, 9am–5pm
Fee: Adult, gold coin donation; children free
Size: Large – 3.6ha (9 acres)
Terrain: Steep & some flat areas
Functions: Dinner by arrangement
Accommodation: Self-contained cottage

during Rhododendron Festival in November

Tupare, meaning "a garland of flowers", was begun in 1932 on a steep hillside wilderness of gorse and blackberry, the boisterous Waiwhakaiho River forming the eastern boundary, with farmland beyond. In 1984 this large, elegant English-style garden became one of two heritage gardens managed by the Queen Elizabeth II National Trust. The Chapman-Taylor designed Tudor-style home of the original owners, the Matthews family, is now a functions centre, and the cottage, built in similar style, is available for accommodation. Tupare is noted for its collection of stately trees. Significant specimens include a Judas tree (*Cercis siliquastrum*), tulip tree (*Liriodendron tulipifera*) and one of the largest dawn redwoods (*Metasequoia glyptostroboides*) outside its native China. The displays of maples, flowering cherries and magnolias are also popular in the spring and autumn. The formal Elizabeth Garden with its goldfish pond and fountain, Cliff's Cascade which spills down the hill in a series of pools, and the many paths that follow the contours of the land, all contribute to the structure for a rich plant collection. In late spring white bracts from the Dove or handkerchief tree (*Davidia involucrata*) float down to the rhododendrons in the Dell, underplanted with woodland anemones. Native trees and ferns also feature year round at Tupare.

PUKEKURA PARK AND BROOKLANDS
New Plymouth

Owner:
New Plymouth District Council

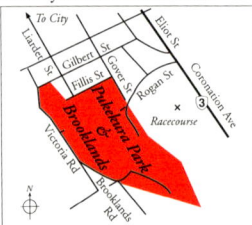

Address: Fillis St, New Plymouth
Postal: Private Bag 2025, New Plymouth
Directions: From City, take Liardet St south to Fillis St. From south, take SH 3 & turn left into Rogan St. Carparks off Fillis, Rogan, Victoria, Brooklands Rds.
Phone: 0-6-759 6060
Mobile: 025 744 961
Fax: 0-6-759 6074
Email: gouldb@npdc.govt.nz
Website: www.newplymouth.nz.com
Open: All year, daily, 8am to dusk
Groups: Guided tours available
Fee: No charge (guided tours at cost)
Size: Large – 50ha (125 acres)
Terrain: Flat & hilly
Refreshments: At Tea House on site
Festival: Festival of Lights, nightly, Christmas to early February

    to flat areas

Pukekura Park was opened in 1876, pathways laid and the first trees planted. The Park was named "Pukekura" in 1908, after the stream that runs through it. This was dammed to form the lake, crossed by Poet's Bridge since 1884, and with clinker-style rowing boats available for hire since around 1890. The second lake was formed in 1893 and the illuminated fountain installed in 1955. The Rhododendron Dell, now featuring over 400 varieties and species, was established, and three caverns of the underground Fernery opened in 1928, with the fourth added in 1939 to display subtropical plants. Further plant collections in the Park today include azaleas, vireyas, camellias, acers, magnolias, woodland bog plants, aloes, a pinetum and herbaceous borders. Adjoining is Brooklands estate of almost 22 hectares which was gifted by Newton King's family in 1934. It contains the chimney of the original homestead, The Gables – a colonial hospital built in 1847, exotic trees such as the ginkgo planted in 1841, and bush walks through a remnant of native forest which includes a 2,000-year-old puriri. Brooklands Bowl, complete with amphitheatre and stage, was opened in 1958, and the illuminated waterfall by the lake was switched on in 1970. A historic water wheel commemorates the Park's centennial, and during the Festival of Lights every summer the Park and trees are lit up at night by thousands of lights.

NGAMAMAKU
Oakura

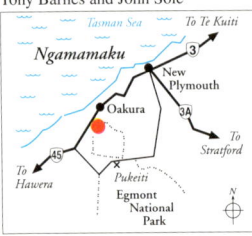

Owners:
Tony Barnes and John Sole

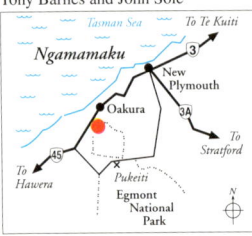
Ngamamaku

Tasman Sea — To Te Kuiti
New Plymouth
Oakura 3A
To Stratford
To Hawera 45 Pukeiti
Egmont National Park
N

Address: 1521 Main South Rd,
Oakura, R D 4, New Plymouth
Directions: Take SH 45 west from
New Plymouth. Travel 4km past
Oakura. Ngamamaku on left, next to
Egmont National Park.
Phone: 0-6-752 7873
Fax: 0-6-752 7873
Email: tony.john@xtra.co.nz
Open: During October/November
Rhododendron Festival; & 1 August
to 31 March, by appointment
Fee: $3 per adult
Size: Medium – 1.2ha (3 acres)
Terrain: Flat & sloping
Functions: Available for functions by
prior arrangement
Accommodation: Homestay by prior
arrangement

   mostly

by arrangement

Ngamamaku, meaning "the Place of the Tree Ferns", is a richly historic site adjoining Egmont National Park. Battles were fought here during the 1864 Wars, and pre-European stone walling is still a feature. It was later the site of an air force radar base and barracks during World War II. The present garden, with rural views to the Tasman Sea from its elevated position, was begun from nothing in 1986. Ngamamaku is now very sheltered and secluded, being developed on different levels as separate garden rooms, combining to create a harmonious whole. A natural bush stream runs through the centre of the garden, the streamside dell planted with a wide range of damp-loving perennials in delicate, restful colours. Magnolias, acers, azaleas, rhododendrons, camellias and hostas in great variety are feature plants, combining successfully with the bush and mamaku tree ferns. Native birds abound, and pathways wind through the bush, across the stream and up to a tranquil pond area. A formal paved rose garden, a memorial to John's parents, features a central statue and seats within a circular ponga pergola. Nearby is a large circular aviary. A rockery and pool are screened by a curved avenue of *Thuja pyramidalis*. A unique arched summer house opens on to a formal lawn, enclosed by roses and box hedges leading to a mirrored pergola. Adjacent is a natural native nikau palm bush walk.

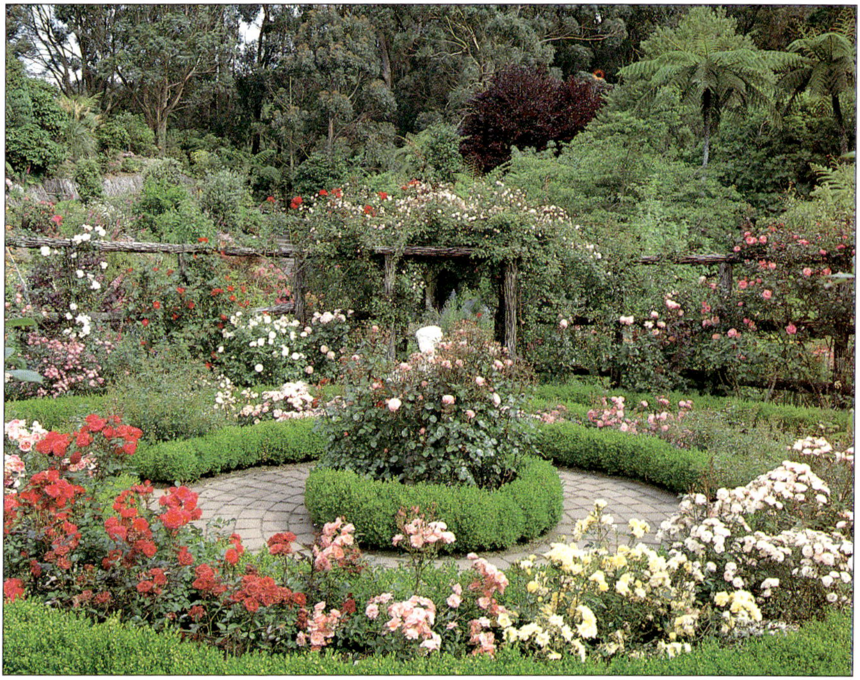

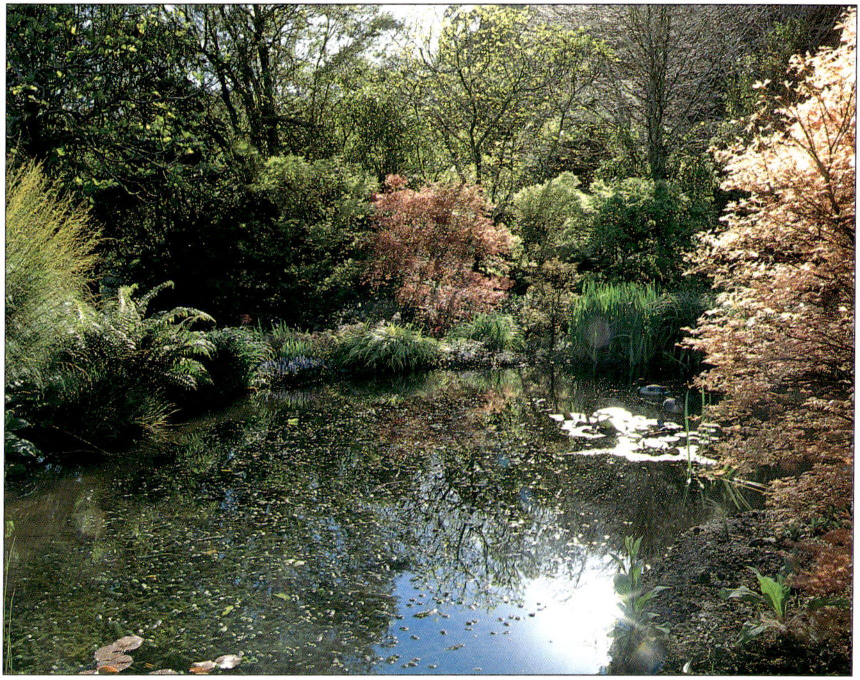

PUKEITI
New Plymouth

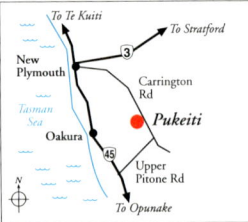

Owner:
Pukeiti Rhododendron Trust

Address: 2290 Carrington Rd, R D 4, New Plymouth
Directions: Travel 20km from City on Carrington Rd. Garden on right.
Phone: 0-6-752 4141 (24 hours)
Fax: 0-6-752 4151
Email: pukeiti@pukeiti.org.nz
Open: All year, except Christmas Day; 9am–5pm October–March, daily; 10am–3pm April–September daily
Groups: As above or by appointment
Fee: $6 per adult, April–September; $8 per adult, October–March
Size: Large – 20ha (50 acres) of garden in 360ha (900 acres) of land
Terrain: Undulating – 5-seat buggy available, only by prior booking
Nursery: Rhododendrons, azaleas, camellias & woodland plants
Restaurant: The Gatehouse on site, available for weddings & functions
Shop: Souvenirs, crafts & other gifts
mostly

Pukeiti means "little hill", referring to its site on the foothills of Mt Taranaki. The first 150 of the present 900 acres were purchased by Douglas Cook in 1951, and a Trust was formed by 25 rhododendron enthusiasts to develop the rhododendron park. Pukeiti now boasts the largest collection of species and hybrid rhododendrons and azaleas in New Zealand. These flower all year, vireya tropical rhododendrons in late summer, autumn and winter, with hardy types continuing in spring and early summer. A covered walk and Perrott House provide shelter for the extensive vireya collection, with orchids and other rare plants. Hybrids are scattered throughout the hills and valleys of Pukeiti, concentrated in the Hybrid Block, with New Zealand-raised hybrids in Stead Block, and large-leafed species in the Valley of the Giants. Founders Garden features native planting, with countless complementary shrubs and plants flowering throughout the year, and rhododendrons underplanted with many damp-loving specimens. Exotic trees include magnolias, viburnums, camellias, cornus, prunus, acers and kalmias. The gardens are surrounded by native rainforest with bush walks throughout, and a rimu plantation flanks Pukeiti Hill. Two garden pools, with viewing platforms, are filled by natural mountain streams that also power a water wheel, which pumps water to the property.

HIKURANGI
Okato

Owner:
Barbara Williams

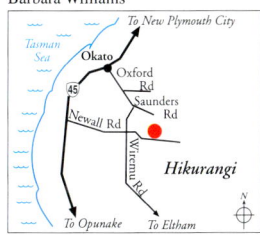

Address: 143 Newall Rd, Okato, R D 37, New Plymouth
Directions: Travel south of New Plymouth to west of Mt Taranaki, on SH 45. Turn left at Okato into Oxford Rd, then right into Saunders Rd. Turn right again into Wiremu Rd, then left into Newall Rd. Hikurangi on left.
Phone: 0-6-752 4058
Mobile: 025 451 422
Fax: 0-6-752 4058
Email: barbiewilly@hotmail.com
Open: Mid October to May, daily; 10am–8pm or dark
Groups: By appointment
Fee: $3 per adult
Size: Large – 2.8ha (7 acres)
Terrain: Varied – hills & vales
Functions: Wedding venue

 x three   partial

by arrangement

Hikurangi, meaning "tall mountain", is an extensive park-like garden with a wonderful backdrop of Mt Taranaki. Pioneered in 1904 from virgin bush, this diverse garden is still being established by Barbara, who has lived here since the early 1950s. Hikurangi comprises a drier area in the older part, with historic points of interest, and newer areas including water gardens. Barbara likes to take her visitors on a tour beginning in the historic 1906 woolshed, which houses a small museum, then walking through the large developing native plantings which include lancewood, pohutukawa and many rare named species. Pathways wind down around the expansive lake which features views of Mt Taranaki, ducks and smaller pond areas. Walkways then continue up past the stream to an old tunnel where a mill supplied electric power in 1906. Glow-worms are an evening attraction along the banks leading to the tunnel. Paths lead up through an alpine rockery to the old garden around the house, then down again to a popular wedding venue with wide grassed walkways between beds of perennials, with azaleas, rhododendrons and a ponga pergola. Colours change with the seasons, camellias and daffodils announcing spring, then lilies, dahlias and annuals flowering in summer, followed by autumn chrysanthemums. A woodland area with tall tree ferns is underplanted with bog plants.

HOLLARD GARDENS
Kaponga

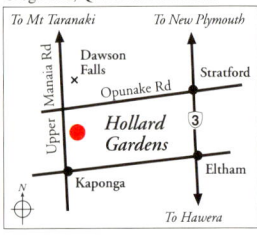

Manager:
Greg Rine, QE II National Trust

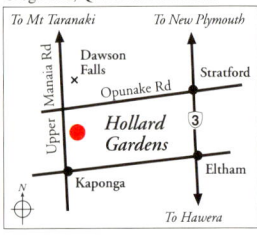

Address: Upper Manaia Rd, Kaponga
Postal: P O Box 40, Kaponga
Directions: From Stratford, travel
14km west along Opunake Rd. Turn
left into Upper Manaia Rd.
Phone: 0-6-764 6544
After Hours: 0-6-764 6616
Fax: 0-6-764 6544
Email: hollardg@clear.net.nz
Open: All year, 9am–5pm
Groups: By appointment preferred
Fee: Adult, gold coin donation;
children free
Size: Large – 4ha (10 acres)
Terrain: Easy contour
Nursery: In spring – rhododendrons
& perennials

  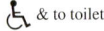 & to toilet

This Queen Elizabeth II National Trust heritage garden is located close to Mt Taranaki, in a mild climate with fertile volcanic soils suited to a variety of native and exotic plants, especially rhododendrons. The late Bernard Hollard collected rare, unusual and attractive plants, particularly species, resulting in a comprehensive range that provides year-round interest. The original two-hectare Old Garden, with its narrow winding paths, was created within a canopy of native lemonwood, tawa and totara in 1927, enclosing tiers of azaleas, camellias and rhododendrons underplanted with perennials and bog plants. The New Garden, with its sweeping lawns and views of the nearby mountain, was developed in 1982. In the same year, Bernard and Rose Hollard gifted the gardens, which represent their lifetimes' work, to the National Trust. Both exotic and native plant conservation of rare and endangered species is continued today. Bernard Hollard's well-known red rhododendron 'Kaponga', and many more, provide vibrant spring displays, along with an old large-leafed *Rhododendron macabeanum*, a mature *R. nuttallii x lindleyi*, azalea hedges, and mollis azaleas. The bog garden is massed with lush spring growth and cardiocrinums. Further features include old-fashioned perennials, clivias and one of the biggest *Pinus radiata aurea* in the country. A bush walk leads through king ferns beneath nikau, and a rare native passion vine climbs tawa.

114

BRIDGER PARK
Eltham

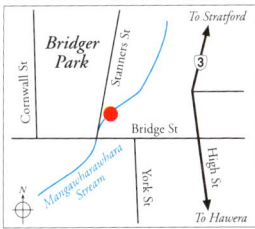

Owner:
South Taranaki District Council

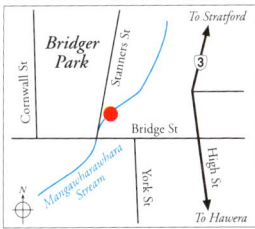

Address: Stanners St, Eltham
Postal: P O Box 902, Hawera
Directions: From Hawera take SH 3 north to Eltham. Turn left into Bridge St, then 1st right into Stanners St. Garden on right. Or from New Plymouth, take SH 3 south to Eltham. Turn right into Bridge St, then as above to Bridger Park.
Phone: 0-6-278 8010
Mobile: 025 462 622
Fax: 0-6-278 8757
Email: john.sargeant@stdc.govt.nz
Open: All year, daily, daylight hours
Groups: As above
Fee: No charge
Size: Medium – 0.8ha (2 acres)
Terrain: Hilly with steps & tracks

Bridger Park is a secluded dell within walking distance of Eltham village. Originally planted in the 1940s, it was named after a prominent councillor of the time. The focal point is Mangawharawhara Stream running through it, bordered by mature kowhai and a bank of established rhododendrons interplanted with native ponga tree ferns. The bank is intersected by metal/gravel pathways, that wind up to the Stanners Street entrance, softened by camellias and grevilleas. The opposite bank of the stream is a grassy lawn sloping up to an ivy-edged garden of rosemary, native flaxes and hebes, punctuated by prunus trees. Picnic tables and seats are provided beneath the cherry trees which offer shade on hot summer days. Steps lead up to the surrounding streets, the Bridge Street entrance edged with camellias and variegated native flaxes. Spring features include the camellias and the yellow native kowhai which attract the tui, as do the flax flowers in summer. The pink prunus blossom is complemented in spring by magnolias dotted throughout the park. Then the red rhododendrons bloom and rosemary with seasonal groundcover. In addition to the kowhai, ponga, hebes and flaxes, native species include pittosporums and an old kauri at the far end beside the stream where agapanthus add their colour in summer. A weir is being installed in the stream, which will enhance the dell as a pleasant picnic spot.

KING EDWARD PARK
Hawera

Owner:
South Taranaki District Council

Address: High St, Hawera
Postal: P O Box 902, Hawera
Directions: Take SH 3 to Hawera.
Turn east into High St. Main gates to
King Edward Park at corner of High
St & Camberwell Rd.
Phone: 0-6-278 8010
Mobile: 025 462 622
Fax: 0-6-278 8757
Email: john.sargeant@stdc.govt.nz
Open: All year, daily, daylight hours
Groups: As above
Fee: No charge
Size: Medium – 1.2ha (3 acres)
Terrain: Flat
Barbecues: 50 cent coin-operated gas
barbecue available
Attractions: Pétanque court,
children's playground & pirate ship

& gas BBQ

Named in the early 1900s after King Edward VII, the park was gifted to Hawera by the early settlers. Its predominant features now include mature English trees and the formal rose garden. The original herbaceous and shrub borders have been revamped and are complemented by the formal annual beds encircling *Magnolia grandiflora* and enclosed by hedging. The focal point of the park is the lake which is only 560mm deep, fringed by weeping willows and featuring ducks and a model boat. Many park seats surround it, enclosed by semi-circular hedges and backed by prunus trees, providing wind-free nooks for relaxing. High hedges separate the park from the road, and long grassy avenues lined with mature trees are petalled with rhododendrons and azaleas underplanted with drifts of forget-me-nots. Magnolias shade further azaleas, cinerarias and forget-me-nots, creating a pink and blue colour scheme. The Goodson Memorial Garden features a sea of blue forget-me-nots beneath pink azaleas in spring. The main entrance is graced by gates erected in commemoration of the Hawera Industrial Exhibition of 1904. A statue of an energetic early settler, Arthur Albert Fantham, who died the same year, is sited adjacent to the scented garden which is shaded by a pergola covered in wisteria and clematis. Nearby is the Chinese Garden and a flax garden. Other natives include mature puriri and some hedges.

Wanganui, Rangitikei and Manawatu

We feature 17 gardens from these regions which extend from Waiouru down through the Rangitikei River Valley to Wanganui on the west coast, south of Taranaki, and the Manawatu, including the inland City of Palmerston North.

On the west coast at Wanganui are two beautiful parks. Virginia Lake, planted with English trees early this century, features an indoor Winter Garden and a fountain illuminated with coloured lights at night. Bason Botanic Gardens are a newer horticultural highlight, with roads intersecting the gardens surrounding the central lake and incorporating a historic homestead garden and contemporary conservatory complex. Fourteen kilometres up Whanganui River is Ohorere with its historic trees, heritage roses and river views. The restored paddle steamer, *Waimarie*, will take visitors on a memorable river trip to this garden, where Devonshire teas are available and accommodation can be arranged.

Immediately north of Waiouru is the Desert Road, leading through a unique alpine area created by volcanic activity. Lookouts provide opportunities to admire this beautiful barren landscape with its desert flora, petrified wood, and backdrop of mountains in the Tongariro National Park. Severe winters, with snow at times, and fairly cool summers provide ideal conditions for growing alpine specimens. Cold autumn conditions favour good autumn foliage, especially seen among the mature trees in the northernmost garden, Waitoka. Other features at Waitoka include a native alpine garden and rose garden, and rhododendrons also flourish in these conditions.

South of Taihape is the region encompassing the Rangitikei River Valley, with a diverse landscape from steep hill country to lush alluvial plains and river valleys. The Rangitikei River carves its course through a plateau, creating extensive terraces and providing rich farming land. The Ruahine Range rises to the east. There are many renowned gardens in this area, as the climatic conditions admirably suit rhododendrons and other plants that enjoy cool nights and summers, a reliable rainfall and above-average altitude.

There are three gardens up in the hills north of Kimbolton, the two-hectare Ruapuna Park at Rangiwahia, the well-known rhododendron garden at Cross Hills and the nearby Heritage Park Kimbolton featuring rhododendrons planted round the focal point of a lake. South of Hunterville on State Highway 1 is The Ridges, with its stunning rhododendron driveway planted in 1924. On the road to Feilding is a woodland garden, Westoe, surrounding the historic home in Italianate style.

Eight Manawatu gardens begin with the classical English terraced garden south of Sanson, planted to accompany the historic home of Pukemarama. Shady Acres is a newer garden featuring roses, a camellia walk and aviary. O'Tara Birch Gardens, located at Rongotea, specialises in dahlias, and de Hoeve 23 is an older garden where roses predominate. In Palmerston North are the Victoria Esplanade Gardens bordering the Manawatu River. English trees date back to the turn of the century and other features include the Rose Garden, Conservatory, Palm Drive, duck pond, aviary and Riverside Walkway. Bloemendaal is a mature city garden with woodland areas surrounding three ponds, while Greenhaugh features trees from the 19th century in a semi-formal country setting. The final garden in the Manawatu is The Herb Farm at Ashhurst comprising 14 theme gardens with herbs as the predominant species.

National Park

48

. Mt Ngauruhoe 2291

Scale

0   30km

Whakapapa
Village

4

2797 . Mt Ruapehu

Cartography by Terralink Ltd

1

Horopito

Lake
Moawhango

Raetihi

Ohakune

49

Tangiwai

Waiouru

Pipiriki

Whanganui R

1

Jerusalem

Moawhango

4

91

Mataroa

Taihape

Utiku

Mangaweka

Ohingaiti

90

88

92

89

WANGANUI

Hunterville

Rangiwahia

3

95

Rata

Rewa

93

RUAHINE

Turakina

1

94

Marton

54

Kimbolton

96

Bulls

Cheltenham

Ohakea

Sanson

Feilding

104

Ashhurst

Rangitikei River

99

Bunnythorpe

3

Tangimoana

97

Rongotea

103

Woodville

PALMERSTON NORTH

100

102

Himatangi

98

101

Mangatainoka

Foxton
Beach

Linton

Pahiatua

Manawatu
River

Foxton

56

Tokomaru

Shannon

N

BASON BOTANIC GARDENS
Wanganui

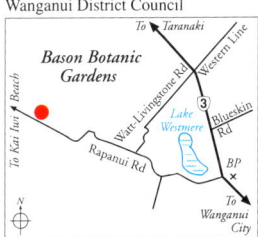

Owner:
Wanganui District Council

Address: Rapanui Rd, Wanganui
Postal: P O Box 637, Wanganui
Directions: From Wanganui, take Great North Rd (SH 3) north towards Kai Iwi. At service station, turn left into Rapanui Rd. Travel 5.5km to Bason Botanic Gardens on right. Sealed roads throughout Gardens.
Phone: 0-6-342 9472
Fax: 0-6-349 0539
Email: erics@wanganui.govt.nz
Open: All year, daily; 7.30am–dusk; conservatory open 9am–4.30pm
Fee: No charge
Size: Large – 25ha (62½ acres)
Terrain: Mainly flat, partly hilly
Picnics: Complimentary gas BBQs
Conservatory, Orchid House & Fern House: Open as above

🚭 🚻 🪑 gas BBQs

♿ conservatory & homestead garden

Stanley and Blanche Bason gifted their farm in 1966, and homestead with traditional English-style garden after Stan's death 10 years later. The roading network was laid throughout the reserve in 1971, thousands of trees and shrubs planted, and Mowhanau Stream dammed to create a lake on the valley floor. The architecturally designed Boothby Bush House and Lookout Tower were erected in 1979, and two years later the award-winning contemporary conservatory complex was built. The Gardens were opened officially in 1982. Springtime features camellia collections, large drifts of daffodils, the iris garden and semi-mature magnolias and flowering cherries. A phoenix palm-lined avenue leads to the homestead garden which peaks in summer with roses, old-fashioned perennials, and a gazebo with views over the lake to hills beyond. Autumn colour is displayed by English trees interplanted through-out the reserve with indigenous species and conifers such as the Norfolk Island pines beginning to dominate the skyline. A group of native hebes features beside the Fern House, and semi-mature native trees include kauri, rimu and those in the revegetation areas of coastal forest, alpine, swampland and rainforest. Other features include the rockery bank planted in succulents, circular bricked herb garden, blood lilies, protea display, fuchsia corner, pergola, bank of marguerite daisies, and the birdlife.

VIRGINIA LAKE RESERVE
Wanganui

Owner:
Wanganui District Council

Address: Great North Rd, Wanganui
Postal: P O Box 637, Wanganui
Directions: From City, take Victoria
Ave north. Continue up St Johns Hill
into Great North Rd (SH 3). Virginia
Lake Reserve on right. Carpark just
past lake.
Phone: 0-6-349 0001
Fax: 0-6-349 0539
Email: erics@wanganui.govt.nz
Open: All year, daily, daylight hours;
conservatories 10am–4pm
Fee: No charge
Size: Large – 20ha (50 acres)
Terrain: Mainly flat, some hilly areas
Refreshments: Restaurant & shop
across road from Lake carpark

   mostly

 complimentary gas BBQ
& coin-operated fountain

Originally named Rotokawau, Maori for "lake of black shags", Virginia Lake was renamed to remind the early settlers of Virginia Waters in Surrey, England. From 1874 it provided water to Wanganui, the roadside gazebo now sited on the disused pumphouse from that era. The band rotunda, opened on the far side of the lake in 1912, is now a lookout framed by exotic trees, with daffodil lawn adjacent. Virginia Lake was officially opened two years later, laid out in Victorian style according to the plan that won the Beautifying Society's competition. The design divided the park into plants from different countries. English species included the mature ashes, liquidambars, oaks and copper beeches that now provide autumn colour. The Australian section resulted in good specimens of gums and wattles. Indigenous species also predominate, with the Kauri Grove, rimu, totara, and sub-storey such as native ferns. Statuary includes two concrete lions, remnants from the ornamental gates that graced the original entrance beside the pumphouse. But the avenue of fine phoenix palms still lines the Virginia Road entrance. The art deco Winter Gardens conservatory was opened in 1940, and the oriental Moongate Garden added in 1974. Other attractions include the walk-in free-flight aviary, and the 1971 Higginbottom fountain in waterlily design, with coloured lights emphasising aesthetic foliage and special features by night.

OHORERE
Wanganui

Owners:
Terry and Carol Delaney

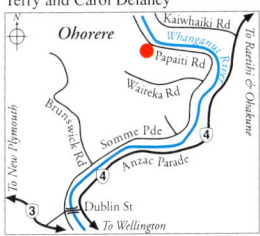

Address: 701 Papaiti Road, Wanganui
Directions: From City, take Somme
Pde along river for 14km, continuing
into Papaiti Rd. Garden on left. Or
arrive by paddle steamer, the *Waimarie*.
Phone: 0-6-342 5848
Fax: 0-6-342 5848
Email: ohorere@xtra.co.nz
Website: www.gardenhomestay.co.nz
Open: Sept.–March, daily, 10am to
5pm; April to August by appointment
Groups: Bus tours & groups welcome
Fee: $3 per adult; children no charge
Size: Medium– 0.6ha (1½ acres)
Terrain: Mainly flat, some slopes
Refreshments: Devonshire teas $2.50;
lunches available; dinners booked
Nursery: Variety of perennials, roses
Shop: Ohorere potpurri, garden trugs,
jams, preserves & produce

Ohorere is Maori for "big surprise", as it must have been over the years to find such an established garden 14 kilometres up the Whanganui River. The garden is the original house block of the almost 90-hectare (224-acre) farm, which was settled in 1860. Many of the existing trees were planted at that time, including an enormous gnarled old Satsuma plum tree that still bears fruit, despite being flooded in 1904 and again in 1990. A large cherry tree shades the parking area, and Devonshire teas and lunches are available on the verandah of the villa overlooking the roses and hollyhocks in the garden, with the river beyond. A mature ginkgo tree overshadows the gazebo where teas can be served, with vistas across the sunken lawn which is popular for weddings. The white 'Wedding Day' roses climbing the gazebo are complemented by more roses and perennials edging the lawn, with views over the Whanganui River. The 30-metre rose pergola links this area to another gazebo for secluded contemplation of the river views. A woodland walk takes visitors through native bush to a pond surrounded with hostas, irises and primulas. A Japanese bamboo water pipe drips into the pool beneath it. The house lawn then connects back through a bush walk and past many camellias to the verandah again. Other predominant species are the 200 heritage roses and the rhododendrons in the woodland with hundreds of spring bulbs and native birds.

WAITOKA GARDENS
Taihape

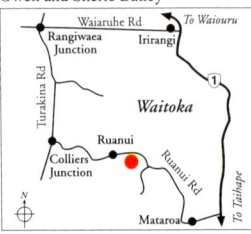

Owners:
Owen and Sherie Batley

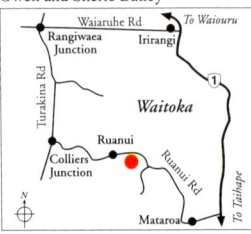

Address: Ruanui Rd, R D 1, Taihape
Directions: From Taihape, take SH 1 north for 3km. Turn left into Mataroa Rd, then right into Ruanui Rd. Travel 10km to Waitoka Gardens on left
Phone: 0-6-388 1112
Fax: 0-6-388 7822
Email: batley.o@xtra.co.nz
Open: 1 October to 31 May, daily, 10am–5pm
Groups: By appointment
Fee: $7 per adult for year pass
Size: Large – 2ha (5 acres)
Terrain: Hilly
Nursery: Cardiocrinum, rhodohypoxis, hosta, gunnera, bergenia, ligularia, peltiphyllum, tricyrtis, desfontainea, leptonella, olearia, campanula, spirea, potentilla, luzula, dwarf conifers, etc

  mostly

English trees planted in 1915, when the homestead was built, provide a framework for Waitoka Gardens today. Spacious lawns unify the gardens, incorporating views to the surrounding hills and mountains. Mature exotic trees, including copper beech, weeping elm, lindens, monkey puzzle and a strawberry tree, are complemented by native bush areas featuring native mistletoe. Owen's favourite is his native alpine garden, while Sherie's is her rose garden. Spring begins with camellias, and masses of bulbs in the woodland garden, shaded by the mature English trees. Rhododendrons provide splashes of spring colour, followed by the old roses which can be viewed from the schist patio where a pergola is clad in 'Wedding Day'. Other features include the formal vegetable garden, the agapanthus collection, cardiocrinums, and of course the native birdlife which is attracted to all the trees. The woodland garden displays shade-loving perennials and shrubs, while in the gully a natural spring flows into two small fish ponds where waterlilies flower in summer. Sited at 670 metres above sea level, the gardens enjoy the cold Taihape climate which produces good autumn colour on the deciduous trees. Drifts of autumn crocuses and cyclamens accompany the late-flowering hydrangeas and early hellebores. Austrian horticulturist, Toby, propagates plants for the well-laid out nursery and trims the topiary.

RUAPUNA PARK
Rangiwahia

Owners:
Ngaire and Alan Hancock

Address: Te Parapara Rd,
Rangiwahia, R D 54, Kimbolton
Directions: 2km north of Rangiwahia,
turn right into Te Parapara Rd.
Phone: 0-6-328 2855
Open: Garden: all year, by appointment
Museum: open by appointment
Groups: By appointment
Fee: $5 per adult
Size: Large – 2ha (5 acres)
Terrain: Mainly flat
Nursery: Perennials from garden eg:
trilliums, fritillarias & *Cardiocrinum
giganteum*
Museum: Granny's Cottage Museum
with colonial cottage of memorabilia
& vintage farm machinery, including
10 working stationary engines

   mostly
by arrangement

Sited at an altitude of 600 metres, Ruapuna Park features an alpine rockery and other frost-hardy plantings. A registered totara tree, almost 1,000 years old, stands amid a woodland area underplanted with large-leafed rhododendron species. Camellias and spring bulbs, including red tulips and trilliums, are followed by a blazing bed of azaleas, then a bank of David Austin roses. Giant lily-like *Cardiocrinum giganteum* flower around Christmas, followed by a stream bank of fuchsias. Two ponds lead into the "moat" spanned by arched bridges. Gunneras, hostas, irises and cerise primulas flourish around the edges, with heaths and heathers growing on an island of clay. Alan was brought up here, his grandfather having farmed the land since 1886. Revamped and expanded since the early 1960s, the resulting parklike garden retains views to the snowcapped Ruahine Range. Alan is keen on conifers, and is also increasing his collection of 20 native olearias, along with acers that survive frost. Stepping stones intersect a garden planted with ornamental grasses, rushes and sedges. Other features include a laburnum archway, a snow gum growing horizontally, two original golden willows underplanted with drifts of blue forget-me-nots and pink primulas, and birdlife, such as pigeons, doves and an aviary of zebra finches, quail, and canaries. Granny's Cottage Museum is adjacent.

CROSS HILLS GARDENS
Kimbolton

Owners:
Rodney and Faith Wilson

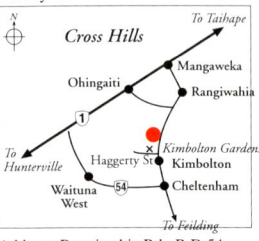

Address: Rangiwahia Rd, R D 54,
Kimbolton
Directions: Take SH 54 to Cheltenham.
Turn into Kimbolton Rd. Travel 14km
to Kimbolton, then continue 5km to
Cross Hills Gardens on left.
Phone: 0-6-328 5797
Fax: 0-6-328 5773
Email: crosshills@xtra.co.nz
Websites: www.crosshills.co.nz & friars.
co.nz/gardens/pages/crosshills.html
Open: Sept.–May, daily, 10.30am–5pm
Groups: Large groups by appointment
Fee: $7 per adult; $1 per child 12
years & over; group concessions
Size: Large – 7.2ha (18 acres)
Terrain: Rolling
Garden café: Oct./Nov., or by request
Nursery: Rhododendrons & azaleas;
mail order nationwide; catalogue $5;
flower souvenirs, videos

This park-like rhododendron garden was developed from the early 1970s by the Wilson family. It now boasts over 2,000 varieties of rhododendrons and azaleas which peak during October and November. Rodney's favourites are the hardy German hybrids and the unusual standards that his father, Eric, originally developed. These standard *R. yakushimanum* are very popular in smaller gardens. Rhododendrons cover the full range of the colour spectrum, more so than other plants, Rodney coordinating them, such as planting pinks with lavenders and purples with oranges. But Cross Hills is not just rhododendrons. In spring, the cherry blossom, magnolias and camellias accompany the early rhododendrons, then a whole host of perennials begin flowering. In December the cardiocrinum walk is in its full glory and the hostas complement the late-flowering rhododendrons. Perennials and dahlias continue into autumn when the mature deciduous trees show off their colours against the crisp blue skies. These include beeches, maples, liquidambars, *Nyssa sylvatica*, parrotia and an original oak, which complement the conifers and natives. Two huge macrocarpa feature by the front gate and kauri are unusual at such an altitude. Other features include the clematis bank above the waterfall and the Azalea Bowl with massed deciduous and evergreen azaleas.

HERITAGE PARK KIMBOLTON
Kimbolton

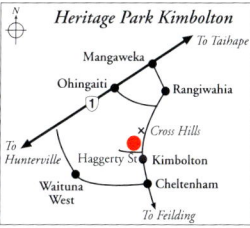

Owner:
The NZ Rhododendron Association

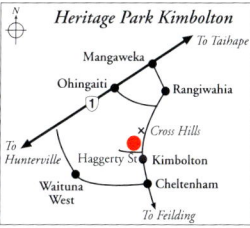

Address: Haggerty St, R D 54, Kimbolton
Postal: c/- Michelle Sims, Parklands, R D 7, Kimbolton
Directions: Take SH 54 to Cheltenham. Turn into Kimbolton Rd. Travel 14km to Kimbolton, then continue 1km & turn left into Haggerty St. Garden 500m on right. Parking on main lawn.
Phone: Michelle Sims 0-6-328 5078
Open: 1st weekend Oct. to mid Dec., daily, from 9am; or by appointment
Groups: By appointment
Fee: $5 per adult; members free
Size: Large – 4ha (10 acres)
Terrain: Undulating
Nursery: Plant sales
For sale: Crafts during season

 limited
large groups please notify

Heritage Park Kimbolton is The National Garden of the New Zealand Rhododendron Association, established in 1970 as a home for its large collection of rhododendrons that were under the care of Dr Yeates at Massey University. The site at Kimbolton was selected for its excellent free-draining soil, good rainfall, altitude and "sharp" seasons. It has become an educational showplace for rhododendron hybrids and species for the general public, as well as New Zealand Rhododendron Association members, to enjoy. There are now over 1,000 mature specimens of rhododendrons and deciduous azaleas in a park-like setting looking across to the Ruahine Range. Spacious open lawns are bordered by rhododendrons with a backdrop of mature trees. Rhododendron-lined grassy avenues lead to three linked ponds which are home to white swans. Rhododendrons are reflected in the waters with hostas, gunneras and trees planted round and waterlilies multiplying in the corners. Some of Dr Yeates' lilium auratum hybrids are grown in the gardens beneath silver birches, chestnut trees, ginkgo, maples, oaks, blue spruce and other conifers as well as native kowhai trees. The rhododendron collection is being expanded to include the best of New Zealand-raised hybrids and species. The peak time for viewing the rhododendrons is during October and November.

THE RIDGES
Hunterville

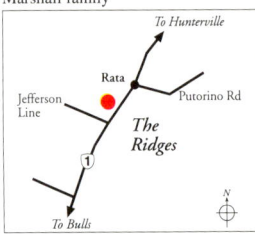

Owners:
Marshall family

To Hunterville

Rata

Jefferson Line

Putorino Rd

The Ridges

To Bulls

Address: SH 1, R D 1, Marton
Directions: 13km south of Hunterville or 21km north of Bulls on west of SH 1.
Phone: 0-6-327 8484
Fax: 0-6-327 8279
Email:(Pending)
Website: friars.co.nz/gardens/pages/ridges.html
Open: Oct.–Nov. daily, 10am–4.30pm; or when sign displayed; or by request
Groups: By appointment, as above
Fee: $6 per adult; group concessions
Size: Large – 2ha (5 acres) & woodland
Terrain: Terraced
Nursery: Specialists in unusual and rare plants, primula, cyclamen, hosta, meconopsis, aquilegia, arthropodium, lilium, rodgersia, rheum, fritillaria, helleborus; mail-order catalogue
Shop: Garden accessories

  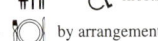 mostly

& by arrangement

Sited on a terrace above the Rangitikei River, The Ridges was originally established by Sally's grandparents from 1924, when the rhododendrons were planted along the driveway. Design elements by Alfred Buxton were added in the 1930s and a sunken garden in the 1950s. The impressive driveway welcomes visitors into this mature garden, where woodland areas are complemented by open lawn with colourful borders. Large trees still allow superb views to the surrounding countryside, Ruahine Range and Tararua foothills beyond. Spring begins with drifts of chionodoxa, dark blue forget-me-nots and dog's-tooth violets under deciduous trees. Flowering cherries, magnolias and dogwoods blossom, underplanted with fritillarias, peonies and early perennials. Masses of rhododendrons and azaleas brighten the green backdrop. Roses and lilies bloom throughout the garden, and summer perennials in the formal sunken gardens frame a central statue of "Spring". Then in autumn pink *Cyclamen hederifolium* carpet the garden beneath the beautiful autumn foliage of notable copper beeches, maples, liquidambars, oaks, and birches. A magnificent *Magnolia campbellii* blossoms in winter, when camellias open. Belladonna lilies stud the entrance, adjacent to a memorable stand of kahikatea and over three hectares of woodland where Sally is planning a bush walk.

126

WESTOE WOODLAND GARDEN
Marton

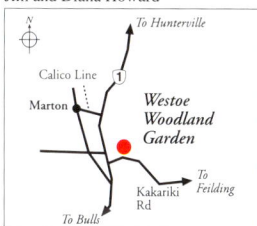

Owners:
Jim and Diana Howard

Address: Kakariki Rd, R D 1, Marton
Directions: Travel along SH 1 north of Bulls or south of Marton turn-off. Turn east into Kakariki Rd. Westoe Woodland Garden on left.
Phone: 0-6-327 6350
Fax: 0-6-327 6358
Open: All year, Tuesday to Saturday, 10am–4pm; other times by appointment
Groups: Coaches by appointment
Fee: $5 per adult; free to nursery only
Size: Large – 4ha (10 acres)
Terrain: Mainly flat, some gently sloping
Nursery: Many plants propagated from garden; unusual trees, shrubs, perennials, old & new species, specialising in NZ native plants

Westoe was laid out in the 1870s by Sir William Fox, who named it after his English birthplace in Durham. Owned by the Howard family since 1885, three generations of keen gardeners have left their mark on this woodland garden surrounding the classical homestead. Jim and Diana have underplanted the mature trees with woodland perennials and rhododendrons. Unusual New Zealand natives are a speciality, including the extensive fernery, with an indigenous area established in 1950 on the valley floor below this sheltered park-like garden terraced down to the Rangitikei River. Native bush surrounds Westoe, which also features magnificent specimens of century-old introduced conifers including redwoods, Italian stone pine (*P. pinea*), Douglas fir, Atlas cedar and Norfolk Island pine. Spring brings prunus, magnolias and dogwoods into blossom, underplanted with drifts of spring bulbs, irises, primulas and clivias. Naturalised annuals have intermixed with the woodland perennials. Rhododendrons are followed by *Cardiocrinum giganteum* and other lilies at Christmas. Autumn foliage includes oaks, maples and cornus underplanted with plectranthus, *Lilium formosanum* and cyclamen. Diana and Jim emphasise winter-flowering species such as hellebores, echiums and camellias, some now 120 years old. Many other exotics, including a copper beech, were planted from 1920 onwards.

PUKEMARAMA
Tangimoana

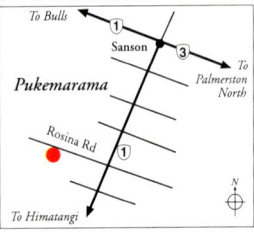

Owners:
Sue and Ian McKelvie

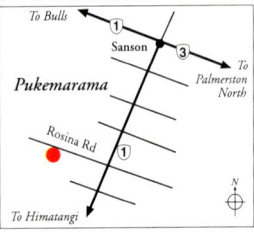

Address: Rosina Rd, Sanson
Postal: R D 3, Palmerston North
Directions: At Sanson, turn west
following SH 1. Take 5th right into
Rosina Rd. Pukemarama 3.5km on
left. From south, take SH 1 to
Himatangi. Continue & take 5th on
left into Rosina Rd. Then as above.
Phone: 0-6-324 8446
Fax: 0-6-324 8446
Email: pukemaramanz@xtra.co.nz
Website:
www.pukemarama.simplenet.com
Open: By appointment only
Closed: Saturdays
Groups: Large groups, all year,
by appointment
Fee: $5 per adult
Size: Large – 3.2ha (8 acres)
Terrain: Terraced

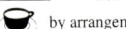   limited

by arrangement

Pukemarama is situated on a hilltop overlooking the west coast. Established at the turn of the century, the gardens are maintained in their original English style by descendants of the McKelvie family. The historic homestead overlooks formal bricked terraces, 51 steps leading down to a sunken garden with adjacent grassed tennis and croquet lawns. Here twin circular parterres, filled with colourful perennials and annuals, are connected by a long rose pergola and edged with English lavender. Trees from the original symmetrical plantings include pairs of Norfolk Island pines, chestnuts, copper beeches, a vast horizontal beech, weeping cherry and an enormous walnut leading into a woodland dell. This features a huge macrocarpa among other mature trees which have been underplanted. Roses both old and new predominate at Pukemarama, from 'Albertine' climbing the verandah to miniatures encircling the central sun-dial in the forecourt. Colourful roses and perennials spill over and soften the concrete steps, while deep red 'Parkdirektor Riggers' climbs the verandah balustrade above box-edged beds of further roses, delphiniums and poppies. Other features include statuary, a summer house, a dove aviary, and Sue's scarecrow, as well as magnificent views over the surrounding countryside. A 1900 eight-stand woolshed can be seen on the farm tours.

128

SHADY ACRES
Oroua Downs

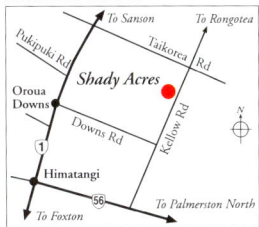

Owners:
Jan and Ian McLean

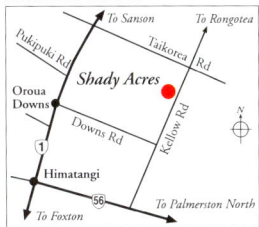

Address: Kellow Rd, Oroua Downs
Postal: Kellow Rd, R D 11, Foxton
Directions: From Palmerston North,
take SH 56 south. Turn right into
Kellow Rd. Travel 4km to garden on
left. From Sanson, take SH 1 south.
Turn left into Taikorea Rd. Travel
4km & turn right into Kellow Rd.
Shady Acres on right.
Phone: 06-329 9767
Fax: 06-329 9767
Open: All year
Fee: $3 per adult
Size: Medium – 1.2ha (3 acres)
Terrain: Flat
Nursery: Camellias, perennials, roses
Craftshop: Includes Jan & Ian's
ornamental message books for sale

    & toilet

  by arrangement

Shady Acres was developed from 1992 as therapy for Jan since her accident in 1991 which left her disabled. The top story of their home was re-positioned beside the lower level, and the garden created on the surrounding paddock. A ride-on mower enabled Jan to establish grassy walkways beween areas and, with Ian's help, five pergolas and two dovecotes were erected. Statuary includes a birdbath, sundial, and Balinese naked lady fountain over one of the goldfish ponds. Garden seats add structure to Jan's design of curved lines. Favourites are roses, from those climbing the pergolas alongside the wisteria, to the standards in the rose ring and many varieties in the rose bed. She also loves her camellia walk which begins to flower in winter just as early spring bulbs open. Prunus and magnolia blossom are followed by pink virgilia and 'Marshwood' lavender encircling the claret ash. Box hedging around trees forms a circle filled with tulips in winter, then stock and petunias in summer. The pink, blue and mauve colour scheme is replaced by golds and russet colours in autumn. A developing native area provides year-round interest as do the aviaries, peacocks and guinea fowl. Recent additions include fowl and hand-fed farm animals such as Highland steer and rare Pitt Island sheep. Jan and Ian enjoy catering for their visitors, and also make ornamental books displaying messages, which they sell from their new craftshop.

O'TARA BIRCH DISPLAY GARDENS
Rongotea

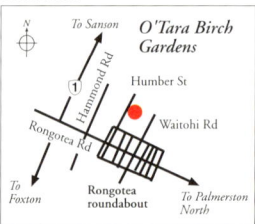

Owner:
Eddie Johns

Address: 72 Humber St, Rongotea
Postal: P O Box 81, Rongotea
Directions: Turn off SH 1 south of
Sanson, towards Palmerston North,
left into Rongotea Rd. Travel 4km
towards Rongotea roundabout. Turn
left into Humber St & travel 400m to
O'Tara Birch Gardens on right.
Phone: 0-6-324 8490
Fax: 0-6-324 8490
Email: otara.birch@xtra.co.nz
Website: www.otarabirch.co.nz
Open: August to mid April, daily,
10am–3pm; evenings by appointment
Groups: By appointment
Fee: $3 per adult, children free
Size: Large – 3.2ha (8 acres)
Terrain: Flat
Nursery & Plant Centre: Dahlias,
grevilleas, hostas, irises & daylilies

  complimentary

Eddie is a dahlia enthusiast, with over 500 different dahlias planted in a formal garden in curving beds. Weeping standardised grevillea encircled by buxus hedging feature in the middle of this garden. Since 1989, hybrids of all shapes and sizes have been grown in the dahlia display garden, creating a mass of blended colour from mid January to the first frosts of May. But O'Tara Birch is not just dahlias. Established exotic trees, including birches, alders, oaks, maples, *Magnolia campbellii* and *Pinus radiata* 'Aurea', surround the garden, separating it into individual rooms. The adjacent rose garden is designed as a formal 16th-century-style open knot garden. A pond area has been developed, with surrounding bog garden featuring over 400 varieties of Japanese irises which flower in late November and early December. These join the Louisiana and bearded irises which begin blooming from early November. The Japanese and Siberian irises at O'Tara Birch comprise the largest collection in the southern hemisphere. The new hosta walk includes massed plantings of the latest hosta varieties available in New Zealand. The series of "gardens of the past for the future" are designed around themes that encompass many exciting visions. Further developments can be observed by regularly visiting the O'Tara Birch Gardens.

DE HOEVE 23
Kairanga

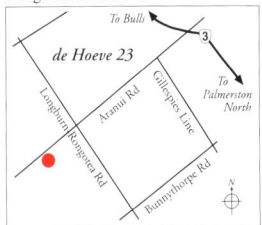

Owners:
Margaret and Jac Bos

Address: Aranui Rd, Kairanga, R D 5, Palmerston North
Directions: From The Square in Palmerston North, take Rangitikei Line (SH 3) north for 7km. Turn left into Aranui Rd. Travel 5km & cross Rongotea Rd to 2nd house on left.
Phone: 0-6-329 0704
Open: September to May, daily, by appointment
Groups: By appointment
Fee: $3 per adult
Size: Medium – 1.2ha (3 acres)
Terrain: Flat
Nursery: Old-fashioned roses & perennials

by arrangement

Dutch for "The Homestead", de Hoeve 23 (pronounced "hoover") was originally planted in 1926 in English style. It has been restored since 1991 and two new areas have been opened up from farm paddocks to provide more room for Margaret's beloved roses which are spilling into her daughter's garden next door. Favourites among the 350 or so roses are the rugosas which were inspired by those in Holland. A walkway edged with low buxus hedging leads to a rose pergola and masses of perennials which complement the roses throughout summer and autumn. Margaret lets the hips ripen on the old roses, which flourish in the Kairanga loam and add to the mixed colours of the garden. Even the white garden has succumbed to other colours. Attractions at de Hoeve 23 include the century-old native kauri tree at the front of the property, the original copper beech, and the flowering tulip tree planted in the late 1980s. Ponds and a stream running through the garden provide water features, and a bridge crossing the stream leads visitors to a small Japanese garden. A developing native area includes the kowhai walk which flowers in spring along with the bulbs and 100 camellias. Recent additions include white fantail doves housed in two dovecotes, as well as a fernery featuring New Zealand native ferns and small indigenous orchids.

THE VICTORIA ESPLANADE GARDENS
Palmerston North

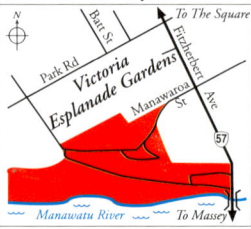

Owner:
Palmerston North City Council

Address: Entrances from Manawaroa St, Fitzherbert Ave, & Park Rd, Palmerston North
Postal: Private Bag 11034, Palmerston North
Directions: From The Square take Fitzherbert Ave south. Turn right into Park Rd or Manawaroa St. Roads throughout Gardens & 4 carparks.
Phone: 0-6-356 8199
Fax: 0-6-351 4454
Open: Daily, October to March 8am–9pm; April to November 8am–6pm
Fee: No charge
Size: Large – 18ha (45 acres)
Terrain: Flat & river terrace
Attractions: Summer concerts; heritage trail; orienteering courses
Education Centre: Environmental information & historic photographs

  & teahouse for functions

Although the land for the Victoria Esplanade Gardens was originally set aside in 1877, the planting of English trees was delayed for 20 years, until the official opening to commemorate Queen Victoria's 60th jubilee. The historic City Post Office, now known as Victoria House, was relocated to the Gardens in 1989 as the teahouse. The large duck pond was formed in 1925, and the original 1930s Cherry Drive was replanted in 1997. A children's paddling pool donated by the RSA was constructed in 1937, and the following year the formal Palm Drive of *Phoenix canariensis* was planted, with annual displays adding colour today. The first aviary, built in 1955, was extended in the 1990s with the Council's participation in a national native bird breeding programme. Indigenous tui are attracted to the flowering eucalypts in winter. The Peter Black Conservatory, erected in 1940, displays subtropical plants, and the more recent Lath House, a collection of shade-loving plants. The 1968 Dugald MacKenzie Rose Garden now features 5,500 roses as well as the International Rose Trial Grounds. The next year, the miniature railway was opened through native bush. The 10.3 kilometre Riverside Walkway and Bridle Track along the Manawatu River are adjacent to five hectares of remnant bush. Other walks lead through mature camellias and rhododendrons. Opened in 1998, the Education Centre provides environmental information and historic photos.

BLOEMENDAAL
Palmerston North

Owners:
Gytha and John Wyatt

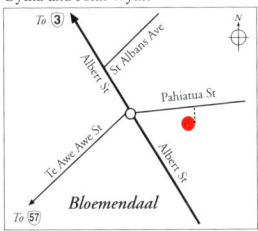

Bloemendaal

Address: 40 Pahiatua St, Palmerston North
Directions: From The Square, take Fitzherbert Ave south. Turn left into Te Awe Awe St. Continue through roundabout into Pahiatua St. Garden on right at end of drive.
Phone: 0-6-358 7268
Website: friars.co.nz/gardens/pages/ bloemendaal.html
Open: Sept.–May
Groups: By appointment
Fee: $3 per adult
Size: Medium – 0.55ha (1⅓ acres)
Terrain: Mainly flat
Nursery: Selection of mainly shade-loving perennials, plectranthus, *Sedum* 'Autumn Joy', *Argyranthemum pacificum, Symphytum grandiflorum, Trachycarpus fortunei* palms, cabbage trees, waterlilies & other bog/water plants. Also fruit in season – persimmons, kiwifruit, citrus, walnuts

Bloemendaal has been in Gytha's family since 1913. John and Gytha began clearing the dense under-growth in 1972 and re-developing the garden of over half a hectare. Walks meander through the woodland area where the Wyatts have retained trees planted round the turn of the century, such as the two ginkgos and mandarin listed as notable specimens, and the liquidambar and grapefruit, all underplanted with a carpet of bluebells and daffodils in the spring. Other woodland trees include mature walnuts, plums, apples and a stand of more than 20 listed *Trachycarpus fortunei* palms. In 1992, many natives were added to the existing kowhai and cabbage trees, including totara, kauri and rimu, which attract the native birds. Shrub and perennial gardens have been planted around the spacious middle lawn, and a lavender garden has been established in the foundations of a glasshouse originally built in the early 1900s by famed vintner, Antonio Vidal. A large pond has been created, in addition to two smaller existing fish ponds, displaying waterlilies in summer which complement Gytha's favourite irises and hostas. Architectural features provide structure, such as the dovecote and rose-covered gazebo and arbour. Recent developments at Bloemendaal include a small persimmon grove where a curved path leads visitors to a rustic garden gate.

GREENHAUGH
Palmerston North

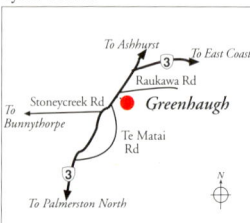

Owner:
Lynne Atkins

Address: 914 Napier Rd, R D 10,
Palmerston North
Directions: From Palmerston North,
take SH 3 northwards. Continue past
100km sign for 6.5km to garden on
right; signpost at gate.
Phone: 0-6-357 3878
Fax: 0-6-357 3868
Website: friars.co.nz/gardens/pages/
greenhaugh.html
Open: All year, Monday to Friday;
weekends by arrangement
Groups: By appointment
Fee: $3 per adult
Size: Large – 2ha (5 acres)
Terrain: Gentle terraced slopes
Nursery: Many perennials, foliage
plants including silver foliage, bulbs,
groundcovers, grasses, & old roses

Greenhaugh, first farmed in the 1870s, has been in the Atkins family since the early 1960s. This large semi-formal country garden was developed from 1986 to extend the colonial homestead's original half acre. Mature trees, over a century old, include two lindens (*Tilia*), copper beech, liquidambar and ginkgo, which provide a wonderful canopy of autumn colour. Old roses clothe a tennis-court length pergola, complemented by clematis and wisteria. Austin roses are also abundant, featured in a salmon, cream and green area close to the house with *Alchemilla mollis* and cream Californian poppies. The roses, clematis, bearded irises and aquilegia steal the scene in spring together with the *Kolkwitzia* and many euphorbias. Then the perennial borders come into their own during summer, with shasta daisies, salvias, penstemons, geraniums, lavateras and lilies. In autumn, the drier Mediterranean gardens take over with their hotter colours and lots of silver and gold foliage. These include *Helianthus*, sedums, Michaelmas daisies and lavenders, with Japanese anemones featuring in the herbaceous borders. Winter brings collections of hellebores to the fore, then the 1940s daffodils lining the driveway bloom, heralding the springtime again. Local limestone is used in the formal pond areas, steps and paths.

THE HERB FARM
Ashhurst

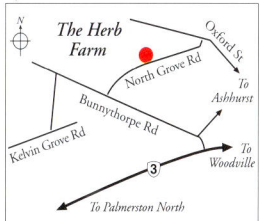

Owners:
Lynn and Bill Kirkland

Address: North Grove Rd, Ashhurst
Postal: R D 10, Palmerston North
Directions: From Ashhurst, take
Oxford St west. Turn left into Nth
Grove Rd. Travel 1km to garden on
right. From PN take Kelvin Grove Rd.
Phone: 0-6-326 8633
Fax: 0-6-326 9650
Email: herbfarm@inspire.net.nz
Open: By appointment, or Nov.–Feb.,
Thurs.–Sun., 10.30am–5pm;
March–Oct., Fri.–Sun., 11am–4.30pm
Groups: Any time, by appointment
Fee: $3 per adult; $4 per adult for
conducted tours (of 10 or over)
Size: Medium – 1.2ha (3 acres)
Terrain: Flat
Nursery: Herbs & cottage perennials
Studio shop: Herbal products, oils
Café: Pantry goods; functions catered

 partial

The Herb Farm comprises 14 theme gardens developed
from bare paddocks since 1992. These display gardens
celebrate the use of herbs, from Lynn's favourite summer-
flowering *Echinacea purpurea* and Japanese menthol
mint to massed lavenders and the chamomile lawn in the
fragrant garden. The woodland garden consists of two
eucalyptus groves where flowering clematis forms a
white wall in spring and gnomes direct the children's
interest. A further children's garden beyond a little gate
features child-sized tunnels and pathways, fragrant plants
and hidden fairies, teddies and animals to discover.
Beyond the woodland is a heritage garden, complete with
an old railway carriage, poppy meadow and potager. A
native area is developing adjacent to a stream-fed dam.
The studio is a unique architecturally designed building
containing the award-winning café where daily delights
are prepared from garden-fresh produce. Functions are
catered for and a wedding garden has been established.
The spring clematis and stoechas lavenders are followed
by the English *Lavandula angustifolia* in summer which
are complemented by the roses and all the herbs. The
Echinacea (coneflowers) bloom a striking purple, then in
April the saffron crop flowers while rosehips develop on
the rugosa hedges. In winter, as the garden is resting, the
surrounding countryside comes more into focus.

TARARUA AND WAIRARAPA

Tararua and the Wairarapa lie south of Hawke's Bay, on the east coast. Pastureland, orchards and vineyards flourish in the typical east coast sunshine of this region. The wide strip of fertile land to the east of the Tararua Range is very dry and almost Mediterranean in its extremes of climate, from hot summers to cold, frosty winters.

The 11 gardens featured in this region extend from Norsewood, through Dannevirke to the Wairarapa. Four gardens are found in the Tararua region. The northernmost is Atholbrae in Norsewood, a park-like garden with a hillside of massed rhododendrons. Then at Dannevirke are three gardens. Laven d'Lane is predominantly devoted to lavender, with many products for sale, the lavender complemented by irises and roses. Victoriana is an urban garden full of rare and unusual bulbs, with a woodland area featuring historic trees. Gardenstone is a rural garden incorporating an extensive bush walk, a Cretan labyrinth and an extensive library of gardening books.

South of the Tararua region is the Wairarapa. There Borderlands is located at the foot of the Pahiatua Track, east of Palmerston North, with its extensive woodland and beautiful creek. Further gardens are found at Masterton, down in Carterton and further south in Martinborough, the wine producing capital of the Wairarapa, as well as south of Featherston by Lake Wairarapa. Altogether these 11 Tararua and Wairarapa gardens feature a great range of plants in different settings, from cottage gardens to sculpturally designed landscapes.

The first of the two Masterton gardens is Tussie Mussie, a small urban garden which developed around an interest in making tussie mussies. Travelling down the road east towards Castlepoint, we come to the Bideford Valley where Dursley is located. This is a restored Alfred Buxton garden featuring large deciduous trees and views to the surrounding hills.

South of Masterton is Carterton, where Awaiti is sited on almost two and a half hectares of land, with a recently restored colonial cottage tearoom. Ten kilometres north of Martinborough is Ngaranui Garden, incorporating mature trees, with a waterlily pond as focal point. South-east of Martinborough is Harakeke where roses, clematis, massed daisies and blue-flowering plants predominate. Lake Wairarapa is located south of Featherston, where another Wairarapa garden is found. Sited on the western shore is Prairie Holm, developed around established natives underplanted with camellias and rhododendrons. Accommodation is also available at Prairie Holm, an ideal stopover for garden visitors to the Wairarapa.

As well as the 11 private gardens featured, public botanical gardens can also be visited in the Wairarapa, including Queen Elizabeth Park in the centre of Masterton, the gardens at Carrington Park in Carterton, which have the historical significance of having been designed by Alfred Buxton early this century, and Greytown's Memorial Park of eight hectares. The steep Rimutaka Range separates the Wairarapa from Wellington.

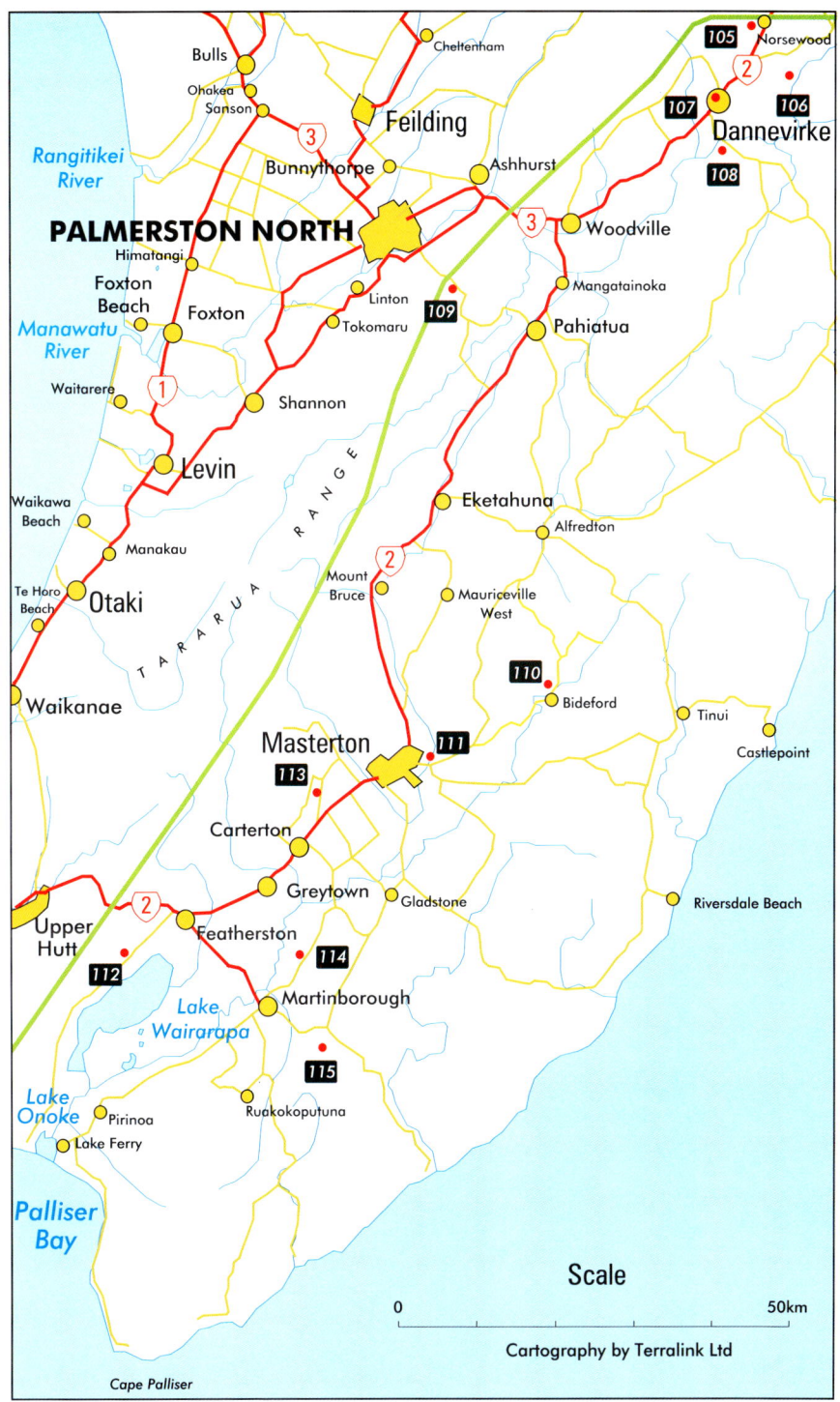

Bulls
Cheltenham
Ohakea
Sanson
Feilding
105
Norsewood
107
Dannevirke
106
3
Bunnythorpe
Ashhurst
108
Rangitikei River
PALMERSTON NORTH
3
Woodville
Himatangi
Foxton Beach
Foxton
Linton
Mangatainoka
Manawatu River
Tokomaru
109
Pahiatua
Waitarere
1
Shannon
Levin
Eketahuna
Alfredton
Waikawa Beach
Manakau
Mount Bruce
2
Mauriceville West
Te Horo Beach
Otaki
110
Bideford
Tinui
Waikanae
Masterton
111
Castlepoint
113
TARARUA RANGE
Carterton
Greytown
Gladstone
Riversdale Beach
Upper Hutt
2
Featherston
114
112
Martinborough
Lake Wairarapa
115
Lake Onoke
Pirinoa
Ruakokoputuna
Lake Ferry
Palliser Bay

Scale

0   50km

Cartography by Terralink Ltd

Cape Palliser

ATHOLBRAE
Norsewood

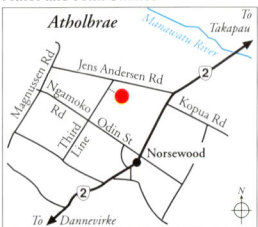

Owners:
Athol and John Staines

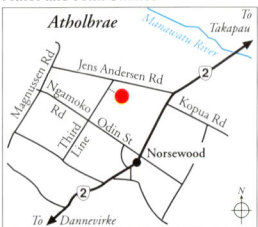

Address: 35 Third Line, Norsewood
Postal: Third Line, R D 11,
Norsewood
Directions: From Dannevirke, take
SH 2 north to Norsewood. Turn left
into Odin St. Travel 0.5km & turn
right into Third Line. Garden on right.
From Takapau, take SH 2 south. Cross
Manawatu Bridge & travel 0.5km.
Turn right into Jens Andersen Rd, &
left into Third Line. Garden on left.
Phone: 0-6-374 0763
Open: All year, daily, dawn to dusk
Fee: Donation
Size: Large –2.4ha (6 acres)
Terrain: Flat to sloping
Items for sale: Rimu furniture & arts
& crafts for sale, samples in The Barn
in Norsewood village

 hot water available

Atholbrae is named after its owner, although her friends call her Kenny! She has developed her large park-like garden since 1989 on a potato paddock, relocating plants from a previous home in Waipukurau. The hillside beside the long driveway is a sea of colour in springtime when the massed rhododendrons bloom. These are accompanied by azaleas, camellias, magnolias and a long row of cherry blossom. Other hillside plantings include lilac trees, ornamental conifers, leucadendrons and native hebes and flaxes. Summer brings the peonies into flower, along with the lilies and hydrangeas. Then the deciduous trees provide autumn colour until June, when the early daffodils and jonquils begin to flower. Occasionally snow falls in winter, but the bare limbs of the specimen trees make it easy to view the birds. Trees have been planted at Atholbrae to attact the native tui and wood pigeons which come down from the bush. The tui feed in the several varieties of eucalypts on the perimeter and nest in the garden too. There is a birds' bath on the lawn, the large grassed areas broken by beds of shrubs, flowers and trees. Wisteria adorns the verandah of the house overlooking the lawn, with views to the Ruahine Range beyond. John sells his furniture crafted from native rimu, samples of which are displayed in The Barn in Norsewood village, three kilometres to the east.

LAVEN D' LANE
Dannevirke

Laven d' Lane

Owners:
Sue and Robert Stephenson

Laven d' Lane

Address: 600 Maunga Road, Dannevirke
Directions: From Dannevirke, take SH 2 north to Rest Area. Turn right into Otanga Rd & travel 4km. At "T" junction, turn right into Maunga Rd. Travel 5km to garden on right.
Phone: 0-6-374 8181
Mobile: 025 539 309
Fax: 0-6-374 8181
Open: October to March, Friday to Sunday, other times by appointment
Closed: April to September
Groups: By appointment
Fee: $3.50 per adult
Size: Medium – 1.4ha (3½ acres)
Terrain: Flat
Nursery: Lavender plants in summer
For sale: Local artwork & crafts & large range of lavender products

by arrangement

A hectare of Laven d' Lane is devoted to lavender. The main species are the English *Lavandula angustifolia* varieties such as 'Grosso' and 'Pacific Blue'. The spiky English lavender produces the best oil and retains the strongest perfume. Sue and Robert sell a large range of lavender products and plan to establish a still on the property in order to process their own oil. They also sell lavender plants in the summer season when the English varieties flower. Most of the garden was originally their daughter's pony paddocks, so has had to be developed from scratch since 1984. Although lavender is the predominant species at Laven d' Lane, almost half a hectare (an acre) is laid out as a cottage garden. Over 400 Dutch irises flower in the spring, followed by 400 old-fashioned roses through the summer months when the lavender is at its peak. Sue has planted the garden mainly in soft pastel colours with separate areas of bright yellows, reds, purples and blues. As well as her favourite Dutch irises, Sue loves the flowering cherries in spring, accompanied by camellias, rhododendrons and clematis. Then, in addition to the roses, summer features include Sue's sunflowers and many other perennials. The foliage of the deciduous trees provides autumn colour. Laven d' Lane is open from October to March and is easy to find, just nine kilometres of sealed road from the main highway.

VICTORIANA
Dannevirke

Owners:
Olive and Les Bayly

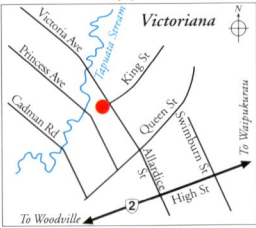

Address: 33 Victoria Ave, Dannevirke.
Directions: Take SH 2 to Dannevirke.
From High St, turn north-west into
Allardice St. Continue across railway
line into Victoria Ave. Victoriana
garden on left.
Phone: 0-6-374 7185
Open: All year, daily, by appointment
Groups: As above
Fee: $3 per adult
Size: Medium – 0.5ha (over 1 acre)
Terrain: Flat with sloping woodland
Nursery: Bulbs, small perennials &
unusual plants for sale
Teas: $2 pp, by arrangement

   on flat

 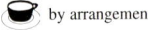 by arrangement

Originally planted in 1915 when the house was built, Victoriana is a classic styled garden developed since 1990 when Olive took it over. Her favourite plants are the rare and unusual bulbs in her alpine beds, the predominant species including fritillarias, which accompany the trilliums, cyclamen and crocuses in spring. Arisaema, miniature narcissus and tulips are also prolific. The focal point of the woodland area is a huge coast redwood that has survived since 1915. Other woodland features include magnolias, camellias and azaleas, with underplantings of hellebores, hostas and groundcovers. As well as the redwood, there are some equally old deciduous trees such as the walnut, silver birch, chestnut, oak. Natives planted since then comprise young kauri, rimu, kahikatea, pseudopanax and New Zealand ferns. Another recent addition is the brick walling – over 22,000 old bricks have been used in walls of varying heights. Roses climb the brick walls, complemented by over 100 varieties of clematis which Olive loves. And in 1999 she won $1,000 worth of pots which also now feature throughout the garden. Many varieties of irises are prominent in season – dwarf, bearded, Evansia and Siberian irises. Seasonal colour and perfume are also provided by magnolias, michelias and *Daphne bholua* in spring, alstromeria in summer, and nerines and hydrangeas in autumn.

GARDENSTONE
Dannevirke

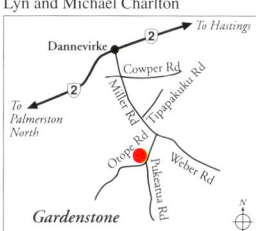

Owners:
Lyn and Michael Charlton

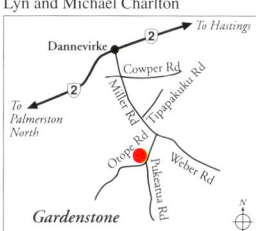

Address: Otope Road, R D 5, Dannevirke
Directions: From Dannevirke, take Miller Rd south-east for 5km. Turn right into Otope Rd. Travel 1km to Gardenstone on right.
Phone: 0-6-374 8259
Mobile: 025 205 4418
Email: charlton@voyager.co.nz
Open: 1 October to 31 May, 10am to 5pm, by appointment only
Closed: 1 June to 30 September
Fee: $3 per adult
Size: Medium – 1ha garden (2½ acres) & large – 2ha bush (5 acres)
Terrain: Flat & undulating

   by arrangement

Gardenstone is a rural garden, just six kilometres east of Dannevirke. The house garden features roses, clematis, perennials and mixed plantings, divided into garden rooms by arches and young hedges of buxus, hornbeam, beech and yew. Local riverstone has been used to build a large well and retaining walls. A kilometre-long native bush walk takes visitors through mature kahikatea, totara and matai, past drifts of arthropodiums and statuary, to seats and a swing by the woodland stream. Gardenstone features mature trees as well as recent plantings such as the lime walk, oak woodlot, maples and other deciduous trees. There is also a formal potager, pétanque court, and extensive library of garden books for visitors to enjoy. A 40-metre Cretan labyrinth is under construction, located near an amphitheatre in the bush, where weddings are held. Hydrangeas, late flowering perennials and shrubs, and the changing colours of the deciduous trees create a welcoming autumn garden. Climbing plants including jasmine, old roses, lonicera, *Hydrangea petiolaris*, Boston ivy, hops and ornamental grapes provide vertical accent and year-round interest. Morning and afternoon teas, lunches and picnic baskets are available on request. Gardenstone is designed for visitors to spend a relaxing day in the country. Animal lovers will enjoy feeding the donkeys.

BORDERLANDS
Pahiatua

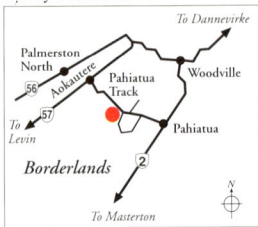

Owner:
Romayne Abraham

Address: Pahiatua Rd, Makomako,
R D 3, Pahiatua
Directions: Turn off SH 2 at Pahiatua
and travel west 17km towards
Palmerston North, to Borderlands at
foot of Pahiatua Track on left. Or
travel 18km from Palmerston North.
Phone: 0-6-376 7071
Fax: 0-6-376 7077
Website: friars.co.nz/gardens/pages/
borderlands.html
Open: By appointment from
September to end April, & when
"open" sign displayed
Groups: By appointment; bus parking
Fee: $5 per adult, $5 for bus groups
Size: Large – 2.5ha (6–7 acres)
Terrain: Flat and steps to lower levels
Nursery: Many perennials & bulbs,
sometimes trees & shrubs

  mostly

When the Abrahams moved to Borderlands in 1961, they inherited roadside oaks, large totara, *Acer palmatum,* poplars, lacebarks, pines and the inevitable macrocarpas. A beautiful creek flowed through the garden, now featuring huge *Gunnera tinctoria* contrasting with delicate maple foliage above. An old brick fireplace converted into a pond area by Romayne's late husband, Nigel, now features standard wisteria and weeping maples above waterlilies, irises, pontederia and hostas. Initial plantings of rhododendrons in 1967 are limbed up to accommodate underplanting. Form, texture and colour are carefully considered, with many deciduous trees chosen solely for autumn foliage, others for sculptural trunks, bark, or fragrance. Borderlands is not a pastel garden, Romayne choosing the full spectrum from gentle colours to vibrant combinations, such as the scarlet Chilean fire-bush (*Embothrium coccineum* 'Longifolium'), entwined with creamy *Pandorea pandorana*. A grassy walkway opens into a glade where waratah, *Telopea speciosissima* 'Flaming Beacon', echoes a red rhododendron. Romayne is fascinated with species of rhododendron, camellia, and rose, rather than the hybrids, although they are often more difficult to grow. In summer, soft light filters through the deciduous trees, adorned with climbing roses, clematis and wisteria. Vistas have been retained to the nearby hills.

DURSLEY
Masterton

Owner:
Judith Callaghan

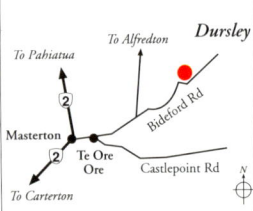

Address: Bideford, R D 11, Masterton
Directions: Turn east off SH 2 into
Castlepoint Rd. Turn left into SH 52,
then up Bideford Valley, past Te Roto
garden. Dursley on left. 18 minutes
from Masterton.
Phone: 0-6-372 4804
Fax: 0-6-372 4804
Email: dursley@actrix.gen.nz
Website: friars.co.nz/gardens/pages/
dursley.html
Open: September to April (Fathers'
Day to Anzac Day), 10.30am–6pm,
daily
Fee: $3 per adult
Size: Medium – 1.52ha (3⅘ acres)
Terrain: Flat with small terrace
Tours: Combined catered tours can be
arranged with Te Roto & Historic
Church

   mostly
by arrangement

In 1916 Alfred Buxton designed the garden, then known as Te Rangi Pai. The name was changed to Dursley in the 1930s, but the lines of Buxton's landscaping are still apparent today. A 1917 arbutus and weeping birch give stature, with some original rose bushes featuring among the 300 now growing throughout the garden. Many other established trees, underplanted with naturalised bulbs, form a woodland carpeted with spring bulbs, including daffodils, bluebells, galanthus and grape hyacinths, then drifts of cyclamens in autumn. Long views under the trees are retained in a natural, not contrived, way, with pathways through deciduous azaleas, rhododendrons, camellias and tree peonies, their bright colours downplayed by shadows from the canopy overhead. In summer, Turk's-cap lilies *(L. martagon)* feature throughout the woodland area, and a very large clump of California "tree" poppies *(Romneya coulteri)* is striking when in full bloom. Three herbaceous borders are sited to provide views from the house. When the Callaghans took over the garden in 1972 they removed seven truckloads of debris before beginning to recover the garden area around the flowing driveway. Care has been taken not to plant out the panoramic views to the hills, appreciated from the seats which abound for visitors to sit and listen to the birds in the quiet, tranquil atmosphere.

TUSSIE MUSSIE GARDEN
Masterton

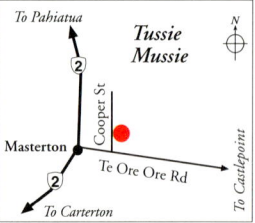

Owners:
Beth and Ross Sutherland

Address: 6 Cooper St, Masterton
Directions: North of Masterton, turn
right down the Castlepoint Rd, then
first left into Cooper St. Tussie
Mussie Garden on right.
Phone: 0-6-377 3473
Open: Most days
Groups: By appointment
Fee: $3 per adult
Size: Small – 0.05ha (⅛ acre)
Terrain: Flat
Nursery: Herbs, lavenders, climbers
& unusual plants from garden
Shop: Beth's paintings for sale;
tussie mussies can be ordered

 by arrangement

This intensively planted garden filled with small flowers and foliage developed around Beth's interest in making tussie mussies. After the Sutherlands left their farm in 1982, Beth established many scented and old-fashioned varieties in this small retirement cottage garden, extending it to include herbs. The flowers inspire Beth's paintings, so she chooses her colours carefully, enjoying rich but not garish combinations, including greens, pinks, blues, wine red, lemon and whites. Spring bulbs are complemented with camellias, apple blossom, *Magnolia stellata*, dogwood, and a Judas tree. Beth's favourite old roses climb over pergolas, arbour, gateways and garage. Bougainvillea brightens the front entrance in summer, when hanging baskets of begonias and many potted plants bloom with Beth's unusual old perennials. Autumn features an ornamental grape and *Prunus subhirtella* 'Autumnalis', which blossoms in winter. A little circular bricked fish pond in the front garden planted with waterlilies and irises provides a tranquil spot where the Sutherlands enjoy watching raindrops on the water on a wet day. Bonsai grow round a birdbath nearby. Ross has developed a native fern area next to a rangiora with banksia climbing through it. Other natives include rata, tree fuchsia, lancewood, kowhai, *Brachyglottis compactus* and *B. greyi* (formerly *B. senecio*).

146

PRAIRIE HOLM NURSERY AND GARDENS
Featherston

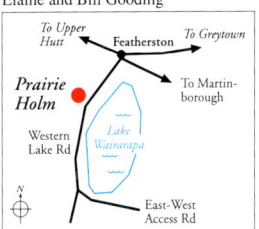

Owners:
Elaine and Bill Gooding

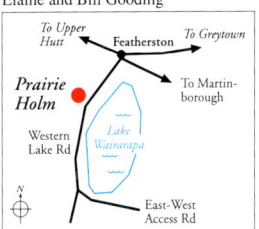

Address: Western Lake Rd, R D 3,
Featherston
Directions: From Featherston, travel
south, taking Western Lake Rd for
13km. Garden on right.
Phone: 0-6-308 9090 after hours
Mobile: 025 374 932
Fax: 0-6-308 9090
Open: All year, daily
Groups: By appointment
Fee: $4 per adult
Size: Large – 2.4ha (6 acres)
Terrain: Flat
Accommodation: Available, in
addition to Elim Waters chalets for
traumatised people under physical or
emotional stress with special needs

 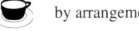 by arrangement

Prairie Holm, named after the children's book *Little House on the Prairie*, has been developed since 1980 around a large grouping of established natives, some planted before World War I. These attract native birds and are underplanted with camellias and rhododendrons. Native tui and wood pigeons feed on tree lucernes planted for shelter from strong northwesterlies and unusual shrubs for windy sites feature. Azaleas begin flowering in winter, with 'Cécile Brünner' roses and *Heuchera* 'Palace Purple' in the sunken garden. Above the sunken garden is a bank of perennials with tall purple and rose echiums, a collection of salvias, penstemons and monardas, which thrive in the wind. Further perennials border the nursery and old roses are planted throughout the gardens. Large plantings of rhododendrons grow in dappled sunlight, including a selection of vireyas. Stone-lined paths wind throughout the woodland, with box edging and local stone walls, to the gazebo in a clearing. A rockery by the house displays dwarf rhododendrons, and another rockery features in the water area, with stonework walls beside two ponds that are connected by a replica water wheel. A young laburnum arch, flowering above with climbing roses, leads through dahlias, lilies and perennials to the Elim Waters chalets. A dovecote stands beside the pines, doves welcoming visitors. Accommodation is also available at Prairie Holm.

AWAITI GARDENS & GIFTS
Carterton

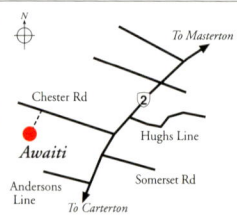

Owners:
Allan and Jeanette Gates

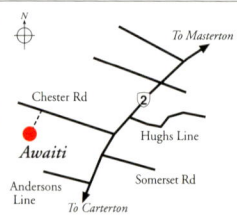

To Masterton

Chester Rd

Hughs Line

Awaiti

Andersons
Line

Somerset Rd

To Carterton

Address: Chester Rd, R D 1, Carterton
Directions: North of Carterton, turn
left into Chester Rd. Travel 2km to
Awaiti Gardens & Gifts on left.
Phone: 0-6-379 8478
Fax: 0-6-379 8478
Email: p.k.jordan@zfree.co.nz
Website: gardens.co.nz/
GardenstoVisit/Gardenpages/
Awaiti.htm
Open: 1 September to 31 May,
Tuesdays to Sundays, 10am–4pm;
plus holiday Mondays;
June to August open by appointment
Fee: $4 per adult for garden only
Size: Large – 2.4ha (6 acres)
Terrain: Flat
Nursery: Small nursery – plants from
garden eg perennials & annuals
Shop: Awaiti Gifts selling silk,
porcelain dolls, pot-pourri, china,
dried flowers, etc

Awaiti, meaning "little stream", has evolved around a meandering stream since 1980. Stones from the surrounding farmland are used for lining the waterways and for hand-made walls, with viewing portholes providing glimpses of Japanese irises and lupins beyond. A weir and waterfall are bordered with primulas and lead into pools edged with hostas, astilbes, Japanese irises and azaleas. Jeanette's favourites are the cottage perennials, which grow in abundance in a riot of colourful beds. A lavender walkway borders a rhododendron garden and old totara railings edge the pathways leading out to the lake. Here Allan has crafted a quaint shingle-roofed brick shed and water wheel backed by swamp cypresses and liquidambars. More than 300 rhododendrons are planted among silver birches, ash trees and maples which provide glorious autumn colour. A formal yew-edged rose garden is shaped like a clover leaf around a central wishing well. Clipped *Thuja plicata* 'Pyramidalis' separate the garden into lobes and provide a backdrop for the many roses. Archways of climbing roses, pink clematis and mauve wisteria provide viewing frames for vistas of cherry blossom. White fantail pigeons, doves and peacock complement the garden. The original farm cottage, built in the 1860s, has been converted into tearooms surrounded by a cottage garden, including two turn-of-the-century camellia trees.

NGARANUI GARDEN
Martinborough

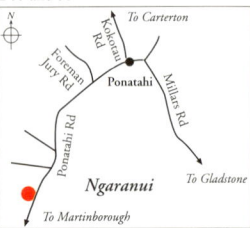

Owners:
Bee and John Blundell

Address: Ponatahi Rd, R D 2, Carterton
Directions: From Carterton, travel east & turn right into Ponatahi Rd. Travel 8km. From Martinborough, turn right into Princess St. Continue into Ponatahi Rd & travel 10km to garden.
Phone: 0-6-306 9140
Mobile: 025 463 248
Fax: 0-6-306 9945
Email: ngaranuigarden@xtra.co.nz
Website: friars.co.nz/gardens/pages/ngaranui.html
Open: Late September to May, 9am–5pm, by appointment
Fee: $5 per adult
Size: Medium – 0.8ha (2 acres)
Terrain: Sloping – flat & rolling
Nursery: Wide variety of seedlings & plants from garden eg roses, salvias, cranesbills, penstomens, euphorbias

  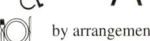

by arrangement

Ngaranui is a relaxed English-style garden, designed with different garden rooms featuring a wide variety of plants. Although the oak trees were planted in the early 1900s, the garden was not begun until 1993, after a tour of the United Kingdom provided inspiration. Fortunately a number of trees were established in the 1970s, creating a framework for the planting. Rustic pergolas, seats, dovecotes and a bridge add further structure, softened by many roses that are a drawcard in summer, interplanted with clematis, irises, delphiniums, euphorbias and salvias. Perennial borders define the boundary, with long vistas to the surrounding Wairarapa countryside. Bee even cut windows in the tennis court netting to frame the view and the historic farmhouse that was built for John's grandfather. A central waterlily pond features a fountain and small waterfall which flows into a stream under the bridge, feeding the hostas, primulas, ligularias and gunneras that thrive in the adjoining bog garden. The old driveway has been transformed into a gravel garden where verbascums, cranesbills, sedums and annuals self-seed each year. Bee's colour scheme is lively, but also includes the quiet green woodland. The spring begins with fritillarias, other early bulbs and trilliums, followed by the lilies, colourful roses and perennials. Recent features include oak and cotinus hedges, a lime walk and maple courtyard.

HARAKEKE GARDEN
Martinborough

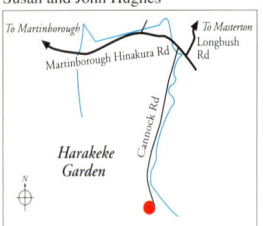

Owners:
Susan and John Hughes

Address: Cannock Rd, R D 4, Martinborough
Directions: From Martinborough, take Oxford St to the east. Travel 12km & turn right into Cannock Rd. Travel 5km to garden on right.
Phone: 0-6-308 8846
Fax: 0-6-308 8247
Open: Labour weekend (end October) to Easter, when "open" sign out or by appointment
Groups: By appointment
Fee: $4 per adult
Size: Medium – 0.8ha (2 acres)
Terrain: Sloping
Nursery: Good selection of perennials from garden.

limited

by arrangement
for groups only

Harakeke is the Maori word for flax, which grew profusely on the property at the turn of the century. It is still evident today, especially in the bog garden where it blends with the yellows, whites and blues. A wooden bridge crosses the bog garden and leads to the tennis court bordered by a dry bank of whites and yellows where the massed daisies are summer favourites of Sue's. She also loves blue-flowered plants such as delphiniums, cornflowers and centurea, grey foliage, hostas and other perennials including the penstemon, foxglove and red wallflower. The predominant species are roses, favourites including 'Dublin Bay' which climbs the entrance to the garden, 'Buff Beauty', 'New Dawn', 'Madame Alfred Carrière', 'Sally Holmes', 'Indica Major', 'Mary Rose', and 'Albertine' on the fenceline behind the clothes-line. The latter is a feature in itself, clad in clematis, another of Sue's loved plants. Harakeke has been gradually developed since 1964 from a bare paddock. Popular for weddings today is the lawn bordered by a semi-cicular bed, where white and blue flowering native olearias join the spring features, the Wairarapa hills forming a tranquil backdrop. Other special areas include a small pond by the bridge, the shadehouse, a small berry cage and the potager supplemented by John's vegetable garden. Harakeke is closed in winter because of heavy frosts and poor drainage.

KAPITI COAST AND WELLINGTON

Over the exposed Rimutaka Range from the Wairarapa are the final nine North Island gardens, in the Wellington region. Here is the capital city of New Zealand, situated on the southern tip of the North Island, separated from the South Island by the Cook Strait.

The Kapiti Coast extends down the west coast from Lindsay Garden just north of Levin, to Waikanae, north of Wellington. Lindsay Garden is notable for its humour and collectables, as well as the trees overlooking its lake. At Manakau, on the coastline is Pukehou Nursery adjacent to Serenity which features an extensive rockery that becomes a mass of colour in spring when the swathe of 'Pukehou' lavender flowers. These west coast gardens are much wetter than those in the east, although they are sheltered from prevailing westerlies by Kapiti Island. The Tararua Range lies to the east of the Kapiti Coast. Market gardening is popular in the Otaki area, and the soil around Waikanae is rich, but generally full of river stones.

Inland from Waikanae are two gardens in the Akatarawa Range, halfway between Waikanae and Upper Hutt. Moss Green is a haven for rhododendrons and other plants that enjoy the cool, moist conditions and Efil Doog (or "Good Life" spelt in reverse) is a sculpture park again featuring the rhododendrons that flourish here. Contemporary sculpture is displayed in this garden and an added attraction for art lovers is its private gallery specialising in early New Zealand paintings. The clear Akatarawa River flows through both these gardens.

North of Wellington at Tawa is The Threshold, an urban garden full of nooks and secluded corners, with water features, roses, gazebos and entertainment areas. Over towards the west coast beyond Johnsonville is Ohariu Valley, where two more gardens are located. Tikara Country Lodge and Gardens is set on a working farm with 300 roses as well as garden and bush walks beside a natural stream leading to the conference centre. Nearby is Sudbury, featuring rhododendrons and natives around a stream-fed lake. The climate in Wellington is notorious for its gale-force winds funnelling through Cook Strait and its steep, hilly terrain. But gardens nevertheless survive, tucked away in sheltered spots or with established trees breaking the winds. The climate here is generally colder than up north, with frosts in winter.

The final two gardens in the North Island are located in Wellington City itself. Both are public botanic gardens, but in total contrast to each other. The first is the extensive Wellington Botanic Garden in Thorndon and Kelburn, established in 1869, and featuring its popular tulip displays in early October, and a summer rose display in the adjoining Lady Norwood Rose Garden, where there is also the Begonia House. Other features include the Herb Garden and tower building housing the Education and Environment Centre. Nearby in Wilton is a native botanic garden, Otari – Wilton's Bush, featuring over 1,200 native species in the Fernery, Alpine Garden, Rock Garden, and the Wild Garden, with 10 kilometres of walks through original native bush. The newest feature is the 75-metre Canopy Walkway through the treetops to the Visitors' Centre.

The South Island is visible from Wellington on clear days and can be reached by the ferry service. Cars are taken on most of the ferries which average about three hours to cross Cook Strait. Advance ferry bookings are advisable. The Interisland ferries land at Picton, giving the motorist the option of travelling down the Marlborough east coast towards Christchurch, or across to Nelson where there are also many attractive gardens. The Marlborough Sounds are directly accessible from Picton, featuring further gardens.

TASMAN SEA

Waitarere

116

Shannon

Levin

Waikawa
Beach

117

118

Manakau

Otaki

Te Horo Beach

Kapiti I

Paraparaumu

Waikanae

119

Paekakariki

120

TARARUA RANGE

Mount
Bruce

2

Masterton

Carterton

Plimmerton

Birchville

Greytown

Mana I

Titahi Bay

Porirua

Paremata

2

Upper
Hutt

Tauherenikau

Featherston

Tawa

121

Martinborough

123

122

Makara
Beach

Petone

Lower Hutt

Port
Nicholson

Lake.
Wairarapa

125

Wainuiomata

124

WELLINGTON

Ruakokoputuna

Cook Strait

Lake
Onoke

Lake Ferry

Baring
Head

Palliser
Bay

Cape Palliser

Scale

0   50km

Cartography by Terralink Ltd

LINDSAY GARDEN
Levin

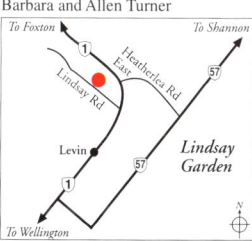

Lindsay

Owners:
Barbara and Allen Turner

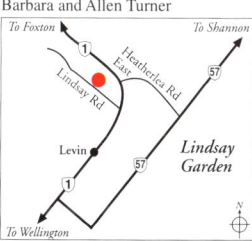

Address: 84 Lindsay Road, Levin
Postal: 113 Renown Road, Raumati
Directions: From Levin, take SH 1 north for 3km. Turn left into Lindsay Rd. Travel 1km to garden on right. Or from Foxton, take SH 1 south for 17km. Turn right into Lindsay Rd. Travel 1km to garden on right.
Phone: 0-4-902 1231
Mobile: 021 210 679
Fax: 0-4-902 1231
Open: October to April, Friday to Sunday, 10am to 6pm
Closed: May to September
Groups: By appointment
Fee: $4 per adult
Size: Medium – 1.2ha (3 acres)
Terrain: Flat with small valley

     partial

The first planting of the native border was undertaken in March 1996. The original site was a gully with farm pond choked with weeds and a big paddock with one huge pine tree, which now shelters a seat overlooking the small lake. The island in the lake is home to a pair of geese and further small pools are edged with bog plants. Many garden rooms of different characters feature varying colour schemes and focal points, such as pools, specimen trees, and planters retrieved from the local rubbish dump! Lindsay Garden is Barbara and Allen's retirement project, notable for its humour and included in the book *Kiwiana*. Apart from the interesting corners and hillside of English trees, there is a formal area, which was planned with herbaceous borders surrounding an oval lawn where weddings, funerals and small functions are held. Spring arrives with the daffodils and blossom on the prunus, malus and cornus trees. Summer features include the colourful flower beds of dahlias, asters and other perennials. Many of these continue into autumn when the deciduous foliage provides added colour. Barbara and Allen's ambition to grow trees and own a garden to roam in is being fulfilled as the bank of native trees and grasses matures and the woodland hillside of exotics grows up. They plan to establish more pathways as Lindsay Garden develops.

SERENITY
Manakau

![Serenity garden]

Owners:
Mary and Dean Robertson

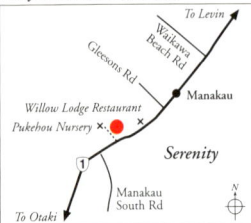

Address: SH 1, Manakau
Postal: Pukehou Nursery, R D 31, Levin
Directions: From Levin, take SH 1 south for 11km to Pukehou on right. From Otaki, take SH 1 north for 6km to Pukehou Nursery on left. Serenity adjacent on right of driveway.
Phone: 0-6-362 6869
Fax: 0-6-362 6865
Website: friars.co.nz/gardens/pages/serenity.html
Open: Aug.–April, daily, 9am–4.30pm
Groups: Welcome by appointment
Fee: $4 per adult; $3 pp for groups 10+
Size: Large – 2ha (5 acres)
Terrain: Easy contour
Nursery: Full range of plants for sale at Pukehou Nursery adjacent

   complimentary

at restaurant nearby

Serenity is enclosed by tall narrow hedges of *Cupressocyparis leylandii* 'Leighton Green', a fast-growing macrocarpa cross. In 1985 Dean and Mary planted a large hillside rockery on a sloping paddock. In spring, hundreds of bulbs cover it, followed by masses of red 'Angel Wing' poppies with touches of blue and white, evoking a Mediterranean atmosphere reminiscent of Monet's painting. Mary uses silvery-leafed plants to break the colour. *Teucrium fruticans* feature again above the rockery under blue Atlas cedars, underplanted with toning *Hosta sieboldiana*. More hostas and ferns fill the box-edged beds by the house. Beyond the rockery are massed borders of the deep purple lavender, *L. pedunculata* 'Pukehou', developed by the Robertsons in 1988. Below these is Mary's favourite garden, "Tranquillity", with its white and pink beds leading through a long wisteria-covered pergola to a small fernery. In summer, Mary's hundred-metre-long perennial borders are a mass of colour, backed by Dean's drystone walls. Mary loves her winter-flowering hellebores, many 'Pukehou Hybrids' in reds, pinks, whites, greens and mixed tonings growing along "Annabel's Amble" which faces the roadside. An avenue of 'Mt Fuji' cherries forms a tunnel of spring blossom nearby, and Dean's bridge, across Manakau Stream below, links a large pond to the highway garden.

MOSS GREEN GARDEN
Akatarawa

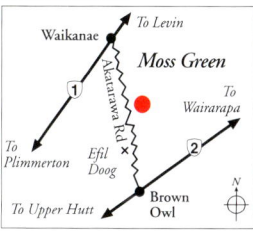

Owners:
Bob and Jo Munro

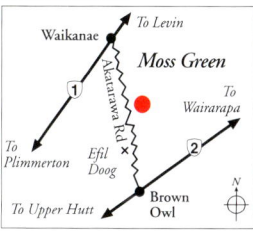

Address: 2420 Akatarawa Rd, Upper Hutt
Directions: 21km from either Upper Hutt or Waikanae on Akatarawa Rd.
Phone: 0-4-526 7531
Fax: 0-4-526 7507
Email: mgg@actrix.gen.nz
Website: www.mossgreengarden.co.nz
Open: Sept.–April, Wed.–Mon, public & school holidays, 10am–5pm
Closed: Tuesday
Groups: Preferably by appointment
Fee: $5 per adult, $1 per child
Size: Medium – 1ha (2 acres)
Terrain: Mostly flat, some hilly
Nursery: Selection of specialist plants eg damp-loving
For sale: Copper & hypertufa garden sculpture
Talks: Available to give talks at other venues

  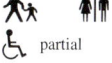 partial

Moss Green Garden is nestled among the bush-clad hills of the Akatarawa valley, and features the clear waters of the Akatarawa River running through it. Native plants, particularly ferns and grasses, have been used throughout the garden, complemented by exotics. Thought has also been given to providing food and habitat for wildlife. Large bog gardens are planted boldly to give an impression of natural water gardens. The marsh marigolds, irises and primulas of spring are followed by successions of other damp-loving plants which extend the season through summer into autumn. There is a large mixed border of shrubs, perennials, annuals and bulbs, where foliage has been used effectively. Although much of Moss Green Garden has been given over to informal woodland and water gardens, there are many other diverse areas on a smaller scale, in damp, dry, sunny and shady situations. Water is a unifying theme of the garden, with numerous water features in addition to the large natural pond and the river. Most of Bob's copper sculptures and hypertufa incorporate water, such as the misting units in his sentinels. Many of Bob's garden sculptures are for sale. He is also skilled at giving talks on various aspects of gardening at other venues. Picnickers are most welcome at Moss Green.

EFIL DOOG GARDEN OF ART
Akatarawa

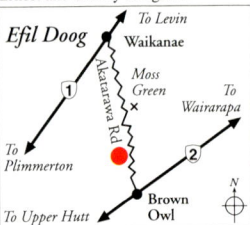

Owners:
Ernest and Shirley Cosgrove

Address: 1995 Akatarawa Rd, Upper Hutt, Wellington
Directions: From Upper Hutt, turn left at Brown Owl into Akatarawa Rd. Garden 12km on left. From Waikanae, travel 27km to garden on right.
Phone: 0-4-526 7924
Fax: 0-4-526 7904
Email: efildoog@xtra.co.nz
Website: www.efildoog-nz.com
Open: 1 Oct.–31 March, Wed.–Sun., 10am–4.30pm; or by appointment
Groups: All year, by appointment
Fee: $12 per adult, $6 per child 6–15 yrs; season tickets $20
Complimentary: Fruit juice/bookmarks
Size: Large – over 4ha (11 acres)
Terrain: Mixed, but mostly easy
Art Gallery: Early NZ original paintings
Functions: Weddings, conferences, etc

cottage   by arrangement

Efil Doog is "Good Life" spelt backwards! And for Ernest and Shirley, life on their large Akatarawa property is good. Embedded in their all-season garden are over 40 sculptures by New Zealand and international sculptors. The cool, moist climate in the hills favours the growth of rhododendrons, with over 2,000 species and hybrids featuring against the borrowed bush landscape. The park-like grounds are bissected by the beautifully clear Akatarawa River, Maori for "Valley of the Hanging Vines". The native vines beyond the garden are now complemented by clematis climbing trees and arbours, laburnum arches, and a wisteria walk. The water theme is extended with five ponds reflecting the colourful blossoms, and home to waterlilies and rainbow trout. A Japanese water feature is the focal point of the sculptured bonsai house and exhibition. The native trees attract countless birds, with over 40 species to be encountered in the wild. Exotics provide summer brilliance and autumn colour. A boardwalk takes visitors through the iris garden with 140 varieties of Japanese and Siberian irises providing massed colour towards the end of the year. Within a pine grove is an enchanted garden of the Akatrolls. Shirley's favourites are the borders of rare and special perennials. The private gallery features an exhibition of early paintings, and guided tours are available of the artworks, sculptures and gardens.

THE THRESHOLD
Tawa

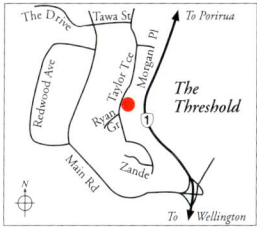

Owners:
Noeline and Derek Thresh

Address: 75 Taylor Terrace, Tawa, Wellington
Directions: From Wellington, travel north for 15 mins towards Tawa. Take Tawa exit. At roundabout turn right into Tawa St. Cross railway line & turn right into Taylor Tce. Garden on left. Or take train from Wellington City to Redwood Station.
Phone: 0-4-232 6300
Fax: 0-4-232 6300
Mobile: 025 451 688
Email: threshn@globe.net.nz
Open: September to March, 10am to 4pm, weekends & public holidays, by appointment
Groups: By appointment, as above
Fee: $3 per adult
Size: Small – 0.1ha (less than ¼ acre)
Terrain: Gently sloping & terraced

Winner of local garden awards, The Threshold is a small urban garden in a sheltered secluded spot, with archways enclosing intimate garden rooms designed for solitude as well as socialising. Originally a gorse-covered slope, turned into a cattery for breeding Burmese cats, the garden was extensively remodelled in 1987. The conservatory opens to decking encircled by a brick planter featuring camellias, azaleas, roses, lavenders, an ancient lemon tree, and a small pond and fountain. This area flows to an upper wooden deck and lawn. An undercover barbecue area offers seating, with a gazebo surrounded by a bricked circle looking out to an ornamental dovecote, grape-covered pergola, and a fish pond with a waterfall. Derek has lit this area at night, with a brazier providing warmth in winter. Waterlilies and Japanese irises thrive in the pond areas and a shadehouse protects Noeline's orchids. The old rambler rose 'Albertine' disguises the hothouse, and almost 300 roses bloom everywhere, including in containers and hanging baskets, along with fuchsias and annuals. Pathways lead to the upper garden where the focal point is a cedar summerhouse, with views over Tawa. Along with the camellias and azaleas, Noeline's rhododendrons and blossom trees predominate in spring, underplanted with hostas. Fruit trees and a small vegetable garden help to supplement the table.

TIKARA COUNTRY LODGE AND GARDENS
Johnsonville

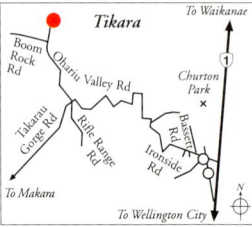

Owners:
Mary and Bruce McCallum

Address: 997 Ohariu Valley Road, R D, Johnsonville, Wellington
Directions: From Johnsonville, turn left into Ironside Rd, then into Ohariu Valley Rd to cross-roads (5km). Turn right & travel 5km to end of road.
Phone: 0-4-477 4646
Mobile: 025 223 6405
Fax: 0-4-473 4084
Email: tikaralodge@xtra.co.nz
Open: 1 August to 30 April, 10am–4pm, by appointment
Closed: 1 May to 31 July
Fee: $5 per adult
Size: Medium – 1.6ha (over 4 acres)
Terrain: Flat & hilly
Lunches: Groups only, by arrangement
Accommodation: (Pending)
Functions: Small private weddings, conferences & meetings catered; Business Retreat Centre available

    by arrangement

This secluded garden is located at the end of Ohariu Valley, providing peace and quietness, with rural views of hills, forest and farmland, yet within easy access of Johnsonville and Wellington City. Based on the site of an old woolshed, the gardens at Tikara have been created from bare paddocks since 1989. The mature trees provided structure, together with the contours of the hillside and valley. The style of the garden is informal and rambling, with walks being established down to the stream at the bottom of the valley. The stream runs naturally through three paddocks which are being developed as garden and bush walks, to link the extended gardens and the Business Retreat Centre where small conferences are held. Tikara is a working farm, with sheep grazing the hillsides. Springtime features bulbs, blossom trees, camellias and rhododendrons. Then 300 roses are the main attraction in summer. Mary's favourites include the camellias, rhododendrons and roses, as well as the poplar trees, lavenders, irises, hostas and Chatham Island forget-me-nots. The bog garden area is lush with these large-leafed *Myosotidium hortensia* and hostas. Weddings are also held at Tikara, with 'Margaret Merrill' and 'Iceberg' roses and lavender edging the wedding area. Native seedlings have been planted in the woodland. Other features include eucalypts, an orchard and vege garden.

160

SUDBURY
Ohariu Valley

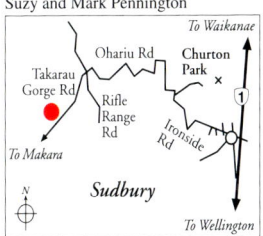

Owners:
Suzy and Mark Pennington

Address: 60 Takarau Gorge Rd,
Ohariu Valley, Wellington
Directions: Turn left at Johnsonville
roundabout. Keep left into Ironside
Rd. At Ohariu Valley crossroads,
continue ahead into Takarau Gorge
Rd. Travel 600m to garden on right.
Phone: 0-4-478 4846
Fax: 0-4-478 4917
Email: suzypennington@hotmail.com
Open: October to April, by
appointment
Groups: By appointment, as above
Fee: $10 per adult, including guided
tour
Size: Large – 2ha (5 acres)
Terrain: Flat and hilly
Nursery: Perennials from garden

  by arrangement

Sudbury is a romantic-style garden planted since 1975, centred around a wooden homestead and overlooking a small stream-fed lake. The garden design blends with surrounding farmland and hills, exotics combining with natives. Irises, primulas, hostas and other bog plants among ferns and ponga line a path following the stream, by two ponds which feed the lake. Rhododendrons, azaleas, kowhai, willows and perennials cover the banks. An arched bridge spans the lake to "Gnomes Island", where kowhai are underplanted with daffodils and gunneras. Behind the lake, walkways meander through a rhododendron dell and woodland area, with hostas, peonies, perennials and bulbs beneath. Kowhai and cherry blossom accompany the spring bulbs, with naturalised fritillaria and *Cardiocrinum giganteum*. Surrounding banks are planted in young kauri. Expansive lawns link the lake with the house garden, featuring roses, perennials and grey-foliaged plants. Nearby, a magnolia walk is underplanted with cream and pink tulips and blue and white forget-me-nots. A wisteria tunnel, formed by a white Japanese floribunda, leads through a perfumed area including many roses, old and new, lavender hedge and philadelphus. An enclosed brick courtyard behind the house is beautiful in late spring with apricot cedrelas, roses and abutilon.

WELLINGTON BOTANIC GARDEN
Kelburn, Wellington

Owner:
Wellington City Council

Address: 101 Glenmore St, Thorndon/
Kelburn, Wellington
Postal: P O Box 2199, Wellington
Directions: From City, take Cable Car
to Garden. Or take Bowen St to
Tinakori Rd. Turn left & continue
into Glenmore St to Garden. Or from
SH 1, exit at Hawkestone St & turn
right. Turn left into Tinakori Rd.
Main entrance from Glenmore St.
Phone: 0-4-801 3071
Fax: 0-4-801 3074
Email: treehouse@wcc.govt.nz
Open: all year, daily, dawn to dusk
Groups: Guided walks by arrangement
Fee: No charge
Size: Large – 26ha (65 acres)
Terrain: Flat to hilly
Treehouse: Surplus nursery plants,
gifts & postcards for sale

   limited

at Café

The Bolton Street Memorial Park at the north-east end
of the Wellington Botanic Garden was first designated
as a cemetery in 1840. Only five hectares was originally
set aside as the Colonial Botanic Garden, as it was then
known. By 1869 stock was removed, destruction of its
native forest stopped, and paths laid out. In the late 1890s
the ornamental gates at the main entrance were erected,
flower beds established and a wide variety of English
trees planted. These exotics are mature specimens today,
complementing the remnant of native trees. Around the
turn of the century the Pukatea Stream that runs into the
garden was dammed to form the duck pond. Then in the
1930s a ravine at the north end of the garden was filled in,
and transformed into the Lady Norwood Rose Garden in
1948. This was opened five years later, and now displays
over 300 varieties of roses arranged geometrically in 106
formal beds in concentric circles around the historic
fountain in the central pool. The adjacent Peace Flame
Garden was completed in 1959, with the Lady Norwood
Begonia House opening the following year. This temperate
house features seasonal displays, complemented by the
tropical Lily House added in 1989. Floral displays begin
in the garden with over 30,000 tulips in early spring and
continue year-round. The Treehouse Visitor Centre offers
information and a range of gifts and postcards for sale.

OTARI – WILTON'S BUSH
Wilton, Wellington

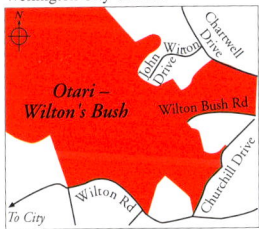

Owner:
Wellington City Council

Address: 160 Wilton Rd, Wilton,
Wellington
Postal: P O Box 2199, Wellington
Directions: From City, take either
Wadestown or Tinakori Rd to Wilton.
Or catch No. 14 bus. 3 entrances from
Wilton Rd, 2 from Wilton Bush Rd &
1 from John Witton Dr into Garden.
Phone: 0-4-801 3071
Fax: 0-4-801 3074
Email: treehouse@wcc.govt.nz
Open: All year, daily, dawn to dusk
Groups: Guided walks by appointment
Fee: No charge for entrance or walks
Size: Large – 76ha (190 acres)
Terrain: Flat, undulating & hilly
Nursery: Native plant sale annually,
each September

   limited

    & 2 gas BBQs

Otari, or Wilton's Bush as it is often known, owes its existence to the foresight of Job Wilton, original owner of the north-facing slopes, who conserved the native forest. In 1904 the City Council bought the land, establishing it as a scenic reserve two years later. Today, Otari is devoted solely to the cultivation and preservation of indigenous plants. A significant proportion of the area is original forest, intersected with 10 kilometres of walking tracks. Predominant native trees include mahoe, kohekohe, tawa, rewarewa, hinau, northern rata with its red summer blossom, and mature rimu, one a 700-year-old specimen. Other features include the Fernery, large Alpine Garden and tarn, Rock Garden with fish pond and collection of native grasses and sedges, Wild Garden with introduced trees, shrubs and herbaceous plants, and in 1999 the 75-metre Canopy Walkway was added through the treetops to the Visitors' Centre. In spring, the flax and yellow kowhai flowers attract native tui, and Chatham Island forget-me-nots flourish in shady spots. The Rock Garden features in summer, when *Hibiscus trionum* flower. The keruru or wood pigeons are abundant in autumn and other native birdlife includes tui, kingfishers, fantails and silvereyes. Otari contains 1,200 different native plants, 500 of which are labelled. Picnics and barbecues are popular in the bush setting beside the creek.

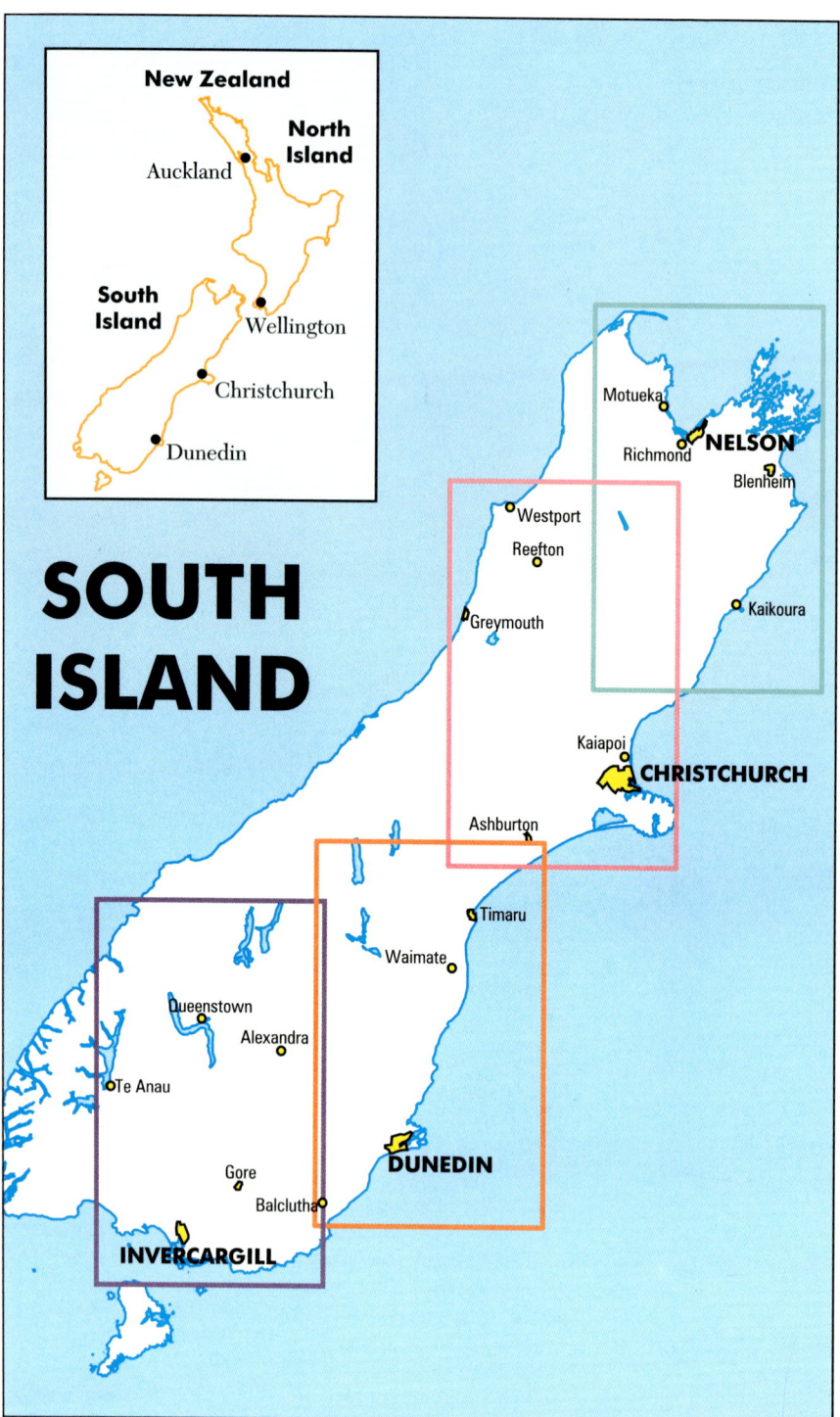

New Zealand

North Island

Auckland

South Island

Wellington

Christchurch

Dunedin

SOUTH ISLAND

Motueka

Richmond   NELSON

Blenheim

Westport

Reefton

Greymouth

Kaikoura

Kaiapoi

CHRISTCHURCH

Ashburton

Timaru

Waimate

Queenstown

Alexandra

Te Anau

DUNEDIN

Gore

Balclutha

INVERCARGILL

MARLBOROUGH AND NELSON

Marlborough and Nelson cover the northernmost tip of the South Island. We present 12 gardens to visit in this region. Marlborough is becoming known as the gourmet province, with its vineyards producing award-winning wines. Marlborough extends from Picton, the arrival point in the South Island for the Interisland ferries, up through the bays and coves of the picturesque Marlborough Sounds, down through the main city, Blenheim, as far south as Kaikoura, famous for dolphin- and whale-watching, and west to Nelson.

The six gardens featured in Marlborough have to contend with the hot, dry summers typical of this region. The gardens stretch from the Sounds down the east coast to Kaikoura. In the Marlborough Sounds themselves is The Nikaus Country Garden and Farmstay with rhododendrons and the nikau palms on the slopes behind.

Blenheim features four gardens: Woodend just north of Blenheim, with its expansive lawn bounded by strong colours, and three Marlborough District Council gardens. Seymour Square is right in the heart of Blenheim and is also known as The Garden of Memories after two war memorials, a clock tower and fountain were erected. This garden is linked by a walkway to Pollard Park, featuring mature trees, a rose garden, annual beds and a stream throughout. McKendry Park is a woodland park comprising plum trees bordered by walnuts and underplanted with thousands of daffodils.

Down the east coast at Kaikoura is Fyffe House, a Historic Places Trust property overlooking the ocean with a backdrop of snowcapped peaks. The cottage is the surviving remnant of an early whaling station, and the garden is being restored to earlier plantings.

Sunny Nelson is renowned for its tramping, fishing and limestone caves and Motueka is famous for its orchards – the most prolific in the country. The region has several national and forest parks, including the well known Heaphy Track in north-west Nelson.

The six gardens featured in Nelson are spread throughout the district. Contrasting with the formal English-style Queens Gardens in Nelson City, just north off the main highway is Miyazu Japanese Garden, a contemplative stroll garden featuring paths, bridges and stepping stones through water gardens (*see front cover*) and a raked gravel Zen garden. South at Richmond are two more City Council gardens: Isel Park and Broadgreen Rose Gardens, both with historic trees. Just south, at Hope, is Etheringtons' Garden Park encompassing "Gardens of the World" around extensive water features. Along the coastal highway towards Motueka is Fable Cottage with rhododendrons, camellias and fruit trees surrounding the cottage.

North at Motueka is Tasman Bay Roses, with the roses thriving in the mild climate. Then over the hill at Takaka are the final two gardens, both appealing to specialist markets. The first is Beautiful Begonias which is worth a visit in summer to see the range of varieties in the tuberous-begonia houses, and the other is Lilies in Bloom overlooking the coast, where a huge range is displayed, including over 10,000 potted lilies.

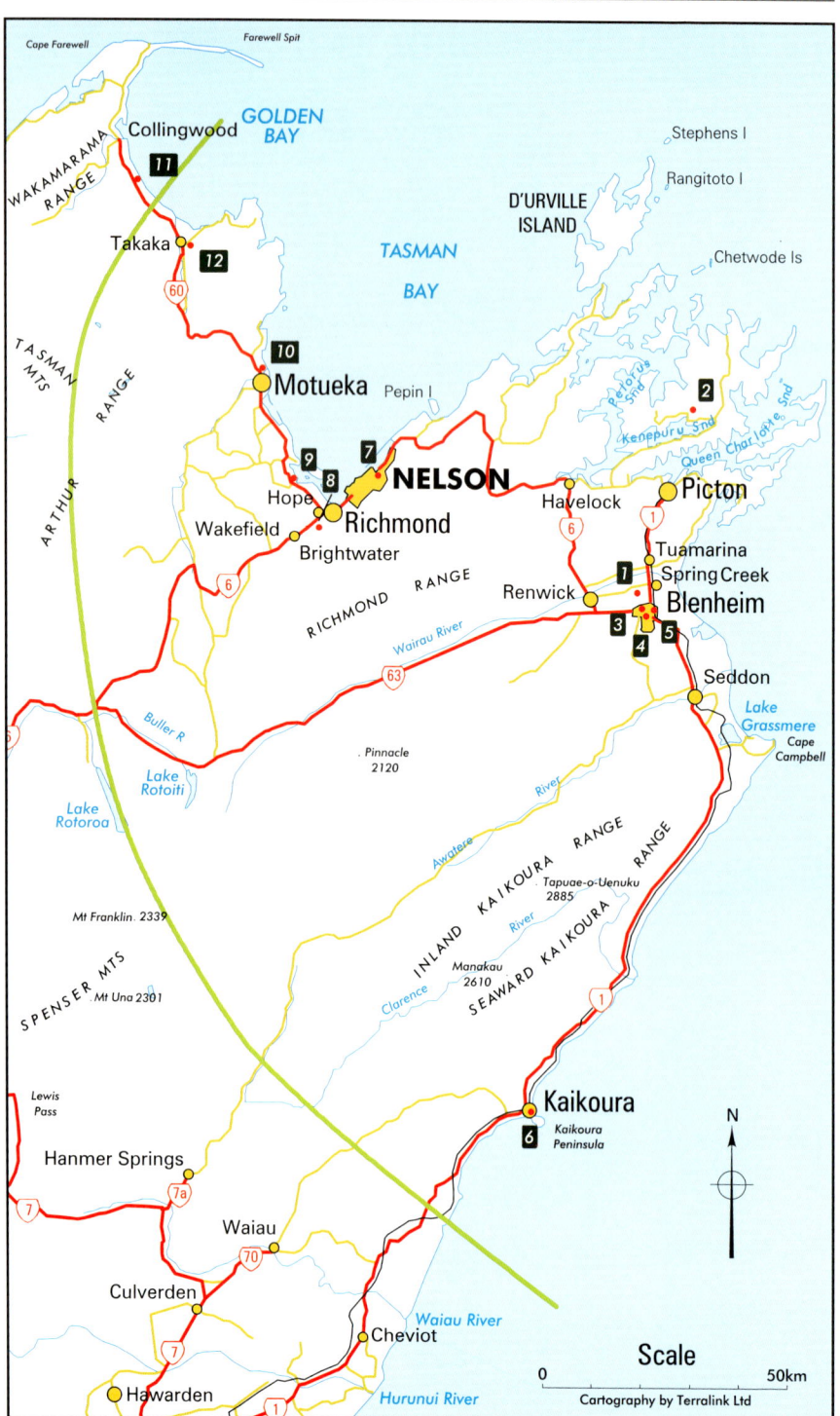

WOODEND
Grovetown, Blenheim

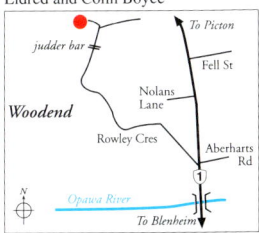

Owners:
Eldred and Colin Boyce

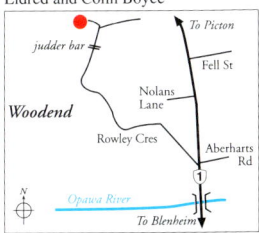

Address: 151 Rowley Cres,
Grovetown, Blenheim
Directions: From Picton, take SH 1
south to Grovetown. Continue 2km &
take 2nd turning on right into Rowley
Cres. Travel to end, past private sign
on left to garden. From Blenheim,
take SH 1 north over Opawa River
bridge. Take next turn left into
Rowley Cres, then as above.
Phone: 0-3-577 8576
Fax: 0-3-577 8506
Open: End August to end April, by
appointment
Groups: By appointment
Fee: $4 per adult
Size: Large – almost 3ha (7 acres)
Terrain: Flat
Nursery: Maybe plants from garden

  x 2

& to toilet ⊙ by arrangement

The driveway to Woodend, lined with golden elms and agapanthus, sweeps along the path of an old river bed. The gravelly soil provides good drainage but requires constant watering – all computerised. The garden has been established since 1993 on a flat two-hectare paddock, treeless except for a grove of century-old gums. These form a woodland backdrop to the garden, now underplanted with hostas, Virginias, hellebores and Chatham Island forget-me-nots and 5,000 spring bulbs such as the daffodils and bluebells which also emerge in the adjacent new rhododendron area featuring 60 specimens. Both Eldred and Colin like strong colours, the dahlias round the boundary being Colin's favourites, while Eldred prefers the roses and clematis climbing the back fence. The clematis walk is at its peak in mid October and the rose pergola, featuring red 'Dublin Bay' contrasting with golden banksia, comes into flower in early November. Eldred also loves the new area of 250 mainly red azaleas, planted in 1996. Deciduous trees such as the dogwoods, flowering cherry walkway and the liquidambar avenue have been chosen for both spring and autumn colour. A wedding area has been planted with oaks, *Robinia frisia*, silk trees, sycamores and zelkovas. The extensive lawn area is Eldred's pride and joy, while Colin looks after the white doves in the dovecote.

THE NIKAUS COUNTRY GARDEN AND FARMSTAY
Waitaria Bay, Marlborough Sounds

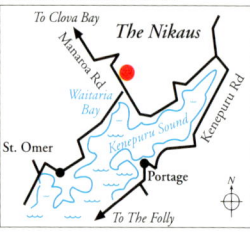

Owners:
Alison and Robin Bowron

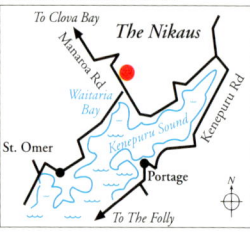

Address: Manaroa Rd, Kenepuru
Postal: Waitaria Bay, R D 2, Picton
Directions: From Picton or Havelock, travel along Queen Charlotte Drive to Linkwater. Turn north into Kenepuru Rd & travel 1½ hours to Waitaria Bay. At intersection take Manaroa Rd. Nikaus Country Garden on right.
Phone: 0-3-573 4432
Fax: 0-3-573 4432
Website: friars.co.nz/gardens/pages/nikaus.html
Open: All year, daily, 10am–5pm
Groups: By appointment
Fee: $3 per adult over 15 years
Size: Medium – 0.8ha (2 acres)
Terrain: Flat
Accommodation: B&B farmstay, by arrangement, dinner optional

Named after the native nikau palms on the slopes behind the house, this garden has been developed since 1992 by Alison, although it was originally designed by another rhododendron lover when it was established two decades earlier. Spring begins with sheets of gold daffodils under the orchard and paulownia, while camellias brighten the pathway and vege garden. Then the pinks, creams and blues take over, with flowering cherries, magnolias and michelia joining the rhododendrons. Clematis climbs the fence surrounding the swimming pool, where Alison has planted ferns and begonias under ponga. In November the lilies begin to emerge, continuing till the end of February with massed displays of Asiatic and Oriental lilies including Alison's favourite apricot Asiatic 'Hartford'. The lilies complement the blue delphiniums and other perennials in the extensive herbaceous borders. Old roses are also summer highlights, followed by chrysanthemums in autumn when the oak leaves turn. Maples shelter a kidney-shaped pond backed by a small rock garden to the side of the house. The views out to sea are marvellous in winter through the deciduous trees, and a *Magnolia campbellii* planted on the lawn in 1970 blooms in early August. Farm walks lead across a creek up to the nikau grove and a waterfall beyond. Bed and breakfast farmstay with dinner is available by arrangement.

SEYMOUR SQUARE
Blenheim

Owner:
Marlborough District Council

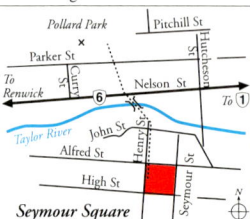

Address: Seymour St, Blenheim
Postal: P O Box 443, Blenheim
Directions: From Picton, take SH 1
south to Blenheim. Turn right into
Alfred St & travel 300m to Square on
left. From Christchurch, take SH 1
north to Blenheim. Turn left into
Alfred St, then as above. From Nelson,
take SH 6 to Blenheim. Turn right
into Hutcheson St, then right again
into Alfred St. Travel 100m to Square.
Phone: 0-3-578 5249
Fax: 0-3-578 6866
Email: mdc@marlborough.govt.nz
Open: All year, daily
Fee: No charge
Size: Medium – 1ha (2½ acres)
Terrain: Flat
Restrictions: No swimming in
fountain

& to toilet

Featured on a 1996 New Zealand postage stamp, Seymour Square is a historic park named after the pioneer Mr A.P. Seymour who gifted the land to Blenheim in 1857. Initially used as a sports ground, the Square was planted as a garden in 1912 by the Beautifying Society. In 1920, the Prince of Wales planted a pin oak which is now one of several notable trees. Seymour Square was also named The Garden of Memories after two memorials were erected to commemorate both world wars. One, a chiming clock tower clad in stone from local riverbeds, was unveiled in 1928. Four diagonally intersecting pathways meet at the other, a multi-coloured fountain built in 1953 in the centre of the Square on the site of the original band rotunda. Many commemorative specimen trees were also planted, including five pink flowering *Prunus serrulata* 'Kanzan' along the eastern border of the Square in 1945 to mark the end of World War II. Seating throughout makes the Square a popular lunchtime meeting place, and stalls are hosted during Garden Marlborough each spring. The formal beds of annuals are renewed every spring and autumn for a year-round display. A wide herbaceous border along the northern boundary is filled with colourful perennials, shrubs and ornamental trees. A marked walkway (*see map*) links Seymour Square to Pollard Park, taking visitors on a 10-minute tour each way.

POLLARD PARK
Blenheim

Owner:
Marlborough District Council

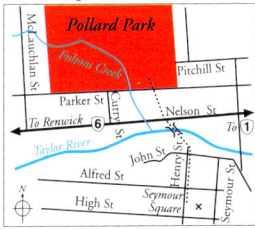

Address: Seymour Street, Blenheim
Postal: P O Box 443, Blenheim
Directions: From Picton, take SH 1
south towards Blenheim. Turn right
into SH 6 then right into Curry St.
Pollard Park at end in Parker St.
From Christchurch, take SH 1 north
to Blenheim. Turn left into SH 6, then
as above. From Nelson, take SH 6
towards Blenheim. Turn left into
Curry St, then as above.
Phone: 0-3-578 5249
Fax: 0-3-578 6866
Email: mdc@marlborough.govt.nz
Open: All year, daily
Groups: By appointment
Fee: No charge
Size: Large – 24.57ha (61 acres)
Terrain: Flat
Children: Large playground
Picnics: Electric BBQs available

🚲 👫 🪑 ♿ & to toilet

Pollard Park is linked to Seymour Square by a scenic walkway (*see map*). The Park was named after William Pollard who donated the funds to buy the land. Originally part of Waterlea Farm, the Park now features four hectares of gardens adjacent to Fulton Creek known as Waterlea Gardens. The Centennial Rose Garden is also bordered by a bend of the creek. In 1914 the Mayor, Mr Corry, initiated the Park's development. Five years later Mr Oliver, the Superintendent of Parks who had designed Seymour Square in 1912, proposed a design for Pollard Park. This was based on the landscape style of 'Capability' Brown, comprising grassland, clumps of trees and creek views. Over the years this plan has been modified as sports facilities have been added and more structured gardens planted around the creek. Today, features of the gardens at Pollard Park include the formal rose gardens, rhododendron dell, camellia bed, native rock garden, potager, gazebo, floral display and perennial border. Mature English trees provide shade and beauty, such as the enormous weeping willows over the creek. Bridges cross the clear water where hundreds of ducks enjoy swimming to a central island. Over 17,000 annuals and 2,000 bulbs flower in spring, followed by the 700 roses. The annuals beds are replanted each year for the autumn display. A large playground includes electric barbecues for picnickers.

MCKENDRY PARK
Blenheim

Owner:
Marlborough District Council

Address: Orchard Lane, Blenheim
Postal: P O Box 443, Blenheim
Directions: From Picton, take SH 1 south to Blenheim. Turn right into SH 6 & travel along Middle Renwick Rd. Turn right into Colemans Rd, then left into Orhard Lane. McKendry Park at end. From Nelson, take SH 6 to Blenheim. Turn left into Colemans Rd, then as above. Footpath access from Aston St & Ward St as well.
Phone: 0-3-578 5249
Fax: 0-3-578 6866
Email: mdc@marlborough.govt.nz
Open: All year, daily
Fee: No charge
Size: Large – 1.06ha (2⅝ acres)
Terrain: Flat
Produce: Plums & walnuts available for picking in season (summer months)

Named after a former mayor of Blenheim who was instrumental in acquiring the land for a recreational reserve in 1995, McKendry Park was historically a commercial orchard. Originally purchased in 1903 by Balfour Clouston, it was planted as an apple orchard with a boundary of walnut trees added 15 years later. In 1939 his son Stewart replaced the apples with more profitable plum trees. He also imported several thousand daffodil bulbs from Holland to provide a spring carpet of yellow beneath the plum blossom. He sold the plum and walnut crops as well as the cut daffodils and bulbs. Later his son Tom, then grandson Tony, invited charity groups to collect daffodils for fundraising each spring. The original 10,000 bulbs have been added to and hybridised over the years to produce an amazing array of different blooms including trumpets, large cups, small cups, doubles and tazettas. These flower prolifically in the woodland beneath the plum trees, along with bluebells, crocus, snowflake, galanthus, and arums. The 185 plum trees include 11 different varieties, while the walnuts comprise 30 common and five French trees. The plums and walnuts can be collected during the summer season. There is also an old quince tree on Murphys Creek which borders the park, edged with Louisiana irises, pseudacorus and arum lilies. It is spring fed and home to many ducks.

FYFFE HOUSE
Kaikoura

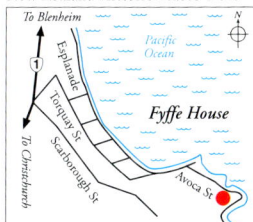

Owner:
New Zealand Historic Places Trust

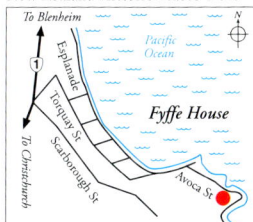

Address: 62 Avoca St, Kaikoura
Directions: From Blenheim, take SH 1 south to Kaikoura. Turn left into Esplanade. Continue into Avoca St. Fyffe House on right. Or from Christchurch, take SH 1 north to Kaikoura. Turn right into Killarney St, then right into Torquay St. Turn right again into Avoca St.
Phone: 0-3-319 5835
Fax: 0-3-319 5837
Email: fyffe.bill@xtra.co.nz
Open: All year, November to April, daily, 10am–6pm; May to October, Thursday to Monday, 10am–4pm
Fee: $5 per adult;
$2 per unaccompanied child
Size: Small – 0.1ha (¼ acre)
Terrain: Flat
Nursery: Wide selection of seeds
Historic Home: Open for viewing

Fyffe House and gardens have historic significance in that they are the only tangible remains of Robert Fyffe's Waiopuka Whaling Station. Originally built as a typical colonial cottage by Robert's cousin about 1860, Fyffe House features extant foundations from whale vertebrae. Only three families lived in the cottage until it was bequeathed to the New Zealand Historic Places Trust in 1980. A Category I listing has since been allocated to the house and grounds. The site is also important archaeologically, revealing evidence of early occupation by moa-hunting Maori. The garden was re-established in 1981 and research will result in earlier plantings being restored. Predominant species in the present garden include roses, lilacs, irises, fuchsias, dahlias, native ngaio trees and perennials such as aquilegias, pelargoniums, daisies, foxgloves, and Japanese anemones, as well as annual marigolds. The peak time for the flowers is spring and early summer when the colour scheme is soft pinks, yellows and blues, featuring bulbs, irises and early perennials. Then the roses emerge, including favourites 'Reine des Violettes' and 'Souvenir de la Malmaison'. These are followed by the Japanese anemones, joined by pineapple sage and succulents in autumn. The panoramic vistas of the snowcapped mountain backdrop and the ocean are most spectacular in winter.

MIYAZU JAPANESE GARDEN
Nelson

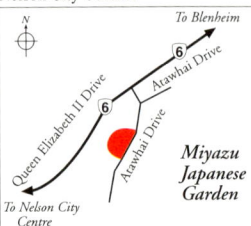

Owner:
Nelson City Council

Miyazu Japanese Garden

Address: Atawhai Drive, Nelson
Postal: P O Box 645, Nelson
Directions: From north, turn left off
SH 6 into Atawhai Drive. Travel past
Miyazu Park for 200m to garden on
right. From south, turn right off
Queen Elizabeth II Drive into
Atawhai Drive. Travel 200m to
garden on right.
Phone: 0-3-546 0376
Fax: 0-3-546 0239
Email: prgrundy@ncc.govt.nz
Open: All year, daily
Groups: As above
Fee: No charge
Size: Large – 2ha (5 acres)
Terrain: Flat

 from carpark

Miyazu Garden is a Japanese stroll garden named after
Nelson's sister city. The first planting in 1990 by the
Japanese ambassador was followed by the official opening
three years later by the Deputy Mayor of Miyazu. The
garden features traditional Japanese aesthetic concepts and
symbolism using water, rocks, gravel and a combination of
New Zealand natives and Japanese plants to create green
on green hues of varying texture, with highlights of
seasonal colour. Cherry blossoms announce the spring when
the camellias, azaleas and the wisteria arbour flower. A
Welcome Gate, with its authentic granite *yukimi-gata*
lantern, overlooks the Dragon Pond. Large granite stepping
stones traverse the still water towards the 25-year-old bonsai
on the far bank, the stone beach contrasting with the water.
A stone cleansing basin or *tsukubai* is adjacent to the pondside pavilion which provides contemplative views of a
century-old camellia. Many bridges and stepping stones
cross the ponds edged with water irises and raupo. A bridge
linking two islands symbolises friendship between the two
cities. Waterfalls, streams and bamboo fountains create
musical sounds and a sense of tranquillity. Many seats
strategically placed throughout the garden allow absorption
of the peaceful ambience and contemplation of the special
features, such as the *Karesansui* Zen Garden where a sea of
raked gravel surrounds asymmetrically placed rocks.

GARDENS OF THE WORLD
Richmond

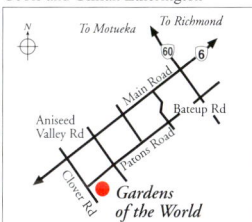

Owners:
Geoff and Gillian Etherington

Address: Clover Rd East,
Brightwater, Nelson
Postal: P O Box 3046, Richmond,
Nelson
Directions: Take SH 6 south of
Nelson. 5 mins south of Richmond,
turn left down Clover Rd. Gardens
just past Patons Rd on left.
Phone: 0-3-542 3736
Fax: 0-3-542 3036
Email: gf&gme@xtra.co.nz
Open: All year, daily, 10am to dusk
Groups: By appointment
Fee: $5 per adult over 12 years;
booked groups $4 per head
Size: Large – 2.4ha (6 acres)
Terrain: Level with landscaped mounds
Functions: Weddings & corporate
functions welcome by arrangement;
concerts in amphitheatre

A grand dream has come to fruition at the Etheringtons' Garden Park, designed to represent "Gardens of the World". Originally a level apple orchard, the garden is landscaped to provide rolling mounds surrounding the more formal central areas. Native plantings from New Zealand, the Orient, the Americas, Europe, Africa and Australia are grouped according to their geographical regions. Avenues of *Fraxinus excelsior* 'Aurea' trees form a square at the garden entrance. Concerts are held in an amphitheatre overlooking the pond, which provides an overview of layered colour between the hedges. Ex-nurseryman Geoff began planting trees in 1990, with some rare African species his favourites. Extensive reticulated water features include a stream with water flowing from the top rockery to a pond, crossed by three diverse bridges. Home to frogs, ducks, white-faced herons, and kingfishers, the pond is edged with Japanese irises and native plantings. Three new ponds will feature fountains. Yew hedges enclose the herb garden with its beds edged in rosemary. Structures include a gazebo and rose pergola in the formal rose garden. A conservatory is planned for the herbaceous garden which is planted in the colours of the rainbow. The Gardens are a popular venue for weddings and garden groups, with a mountain backdrop framing the various sections of the world which swirl around grassed areas.

FABLE COTTAGE
Nelson

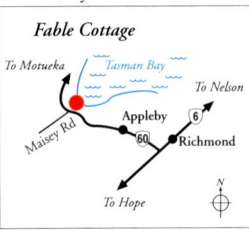

Owner:
Trina McKay

Fable Cottage

Address: Coastal Highway 60, R D 1,
Richmond, Nelson
Directions: Take SH 6 south of
Nelson to Richmond. Continue south
to SH 60 (Coastal Highway), turn
right towards Motueka. Travel to
Maisey Rd on left. Fable Cottage is
opposite, on right.
Phone: 0-3-544 2657
Fax: 0-3-544 2657
Email: pholdsworth@clear.net.nz
Open: 1 September to 30 April,
Friday to Monday, 10am–4pm;
Tuesday to Thursday by appointment
Fee: $2 per adult
Size: Medium – 0.8ha (2 acres)
Terrain: Flat
Nursery: Rhododendrons for sale

Almost a hectare of ornamental garden, lawn, vegetable garden and fruit trees surrounds Fable Cottage, overlooking the estuary. Primarily a spring garden, Trina's favourite plants include her white clematis, magnolias, michelia and maples. The predominant species in the garden are the rhododendrons, which Trina is specialising in, camellias – a white camellia hedge now replaces a line of pencil willows – and roses. Trina has introduced a lot of white-flowering plants and evergreens into the predominantly pink garden, with colour tonings grouped together, separated from the yellow-orange spectrum planted out by the estuary. A stream runs beside the garden, crossed by a bridge. Daffodils, grape hyacinths and white tulips announce the spring, with the camellias, cherry trees, clematis, irises and azaleas. In summer the roses bloom with perennials such as foxgloves, delphiniums, aquilegias, lavender and hostas. Dahlias add summer colour interspersed with white summer flowers. Trees consist of native pittosporums, conifers such as the recently planted Douglas firs, eucalypts and other exotics including maples, willows, and poplars. Trina has developed a herb garden, and fruit trees including mandarins grow near the garden cottage.

TASMAN BAY ROSES
Motueka

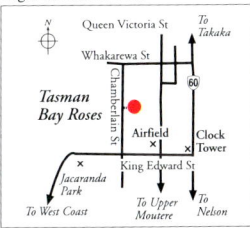

Owners:
Nigel and Judith Pratt

Address: 45 Chamberlain St North, Motueka
Postal: P O Box 159, Motueka
Directions: From Nelson take SH 60 to Motueka. Turn left at clock tower. Travel 3km. Turn right into Chamberlain St. Garden 500m on right.
Phone: 0-3-528 7449
Fax: 0-3-528 7449
Email: tbr@xtra.co.nz
Website: www.tbr.co.nz
Open: Garden: open from mid Nov. all summer; or groups by appointment Nursery: open daily, 10.30am– 5pm
Fee: No charge
Size: Medium – just over 1ha (3 acres)
Terrain: Flat
Nursery: Roses – old & unusual to latest modern varieties; potted roses for summer visitors; perennials; complimentary mail-order catalogue or on-line catalogue

At Tasman Bay Roses, a growing collection of old and rare roses is set among mature trees, with the Arthur Range as backdrop. The main garden features a long double border of old roses leading to a summer house covered in 'Pax', 'Francesca', and 'Crépuscule'. To one side is a mixed border with further roses, perennials and shrubs, backed by a shelter hedge of conifers. A lavender walk leads between beds of predominantly purple and red roses to another formal garden. Roses climb and ramble through an adjacent orchard, and every available wall and building is covered in roses, forming their own shapes and reaching spectacular heights. Old roses create a colourful spectacle in November and December, with repeat-flowering varieties such as 'Bantry Bay' and 'Michèle Meilland' providing interest all summer. A tree-lined driveway leads to the barnyard featuring a historic hop kiln, where roses and perennials are available for sale. Native birds abound, with doves nesting in a large macrocarpa and pheasants, quail and fantails also making their homes in the garden. Visitors are welcomed by 100 climbing roses along the boundary and another 50 cover a massive arbour beside the carpark. The roses enjoy the mild Nelson climate and abundant water supply. The Tasman Bay Roses website features an on-line catalogue.

LILIES IN BLOOM
Golden Bay

![Lilies in Bloom photograph]

Lilies in Bloom

Owners:
Gordon and Bess Hampson

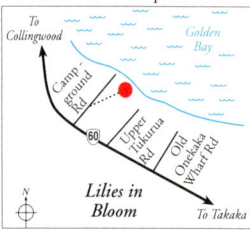

Lilies in Bloom

Address: Campground Rd, Tukurua, Golden Bay
Postal: Takaka, R D 2, Golden Bay
Directions: From Motueka, travel north on SH 60 to Takaka. Continue for another 18km. Garden sign on right, then turn into Campground Rd. Lilies in Bloom garden on right.
Phone: 0-3-525 8353
Fax: 0-3-525 8353
Email: info@bloom.co.nz
Website: www.bloom.co.nz
Open: All year, Mon.–Sat, 9am–6pm
Groups: By appointment
Fee: No charge
Size: Medium – 1.5ha (4 acres)
Terrain: Flat
Nursery: Potted lilies in flower; lily bulbs; mail-order catalogue free, or $2 for colour catalogue – send SAE; raspberries for sale during January

In 1984, Gordon and Bess purchased a gorse-infested block of land right on the water's edge in Golden Bay. There they developed Lilies in Bloom which is open all year, and features more than 150 varieties of lilium. Bounded by a stream, with picnic area overlooking the sandy beach, this coastal garden is a pleasant drive from Nelson City. The peak viewing time for the lilies is from spring until March. The predominant species are Asiatic, Oriental and Longiflorum /Asiatic hybrid lilies. Many of these are exclusive imports, selected for their diverse form and colour, and ease of growing. Lilies are amazingly tolerant of wind and salt-spray as evidenced by this exposed seaside site. In spring, a hectare (over two acres) of Asiatic lilies comes into bloom. These are followed by the large perfumed blooms of the Oriental hybrids. The major attraction of the gardens is the potted lilies which are planted to give a succession of flowering plants, effectively producing a continuous living catalogue of varieties from December until March. At this time both lily plants and bulbs are available for sale and there is a covered display area, accessible in all weather. But even during the winter months the colour catalogue enables visitors to select bulbs to buy. Gordon's website provides viewers anywhere in the world with the opportunity of ordering bulbs. Fresh raspberries are an added attraction in season during January.

178

Lilies in Bloom

BEAUTIFUL BEGONIAS
Takaka

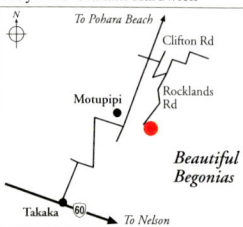

Beautiful Begonias

Owners:
Robyn and Graham Hardwick

Address: Rocklands Rd, Clifton, Takaka
Directions: Take SH 60 from Nelson. Turn right at Takaka, towards Pohara Beach. Follow signs, turning right into Clifton Rd, then right again into Rocklands Rd. Garden on left.
Phone: 0-3-525 9058
Fax: 0-3-525 9058
Open: November to May, daily, 10am–6pm
Groups: As above
Fee: No charge
Size: Small – 1,000 square metres of covered begonia houses (¼ acre)
Terrain: Hilly
Nursery: Tuberous begonias & succulents, fertiliser, flower-supports & mail-order catalogue

Beautiful Begonias is situated near Takaka with superb scenic views across Golden Bay. Graham and Robyn have been selling tuberous begonias every summer since 1983, their collection expanding into numerous shadehouses. The seedlings appear in spring, with the peak flowering time from February to April, when thousands of begonias provide a massed display of all the sunset colours in full flower. The blooms come as standard uprights and hanging-basket varieties, ruffled, frilled or picotee in singles or doubles. Special named begonias include 'Sweetie', a rare scented begonia with soft-yellow, double hanging flowers. Contrary to popular opinion, tuberous begonias are not difficult to grow. As long as they are given appropriate conditions, they can be easily grown in pots or even in the garden outside in sheltered areas with filtered light. The tubers sprout in early spring and are ready to pot up or plant out by late October. The flowering season is late summer, from January through to April, when the plant dies off and the tubers can be dug up, dried and stored ready for the following season. Robyn also raises begonias from imported seed, which requires quite a degree of skill. The new succulent gardens and an aviary of budgies are added attractions.

WESTLAND, NORTH TO MID CANTERBURY, CHRISTCHURCH AND BANKS PENINSULA

Rugged Westland is a beautiful and untouched coastline, with few gardens to visit throughout its length. One garden features at Westport: River View Lodge overlooking the dramatic Buller Gorge on a farm, also offering accommodation. Down the coast at Hokitika are another two gardens. Seaforth features panoramic views over the west coast and a bush walk linking the house garden to the terraced hillside below. Killinchy Woods is a country garden with a stream running through it, on family land since the pioneering days.

Two-thirds of the population of the South Island lives in Canterbury, which includes the largest city, Christchurch. Twenty-eight gardens are featured in this region. From coastal Kaikoura, North Canterbury stretches down to Rangiora, just above Christchurch, then Central Canterbury extends south to the Rakaia River. Mid Canterbury reaches from Rakaia down through Ashburton. Many Canterbury gardens incorporate views of the spectacular Southern Alps which cause rain to fall on the West Coast rainforests, and contrast strikingly with the Canterbury Plains stretching out flat and broad to the Pacific Ocean on the east.

South of Hanmer Springs is the woodland garden of Lowry Peaks at Culverden. At Amberley are two gardens: Brikton, a seasonal garden, and Hunters Garden divided into "rooms", with many planted walkways. Inland from Kaiapoi, at Ohoka on the Canterbury Plains, is Cashel, a formal garden surrounding a Palladian house with long vistas created from axes of hedging. Nearby is Wilsons Mill Garden also featuring architectural planting and tree-lined avenues. To the west in Cust is the rose display garden at Littlerose Nursery.

English-style Christchurch is often called the "Garden City". The picturesque Avon River flows through this flat city, crossed by countless bridges. On the banks of the Avon is the well known Edwardian garden at Mona Vale, and nearby is The Chateau on the Park, with its formal rose gardens and moat. The Avon flows through the Christchurch Botanic Gardens, located within Hagley Park, featuring massed daffodils in spring. The focal point at Fairleigh Garden Guest House is a 10-metre pond. Rose Cottage is an urban garden crammed with roses around a historic cottage. Overlooking Sumner is Gethsemane, a unique garden with a Christian theme. Banks Peninsula features four gardens: at Governors Bay is the well-known formal garden of Ohinetahi, alongside a woodland gully, and on the Akaroa Highway is Ataahua, a country garden with formal hedging and walled Mediterranean-style gardens. At Okains Bay are the Heaton Rutland Gardens with gullies of rhododendrons, and at Pigeon Bay, Annandale is a historic garden with mature trees and hedges on the water's edge.

Towards Lincoln is Ballymoney, a woodland garden offering accommodation. Then south of Christchurch at Broadfield is Grumpy's New Zealand Garden comprising 20 different gardens of natives or New Zealand raised exotics. Nearby is Weedons, where Willow Tree specialises in herbs. In Central Canterbury near Darfield are three gardens: The Gums with banks of colour, Tudor Rose, a semi-formal English-style garden, and Homebush, a historic garden surrounding a river and stables converted to museum and shop. Then at Dunsandel is Marsal Paeonies where peonies predominate and at Southbridge is the woodland garden of Wendrum. Crossing the Rakaia River, we come to Suzette Gardens with its seasonal colour and accommodation. In Ashburton itself are two gardens: Coniston, a mature woodland garden surrounding a lake, and the more formally designed Trotts' Garden. The final garden, Stonehaven, is at Ruapuna, featuring dry stone walling and meandering woodland paths.

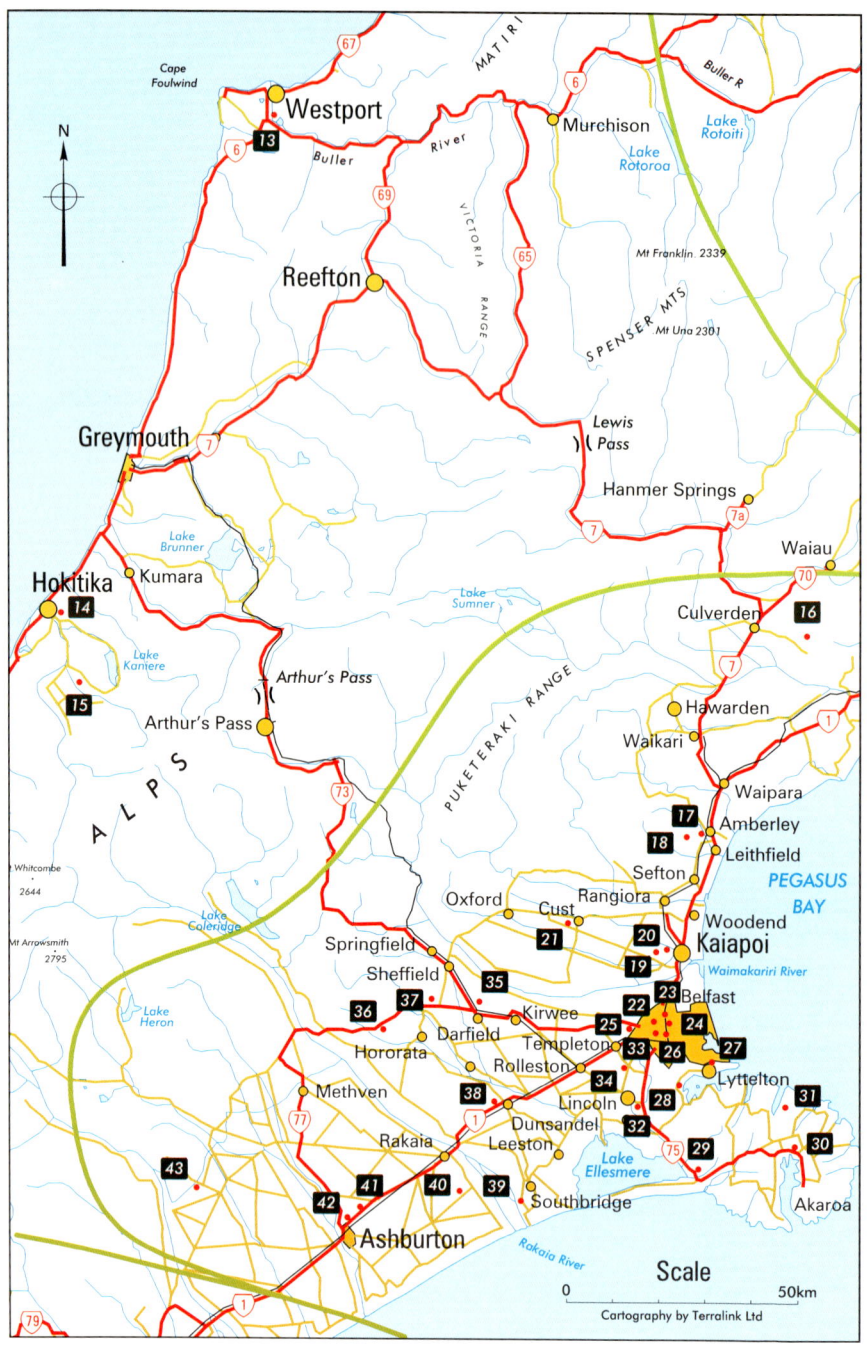

Scale

0 _____ 50km

Cartography by Terralink Ltd

RIVER VIEW LODGE
Westport

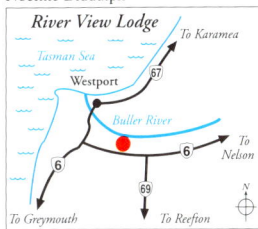

Owner:
Noeline Biddulph

Address: Buller Gorge Rd, Westport
Postal: P O Box 229, Westport
Directions: From Nelson, take SH 6
west, for 40km towards Westport.
Travel through Buller Gorge, past
Reefton turn-off for a further 1km to
garden on right, 7km from Westport.
Phone: 0-3-789 6037
Fax: 0-3-789 6037
Email: rivervie@voyager.co.nz
Website: friars.co.nz/gardens/pages/
riverviewlodge.html
Open: November to May, daily,
by appointment
Groups: By appointment, as above
Fee: $2 per adult
Size: Medium – 0.4ha (1 acre)
Terrain: Gently sloping
Accommodation: By arrangement

by arrangement

River View Lodge overlooks the Buller River, seven kilometres up the Buller Gorge from Westport. The English-style cottage garden is bounded by native bush leading via tracks to the river below on one side and backed by the 14-hectare sheep and deer farm behind. Noeline has been developing the garden since 1994, extending it further around the ridge to the gazebo which looks right over the river. The predominant species are roses and perennials which peak in summer, although the banksia and old English roses on the pergola tend to flower earlier, after the adjoining clematis. Noeline finds that miniature standard roses withstand the possums best and many of her roses flower until June. Exotic trees being established include oaks, chestnuts, elms and ashes. River View Lodge receives lots of rain which replenishes the water garden. Noeline has built a small fish pond at the top of the terrace, with two large waterlily ponds further down. She has edged the ponds with hostas, Chatham Island forget-me-nots and agapanthus. Noeline plans to continue extending the garden. She has planted pines that will be underplanted with rhododendrons and other shade-loving species. Noeline also provides quality accommodation, the guest wing verandahs opening out to the garden, and meals served alfresco in warm weather.

SEAFORTH
Hokitika

Owner:
Helen Love

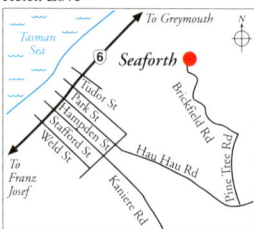

Address: Brickfield Rd, Blue Spur,
R D 2, Hokitika
Directions: Take SH 6 to Hokitika.
North of bridge, turn east into
Hampden St. Continue into Hau Hau
Rd & travel 2km. Turn left into
Pinetree Rd. Continue left into
Brickfield Rd & travel 1km to
Seaforth garden at end of road.
Phone: 0-3-755 7844
Open: October to April, 10am to 4pm,
or by appointment (ring after hours)
Groups: By appointment, as above
Fee: $3 per adult
Size: Large – 2ha (5 acres)
Terrain: Steep, hilly & flat
Plants for sale: Propagated from
garden
Teas: $2 pp, by arrangement

partial

by arrangement

Seaforth comprises a house garden and terraced hillside with two separate garden areas linked by a bush walk. Located at Blue Spur, just five minutes' drive from Hokitika, Seaforth offers panoramic views over the coast in one direction and to the snowcapped Southern Alps and Mount Cook in the other. Developed since 1995 from gorse and virgin bush, the garden has retained the bush and remnants of shafts and tunnels from the old gold mining days. The terraced gardens are linked by grassed pathways and wide stone steps. Rock walls support the terracing and other architectural structures include seating areas, with stone steps leading beneath the pergola to the valley below where bridges cross the creek and pond to a gazebo. Helen also plans to incorporate a natural waterfall. Gunneras and other bog plants enjoy the wet conditions resulting from the high rainfall. The house garden has been designed so as not to obscure the vistas, without vertical plantings. Chatham Island forget-me-nots grow against the brick house and white wisteria climbs the verandah, framing the view. Predominant species at Seaforth are the maples, rhododendrons and the native bush, with specimens of rimu, totara, miro, kamahi, kowhai, kakabeak, ponga tree-ferns, pittosporum, lemonwood, astelia and ferns. Spring blossom includes magnolias, dogwoods and cherries, which also provide autumn colour.

KILLINCHY WOODS
Hokitika

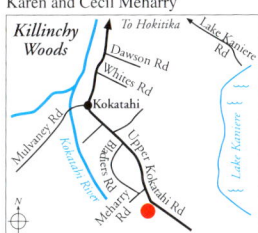

Owner:
Karen and Cecil Meharry

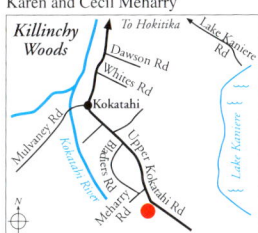

Address: Kokatahi, R D 1, Hokitika
Directions: From Hokitika, take
Stafford St east. Continue into
Kaniere Rd & through Kaniere. Take
right fork & travel 10km to Kokatahi.
Continue 5km to garden on right.
Phone: 0-3-755 6089
Open: October to April, daily,
by appointment only
Groups: By appointment, as above
Fee: $3 per adult
Size: Medium – 1.6ha (4 acres)
Terrain: Flat & rolling
Plants for sale: Perennials & bulbs
propagated from garden
Teas: $2 pp by arrangement

   partial

  by arrangement

The garden at Killinchy Woods has been gradually developed since 1979 from farm paddocks. This land was farmed by the first pioneers of the valley, the Meharry family four generations ago. Located in Kokatahi Valley, 20 minutes east of Hokitika, this large open country garden is planted against a backdrop of old pines planted circa 1860, with views of the bush and snow-clad mountains of the Southern Alps beyond. A weeping willow shades the stream, crossed by bridges, that runs through the garden and into ponds, edged with irises and other water-loving plants. Extensive lawn areas create a spacious feel and architectural features include rose bowers, pergolas, archways, gazebo, seating, stone walls and steps. There is also a bird aviary, ducks and hens, and the trees attract a variety of birdlife including native pigeons. Karen's favourite rhododendrons are underplanted with hostas in springtime. Magnolias, cornus and maples also feature, along with the flowering cherries, camellias, azaleas and the spring bulbs and groundcovers. The old roses in summer are accompanied by peonies, dahlias, penstemons and other perennials and annuals. Tuberous begonias thrive under cover. In autumn the maples, pin oak, scarlet oak, prunus and copper beech provide colourful foliage. Clematis climbs the native bush and its pathways are edged with variegated lamium.

LOWRY PEAKS
Culverden

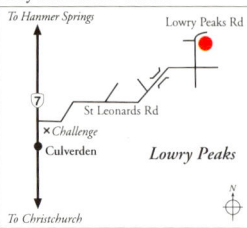

Owners:
Jossy and David Davison

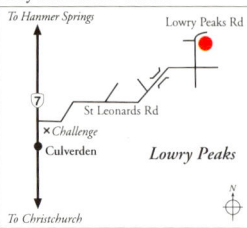

Address: Lowry Peaks, 118 Lowry Peaks Rd, R D, Culverden
Directions: At Culverden, turn east at Challenge Garage into St Leonards Rd. Travel about 10km to cross-roads. Turn left into Lowry Peaks Rd. Continue about 1.5km to Lowry Peaks garden on right.
Phone: 0-3-315 8172
Fax: 0-3-315 8014
Open: September to May, daily, by appointment
Groups: By appointment, as above
Fee: $5 per adult
Size: Medium – 1.4ha (3½ acres)
Terrain: Flat
Functions: Garden weddings by arrangement

Lowry Peaks is a woodland garden planted in 1979, although its origins reach back 66 years earlier to when the house was built in 1913. A vitis vine festoons the verandah and expansive lawns stretch to borders of golden luteum azaleas, underplanted with a sea of blue forget-me-nots, and the focal point of the Gothic gazebo beyond. Prominent species include davidia trees and David's favourite rhododendrons and magnolias, such as a lovely shaped *Magnolia sieboldii* and *M. loebneri* 'Leonard Messel' with its frothy pink stellata-like blooms. Rhododendrons include the fragrant pastel shell-pink 'Loderi Pink Diamond', golden-yellow 'Crest', and pale-lemon 'Unique' under a 'Jack Humm' malus. Other spring features to catch are the 25 different old varieties of daffodils under the silver birches along the driveway in September, and the blossom trees – cherries, quinces and crab-apples. David is replacing some original pines with quinces and red oaks, which provide autumn colour along with maples and claret ashes. Other exotics include four catalpa or Indian bean trees, both golden and green, with their large leaves. Summertime features perennials, lilies and roses. A pergola is clad in white, the climbing 'Iceberg' rose intertwined with the evergreen *Clematis armandii*, hybrid 'Madame Le Coultre', and a native clematis, while a geometric stone pond is planted in blues and yellows.

BRIKTON
Amberley

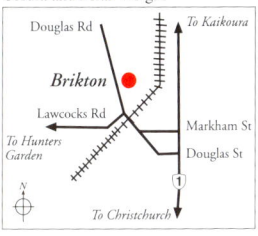

Owners:
Ursula and Brian Wright

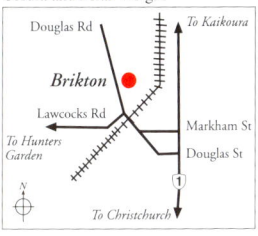

Address: 45 Douglas Rd, Amberley
Directions: Turn off Carters Rd
(SH 1) west into Douglas St.
Continue across railway line into
Douglas Rd. Brikton garden on right.
Phone: 0-3-314 8771
Open: September to autumn, daily,
by appointment
Groups: By appointment, as above
Fee: $2 per adult
Size: Small – 0.2ha (½ acre)
Terrain: Flat
Nursery: Occasional plants from
garden

 by arrangement

Since 1990, Ursula has transformed a bare paddock into a flowering garden sectioned into separate rooms. She chooses reds and subtle pinks, using white, cream, gold and deep blues to harmonise with the recycled-brick house. Ursula's favourite plants include flowering cherries, camellias and rhododendrons in spring, followed by old roses and pickable perennials in summer. She is not keen on bedding plants, preferring grouped container planting and foliage, succulents or flowers she can pick. These include the many varieties of leucadendron she is collecting that look so good against the brick. Proteas, too, feature in early spring, then drifts of spring bulbs, wild primroses and forget-me-nots provide a colourful carpet beneath the prunus and malus blossom. Heritage roses ramble over fences and archways, with a summer house and hedges contributing structure and interest to the garden, and dividing it into rooms. Old bricks matching the house have been used to construct patios and edge the pathways that link the different areas. Native lancewoods provide height down the side of the garden and conifers are interplanted with the exotics. Autumn colour is provided by rosehips and the foliage of the cherries, crab-apples, maples and liquidambars.

HUNTERS GARDEN
Amberley

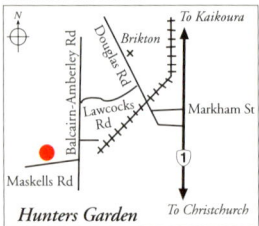

Owners:
Freda and Ian Hunter

Hunters Garden

Address: 162 Maskells Rd, R D 1,
Amberley
Directions: Turn off SH 1 at Amberley
Hotel west into Markham St. Turn
right into Douglas Rd, then left into
Lawcocks Rd. Turn left into Balcairn-
Amberley Rd, then right into Maskells
Rd. Hunters Garden 4th on right.
Phone: 0-3-314 8391
Fax: 0-3-314 8391
Open: September to May, daily,
by appointment
Groups: 10 or more preferred
Fee: $4 per adult
Size: Medium – 1ha (2½ acres)
Terrain: Gently sloping
Nursery: Floral art supplies for sale
*Floral art demonstrations or garden
talks*: For groups by arrangement

by arrangement

The entrance garden features a small waterlily pool set in a rock and alpine garden, with a border of mainly camellias backed by natives. A grape and ivy-clad fence separates off the summer house and "Garden Room" which is planted in trees and shrubs, with white sprays of agonis blossom and standardised choisya in tubs. A woodland path leads to the "View Garden" where rhododendrons and azaleas underplanted with hostas, rodgersias and Japanese irises frame a view to Mt Grey and the surrounding hills. A pathway leads through an archway to the front garden where modern and heritage roses are complemented by fuchsias and dwarf maples. White prunus 'Shirotae' is underplanted with pastel roses and dwarf delphiniums. Rock plants complement a sundial backed by a weeping pink prunus, while a pottery fountain is surrounded by greys, whites and blues. Curving grassy walkways lead to semi-formal gardens where old roses predominate. A "Pergola Walk" ends at the focal point of a rose-clad Bell House featuring a historic bell from 1865. Beyond is the pond which is home to a pair of black swans. Finally, a fernery provides a restful area beneath the maple trees. Freda is happy to give floral art demonstrations and garden talks to groups by arrangement.

188

CASHEL
Ohoka

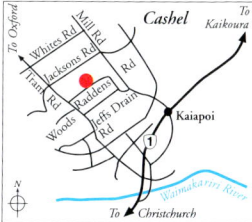

Owners:
John and Pauline Trengrove

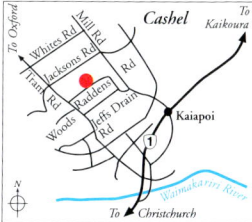

Address: 121 Raddens Rd, Ohoka,
R D 2, Kaiapoi
Directions: From Christchurch, take
SH 1 north. Exit off motorway into
Tram Rd. Travel towards Oxford &
turn right into Raddens Rd. Cashel
garden on left.
Phone: 0-3-312 6123
Fax: 0-3-312 6123
Open: 1 November to 28 February, by
appointment only
Closed: 1 March to 31 October
Groups: Bus tours by appointment
Fee: $10 per adult; $7 pp for groups
10+
Size: Large – 4ha (10 acres)
Terrain: Flat

Located on the Canterbury Plains, Cashel comprises a flat four-hectare (10-acre) formal garden surrounding a Palladian house. Both house and garden were designed as one, to create a unified whole, with views to the Southern Alps beyond. In 1993, the original bare paddock was transformed into long axes with the planting of hornbeam and macrocarpa hedging to form long vistas from the house. The hedges divide the garden into three rooms, with diagonal and cross axes creating interesting patterns. Viewed from upstairs, the teucrium topiary balls and lavender can be seen to form mosaic squares. The colour scheme is very controlled, with one garden room restricted to whites, another confined to yellows, and the third to purples. Long borders include double herbaceous borders, and two of New Zealand natives 750 metres long and five metres wide. A hornbeam avenue encloses a reflective 50-metre canal. Further water features include a stream and two ponds planted with gunnera and other water-loving species. Vast lawn areas enhance the spacious peaceful ambience, edged with the clipped shaped macrocarpa. A bluebell wood has been planted for spring colour, followed by roses and perennials in summer. Many shrubs and grasses complement the variety of deciduous trees and woodland area. Future plans include a parterre and vertical focal point.

WILSONS MILL GARDEN
Ohoka

Owners:
Ann and Alan Izard

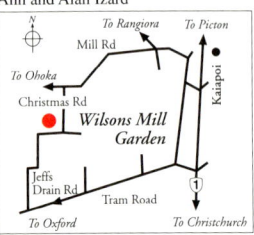

Address: 3 Christmas Rd, Ohoka,
R D 2, Kaiapoi
Directions: From Christchurch, take
SH 1 north. Take 2nd exit off
motorway, towards Ohoka. Travel
along Mill Rd, then turn left into
Christmas Rd. Garden on right.
Phone: 0-3-327 8113
Fax: 0-3-327 8113
Email: wilsonsmill@xtra.co.nz
Website: friars.co.nz/gardens/pages/
wilsonsmill.html
Open: 1 October to 31 May, daily,
10am–4pm; or by appointment
Groups: Bus tours by appointment
Fee: $8 per adult (for 2000/2001)
Size: Large – 5.5ha (13–14 acres)
Terrain: Flat and gently undulating
Nursery: Plants from garden
sometimes available

by arrangement for groups

The Izards began developing their garden in 1987. Strong lines define the structure, with Alan's favourite trees framing vistas and forming axes. Ann's exuberant plantings soften these lines and provide seasonal colour, with apricots and yellows in profusion, punctuated with accent colours. A colonnade of classical pillars is echoed by rows of columnar trees and clipped hedges such as hornbeam and low buxus. An avenue of cabbage trees leads from the entrance courtyard to the lake, where waterfowl swim among the lilies and fountain. Gunneras edge the banks beside a grape and rose pergola walk. The westerly axis from the house and lake is extended by an avenue of Tasman poplars, divided by The Long Lawn to the mound beyond. Two fastigiate oaks and a golden gleditsia are the focal points of the northerly axis of Leyland cypress. Ginkgos lining the driveway turn golden in autumn, and the pin oak grove turns scarlet. Clematis climbs through many of the maturing trees, underplanted with rhododendrons and other shrubs. Spring highlights include a variety of flowering cherries, then hundreds of roses take centre stage in summer. A rose arbour is the central focal point of a formal circular peony garden edged with catmint and enclosed in cypress hedging. Wilsons Mill is named after an original flax mill, the flax now replaced by deer and cattle in adjacent paddocks.

LITTLEROSE GARDENS AND NURSERY
Cust

Owners:
Jill and John Hughes

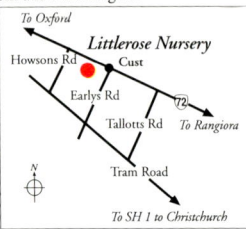

Address: 1771 Main Rd (SH 72), Cust
Postal: P O Box 32, Cust
Directions: From Christchurch take
SH 1 north. Take motorway exit left
into Tram Rd towards Oxford. Travel
23km then turn right into Earlys Rd.
At Cust, turn left on to SH 72. Travel
1km to Littlerose garden on left.
Phone: 0-3-312 5704
Fax: 0-3-312 5704
Open: All year, daily, 9am–5pm,
or by appointment
Groups: By appointment
Fee: $2 per adult
Size: Medium – almost 1ha (2½ acres)
Terrain: Flat
Nursery: Rose specialist –
old-fashioned, patio, miniature &
Austin roses

The Hughes have developed their rose gardens since 1988. They started by planting miniatures in alphabetical order, now numbering over 500 different varieties in bush, climbing and standard forms. Then they planted old roses, including shrubs, climbers and ramblers, in family groups. The roses are all named and arranged in shaped raised beds edged with half-rounds and bordered with low-growing groundcovers. A weeping silver pear provides height and contrast. The most recent garden of one acre was begun in 1994, with a rose walk of 30 climbers connecting the old and new areas. The new garden features a copper beech underplanted with shrub groundcover or "colourscape" roses, and bordered with low box hedging. David Austin roses are a popular attraction in this garden, with 100 different varieties now planted and new ones added as they become available. Wide grass paths set off the beds of old roses and lead through archways covered in climbing roses. To one side of this garden is a rose-framed seat where visitors can relax and enjoy the pool with its fountain playing. The miniature rose 'Patio Cloud' surrounds the pool and lavender hedging edges the outer paving. The peak time for viewing the garden is from mid November. The species and 'Frühlings' roses open first in October, while the patios, Austins and miniatures flower until the first frosts in April.

192

MONA VALE
Fendalton

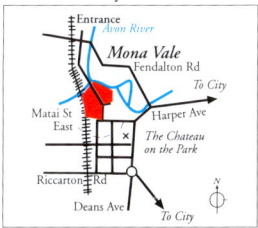

Owner:
Christchurch City Council

Address: 63 Fendalton Rd,
Christchurch
Postal: P O Box 237, Christchurch
Directions: From City, take Harper
Ave along northern boundary of
Hagley Park. Turn right into Fendalton
Rd. Mona Vale garden on left.
Phone: 0-3-366 1701
Fax: 0-3-366 6836
Email: richard.doyle@ccc.govt.nz
Open: All year, daily, 7.30am till
1 hour before sunset
Groups: As above; buses to park
outside grounds
Fee: No charge
Size: Large – 5ha (12 acres)
Terrain: Mainly flat, contoured to river
Homestead: Teas & lunches;
also available for private functions

Mona Vale is a historic garden surrounding a turn-of-the-century homestead on the banks of the Avon River. The Edwardian character of the garden has been retained, despite a succession of owners and garden designers. Alice Waymouth originated the garden in 1900; Annie Townend's additions in the next decade included the Fernery purchased from the 1906 Christchurch Exhibition, the Bathhouse and Fendalton Road Gatehouse. Tracy Gough engaged Alfred Buxton to revamp the garden in 1939, resulting in extensive plantings of rhododendrons, azaleas and English trees. The Buxton rose garden was later replaced by Gough with the current lily pond and fountain. Buxton was also responsible for the mound lawn, and the surprise approaches to the homestead seen through weeping trees are a favourite Buxton feature. Mature trees of note include the weeping elms flanking the house, a liriodendron, Lebanese cedar, and weeping willows bordering the river. Native plantings are another feature. Mona Vale was saved from demolition in 1967, when the Christchurch City Council and Riccarton Borough Council purchased and restored it for public use. Improvements since then include the establishment of rose gardens, transformation of the Bathhouse into a conservatory, restoration of the Fernery, and extensive additions to the many plant collections.

THE CHATEAU ON THE PARK
Riccarton

The Chateau on the Park

Manager:
Jan Stuart

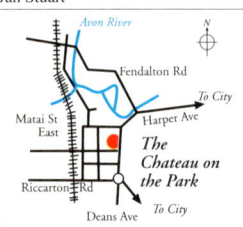

Address: 189 Deans Ave, Riccarton, Christchurch
Postal: P O Box 8161, Christchurch
Directions: From City, take Harper Ave. Turn left into Deans Ave. Garden on right. From Riccarton Rd, turn left into Deans Ave. Garden on left.
Phone: 0-3-348 8999
Fax: 0-3-348 8990
Emails: res@chateau-park.co.nz or salesmgr@chateau-park.co.nz
Webiste: www.chateau-park.co.nz
Open: All year, daily, any time
Groups: By appointment
Fee: No charge
Size: Large – 2ha (5 acres)
Terrain: Flat
Restaurant: Garden Court Brasserie – dinner available
Accommodation: Available

The garden at the Chateau on the Park has been redeveloped since 1992 around existing mature trees. The predominant species are roses, camellias and rhododendrons, the formal rose garden being a special attraction. Courtyards provide structure, with a moat bordering the reception area, which can be viewed from inside through glassed walls. The water garden around the moat is planted with moisture-loving species such as hostas, native ferns and water fuchsias. Weddings are popular in the inner courtyard at any time of the year, plantings providing seasonal colour mainly in pinks, blues and whites. Spring bulbs and beds of spring flowers accompany the camellias and rhododendrons. Protected trees include a large magnolia which adds to the spring display, and an English oak contributing to the lovely autumn colour. A woodland area attracts many birds to enhance the spring atmosphere. The rose garden is the prime summer feature with the Garden Court Brasserie looking out on to the roses. Summer also features prolific cottage plantings of perennials including candytuft, phlox, lobelia and salvia which complement the annual begonias, alyssum, pansies and polyanthus. This unusually extensive garden in a hotel setting borders Christchurch's famous Hagley Park.

194

CHRISTCHURCH BOTANIC GARDENS
Christchurch City

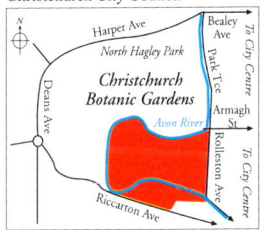

Owner:
Christchurch City Council

Address: Rolleston Ave, Christchurch
Postal: P O Box 237, Christchurch
Directions: From City, take Armagh
St, Rolleston or Riccarton Aves to
Hagley Park. Carparks in Armagh St
& Riccarton Ave; No. 17 bus & trams
to Rolleston Ave entrance to Gardens.
Phone: 0-3-371 1782
Fax: 0-3-371 1987
Email: richard.doyle@ccc.govt.nz
Open: All year, daily; Gardens: 7am
till 1 hour before sunset;
Conservatories & Information Centre:
10.15am–4pm (or 11am–3pm winter)
Fee: No charge
Size: Large – 33ha (over 82 acres)
Terrain: Flat
Tours: Vehicle departs restaurant
11am–4pm daily, September to May
Nursery: Plants often available

    mostly
restaurant

Although the land was set aside for the gardens in 1849, when the first settlers arrived it was uninspiring, with sand dunes, shingle beds, tussock, swamp and no trees, and the Avon River which borders the gardens was choked with flax and toetoe. In 1863, the first oak tree was planted to commemorate the marriage of Edward VII to Princess Alexandra. Development continued, with the native New Zealand Garden established in 1872, then the Cockayne Memorial Garden of native alpines added around 1939. The renowned Central Rose Garden was created in 1909, originally based on an English pattern, but redesigned into its present circular form in 1936. In the early 1900s, the extensive Herbaceous and Rhododendron Borders were planted. A floral conservatory was bequeathed in 1914, and the following year a larger tropical plant conservatory. A fernery was added to the complex in 1955 and three years later a house for desert plants. The Alpine House was next to be built, then a house for orchids and bromeliads in 1981. The elaborate Peacock Fountain, recently restored, was originally erected in 1920, about the time when large gravel pits were transformed into a series of ponds for bog, water and rock gardens. In the 1930s the Azalea and Magnolia Garden was extended and thousands of daffodils planted in the Woodland south of the Avon. Beyond are the Heritage Rose Gardens, established after World War II.

FAIRLEIGH GARDEN GUEST HOUSE
Harewood

Fairleigh

Owners:
Valerie and Allan Carleton

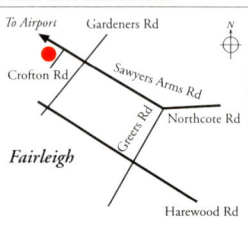

Address: 411 Sawyers Arms Rd,
Harewood, Christchurch
Directions: From Christchurch City,
take Harewood Rd. Turn right into
Greers Rd. Turn left at island into
Sawyers Arms Rd. Fairleigh Garden
towards airport on left.
Phone: 0-3-359 3538
Freephone: 0800 611 411 for bookings
Mobile: 025 224 3746
Fax: 0-3-359 3548
Email: fairleighgardenbb@xtra.co.nz
Open: 1 September to 30 April;
by appointment
Fee: $3 per adult; $5 includes teas
Size: Small – 0.3ha (¼ acre)
Terrain: Flat
Nursery: Perennials & herbs
Accommodation: By arrangement

& to toilet
by arrangement

In 1987 the former market garden was transformed into the Fairleigh garden. Valerie and Allan have added new developments since they took over in 1998. Camellias and bulbs usher in the spring, the main feature being an old 'Mt Fuji' cherry blossom tree from the 'forties, in an outdoor room. Many clematis including native varieties, magnolias, lilacs, azaleas and rhododendrons enhance the spring ambience. A gazebo is reached by a bridge across the 10-metre pond that features goldfish, waterlilies and a waterfall over rocks, and is edged with bog plants, miniature bulbs and irises. In summer, Valerie's favourite roses, herbs and other perennials take over, with archways covered in climbing roses. The croquet and pétanque lawn separates the white, blue, lilac and pink colours from the red, white and blue areas, and Valerie adds splashes of yellow for accent. Hydrangeas contribute to the summer colour and lupins border the pathways that meander through the garden. Autumn brings the deciduous foliage into colour and the potager continues to bear fruit and vegetables. Other attractions include a dovecote, worm farm, compost making, and vintage farm tractors. A raised garden is planned as a floral arrangement, and fuchsia and fern walks are to be established. Quality accommodation is also available; freephone bookings are welcomed.

196

ROSE COTTAGE
Hillmorten

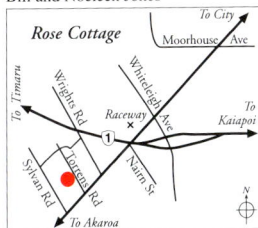

Owners:
Bill and Noeleen Jones

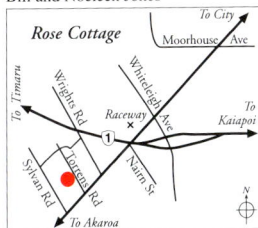

Rose Cottage

Address: 23 Torrens Rd, Hillmorten, Christchurch
Directions: From Christchurch City, turn right into Moorhouse Ave. Turn left into Lincoln Rd & travel south towards Akaroa. At Caltex Service Station, turn right into Torrens Rd. Travel 100m to garden on left.
Phone: 0-3-339 0878 after 3.30pm
Fax: 0-3-339 0878
Open: November to April, by appointment only
Closed: May to October
Fee: $4 per adult
Size: Small – 649 sq metres (⅙ acre)
Terrain: Flat

When Bill and Noeleen began their garden in 1995, it was just a mass of noxious weeds around 38 large trees. They had no experience in gardening, but loved roses, so began their award-winning rose garden that surrounds their historic cottage, which features the original leadlight windows from 1883. This small urban garden is crammed full of roses of every variety – from old-fashioned to modern, climbers to bush, with many David Austins. The old peach 'Albertine' cascades over the front verandah, while red 'Dublin Bay' climbs the verandah poles. The rose pergola is covered with another red rose 'Santana', as well as golden 'Friesia' (also known as 'Korresia'), and white 'Margaret Merrill' perfuming the air as visitors walk beneath. Bill even propagates new roses from seed. But the garden at Rose Cottage is not just roses. Thousands of spring bulbs, including daffodils and tulips, are followed by anemones and ranunculus. Then peonies complement the 380 or so roses. Christmas lilies are another summer feature. A cool spot is beside the goldfish pond with its old-fashioned pump. Now that problem trees have been removed and the convolvulus and oxalis eradicated, Bill and Noeleen can relax and enjoy their roses – from the seats near the pond and on the front verandah. But they plan to continue planting roses as long as space permits.

GETHSEMANE GARDENS
Sumner

Owners:
Bev and Ken Loader

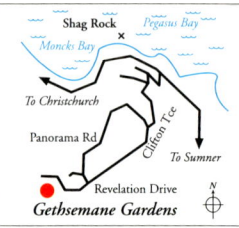

Gethsemane Gardens

Address: 27 Revelation Drive (end Clifton Tce), Sumner, Christchurch
Directions: From Christchurch take Ferry Rd and Main Rd to Clifton. Past Shag Rock turn right up Clifton Tce. Keep left and continue to Revelation Drive (no exit). Gethsemane Gardens on left.
Phone: 0-3-326 5848
Fax: 0-3-326 5849
Open: All year, daily, 9am–5pm
Closed: Good Friday, Anzac morning (25 April), Easter & Christmas Days
Groups: By appointment
Fee: $5 per adult
Size: Medium – 1.2ha (3 acres)
Terrain: Hilly
Teas: For groups by arrangement
Weddings: Chapel & reception tabernacle available

 partly

for groups by arrangement

The Christian theme of this garden is spelt out in garden rooms representing each of the letters of the garden's name G-E-T-H-S-E-M-A-N-E. "G" is a curving herbaceous border, "E", "T" and "H" are herb gardens, a knot garden forms the Star of David in the lower half of "H", with the Star of Bethlehem in the top half, "S" is a scented curving pergola, and the second "E" is a rock garden. "M" is another herbaceous border, with the summer house at the apex, and "A" contains a water garden in the lower section, with a white garden in the top triangle. "N" is a larger rock garden and the final "E" is a shadehouse, each arm filled with shade-loving plants. The dry hill behind is the Mount of Olives featuring recently planted olive trees and lavender. Beyond is a colourful daisy bank with kniphofias massed behind. A lookout provides panoramic views over the coastline and a trellis-built chapel is sited to take advantage of the view. Wedding parties wend their way through the colours of the rainbow in the Bridal Walk towards it. A new reception centre furnished in the red, blue and gold colours of the tabernacle is available for weddings and also group morning or afternoon teas by arrangement. A Rosary Maze features old roses, while a potager is Bev's recent addition. Gethsemane is full of graduated colour all summer, with Marguerite daisies the mainstay in winter.

OHINETAHI
Governors Bay

Owner:
Sir Miles Warren

Address: Teddington Rd, Governors
Bay
Postal: Governors Bay, R D 1,
Lyttelton
Directions: From Christchurch, take
Colombo St over Dyers Pass to
Governors Bay. Continue on Main Rd
1km past shop in Governors Bay.
Garden on left opposite sign
"Ohinetahi Valley" in grassed triangle
at curve in road.
Phone: 0-3-329 9852
Fax: 0-3-329 9842
Open: Mid September to 23 December,
then 7 January to end of March,
10am–4pm, on weekdays only
Groups: By appointment
Fee: $10 per adult; $8 groups of 10+
Size: Medium – 1.2ha (3 acres)
Terrain: Flat & steep with steps

    flat area

Ohinetahi is nestled into the hillside overlooking
Governors Bay, within a framework of mature trees
planted in the 1860s by T.H. Potts, an early botanist.
An original orchard of Burbank plums provides spring
blossom and leads to a double herbaceous border in pinks,
mauves and blues, which ends at the focal point of an ogee
dome-shaped gazebo, reflecting the arches along the
verandah of the historic stone house. This major axis is
one of four which provide strong architectural lines
softened by exuberant plantings. The axes are formed by
clipped hedges, brick pathways and steps, creating vistas
that lead to focal points and views over Lyttelton
Harbour. Within rectangles of topiaried box, a formal
parterre rose garden in white, yellow and terracotta
complements the stone walls of the house. Beyond is
a water garden, with a cross-axis leading up to a walled
red garden. A pleached hornbeam walk extends to a grass
oval, with a geometric "half" garden on the same axis.
A swing bridge crosses a stream running through the
woodland garden which features old camellias and
rhododendrons. The stream is interrupted by small
pools and edged with bog plants. This woodland valley
contrasts with the formality of the terraced garden
rooms above.

ATAAHUA
Banks Peninsula

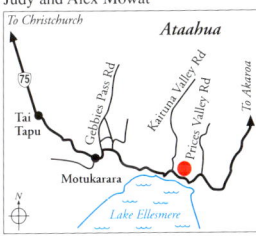

Owners:
Judy and Alex Mowat

Ataahua

To Christchurch

Gebbies Pass Rd
Kanuna Valley Rd
Prices Valley Rd
To Akaroa

75
Tai
Tapu

Motukarara

N

Lake Ellesmere

Address: Main Akaroa Highway,
SH 75, Banks Peninsula, Canterbury
Postal: Ataahua, R D 2, Christchurch
Directions: From Christchurch, take
SH 75 towards Akaroa. Travel 38km
to garden on left. (20km from Tai
Tapu.) Ataahua signposted, with bus
access & separate exit.
Phone: 0-3-329 0898
Fax: 0-3-329 0088
Open: November to March, 10am to
4pm; other times by appointment
Closed: Wednesdays
Groups: By appointment
Fee: $5 per adult
Size: Medium – 1.2ha (3 acres)
Terrain: Flat
Teas: $5 pp with muffins, by request

by arrangement only

Meaning "good and beautiful" in Maori, Ataahua was first planted in 1935, then revamped in 1985 and again in 1994 when Judy and Alex took it over. Ataahua is an open country garden with formal areas. Judy's favourite established deciduous trees, such as the silver birches, oaks and beech, the extensive plantings of old-fashioned roses and the formal hedges give it an English ambience. The Mowats opened up the garden by removing a large macrocarpa hedge and constructing a 100-metre long ha-ha, then planting a 220-metre avenue of ash with vistas to the poplars and hills beyond. Other axes are formed by a 75-metre herbaceous border backed by climbing roses behind a long pleached privet hedge, and a similarly long pleached hornbeam hedge, set off by massed plantings of white agapanthus. Other parts of the garden have a Mediterranean feel enhanced by walled gardens, including the white garden with its Italian splash fountain enclosed within brick walls. Judy plans to extend this look with gravelled courtyards and large pots. As well as whites, she has continued the existing restricted colour scheme using blues, mauves, yellows and greens to create a cool spacious feeling, with occasional bright highlights. White and yellow spring bulbs and bluebells accompany massed hellebores and camellias. Then the roses flower with aquilegias and many other perennials.

HEATON RUTLAND GARDENS
Akaroa

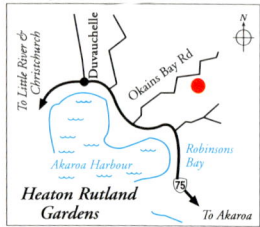

Owners:
Heaton Rutland and Alison
Collingwood

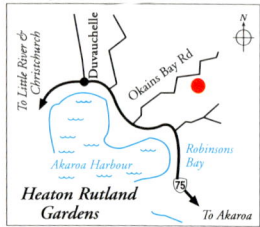

**Heaton Rutland
Gardens**

Address: Okains Bay Rd, R D 1,
Robinsons Bay
Directions: From Christchurch, take
SH 75 towards Akaroa. Past
Duvauchelle, take 2nd turning on left
into Okains Bay Rd. Follow signposts
& travel 2km to garden on right.
Phone: 0-3-304 7096
Open: All year, daily, 9am–5pm
Groups: By appointment
Fee: $4 per adult or purchase from
nursery
Size: Large – 8ha (20 acres)
Terrain: Hilly, gently contoured paths
Nursery: Rhododendrons, shrubs,
alpines, natives, & perennials from
garden

    partly

 & groups by arrangement

Begun in 1987 in the crater of an extinct volcano, Heaton Rutland's gardens keep spreading. When he filled up the first gully with his favourite rhododendrons, he began on the adjacent valley. Now he is over the hills, planting trees and letting perennials naturalise to provide extensive drifts of groundcover. Heaton has designed his gardens for seasonal colour, although the spring is hard to beat with his massed rhododendrons blooming, underplanted with drifts of trilliums, groundcover and perennials to form carpets of colour. Roses intermingle with a great range of trees and shrubs, many rare and unusual. Spring and autumn display the glory of the cherry trees, dogwoods, elms, maples and birches against the hills and harbour vistas. A native kauri grove is complemented by other indigenous trees being established throughout the gardens. This is planting on a large scale, with always another basin beyond, each valley providing new panoramic views over Akaroa Harbour. Every season is quite distinctive, with many flowers continuing through the winter. Heaton doesn't consciously plant according to colour; if a plant feels right in a given place, that is where he puts it. Peacocks strutting, displaying, flying and calling add to the colourful spectacle. Heaton Rutland Gardens also now cater for visitors with light refreshments, and groups by prior arrangement.

202

ANNANDALE
Pigeon Bay

Owners:
Jane and Frank Davison

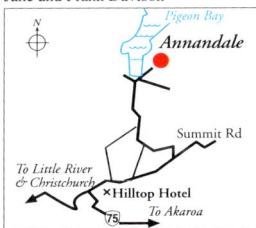

Address: Pigeon Bay, Banks Peninsula
Postal: P O Box 19, Pigeon Bay, Banks Peninsula
Directions: From Christchurch, take SH 75 towards Akaroa. At the Hilltop Hotel turn left into Summit Rd. Take 3rd roadway on left. At Pigeon Bay turn right across bridge & continue to garden at Annandale.
Phone: 0-3-304 6800
Fax: 0-3-304 6893
Email: frankd@clear.net.nz
Open: October to April, by appointment
Fee: $5 per adult
Size: Medium – 0.6ha (1½ acres); original 1.6ha (4 acres) accessible
Terrain: Sculptured
Accommodation: Shearers' cottage sleeps 14 backpackers, $12 per person

by arrangement

In 1925 James Gibson designed the Davisons' fifth-generation garden on the water's edge, incorporating two cabbage trees and box hedging planted over 40 years previously when the house was built as a hotel. Gibson's training by Alfred Buxton still shows in the layout and lines. Overgrown wattles and blue gums were removed and Gibson's elm trimmed to spread elegantly over the sweeping lawn to a perennial border beside the rose pergola, where Jane grows some of her favourite old roses. The original shaggy, two-metre-high hedge of *Lonicera nitida* has been clipped to neatly edge the sweeping lawn. The Davisons created windows through the trees for sea views, with sizeable eucalypts and wellingtonia providing privacy and a windbreak. An enormous golden banksia rose hedge stretches along the far side of the lawn. Formal box hedging flanked by the ancient cabbage trees still borders a straight path, creating a vista seawards. An old Judas tree rises from the adjacent perennial bed, its cerise spring blossom contrasting with the predominantly green colour scheme. Jane groups her pinks and blues together, with reds and blues elsewhere. She restricts yellows to the far end, where the fernery "wilderness" is now fenced off from the garden.

BALLYMONEY
Taitapu

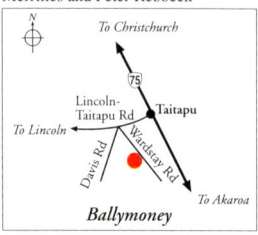

Owners:
Merrilies and Peter Rebbeck

Ballymoney

Address: Wardstay Rd, Tai Tapu,
Christchurch
Postal: Wardstay Rd, R D 2,
Christchurch
Directions: From Christchurch City,
take SH 75 to Taitapu. Turn right
towards Lincoln. Turn left into
Wardstay Rd. Garden on right.
Phone: 0-3-329 6706
Fax: 0-3-329 6709
Email: rebbeckpandm@hotmail.com
Open: All year, daily, by appointment
Fee: $5 per adult including tea/coffee;
$4 pp for groups 10+ including teas
Size: Medium – 0.8ha (2 acres)
Terrain: Flat
Accommodation: Featured in *Friars'
Guide to NZ Accommodation for the
Discerning Traveller – 2001*

by arrangement

Ballymoney was the name of the property the Rebbecks owned in Ireland. The trees and hedges they planted in 1980, to break the Canterbury winds, now divide the garden into different areas. Once the trees were established, lots of camellias and rhododendrons were planted, then old roses, perennials and groundcover. Silver birches have self-seeded everywhere along with the oaks, creating a woodland. Daffodils, bluebells and other spring bulbs beneath these trees are followed by the camellias and rhododendrons underplanted with white forget-me-nots, foxgloves, violets and trilliums. Summertime is the peak for the David Austin and old roses underplanted with perennials, and the large area of hostas under the trees. Recently planted is a spring avenue of quinces leading to the pond, where reflections of foliage and berries brighten the autumn. Merrilies keeps colour out of this area, so as not to distract from the surroundings. The pond hosts a large collection of domestic and wild ducks, with guinea fowl and peacocks nearby, and a dovecote housing pigeons. Many rare breeds of animals and birds add interest. The windbreaks such as beech hedges feature in the winter.
A small knot garden, summer houses and pergolas provide structure. A potager is being established and the orchard underplanted with lavender. Quality bed and breakfast and farmstay accommodation is available by arrangement.

GRUMPY'S NEW ZEALAND GARDEN
Broadfield

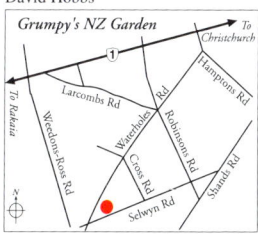

Owner:
David Hobbs

Grumpy's NZ Garden

Address: Selwyn Rd, Broadfield, Christchurch
Postal: P O Box 13 632, Christchurch
Directions: From Christchurch, take SH 1 south to Hornby Mall. Turn left into Shands Rd. Travel 6km & turn right into Selwyn Rd. Travel 2km to garden on right. Or continue on SH 1, then turn left into Waterholes Rd. Veer right, travel 6km & turn left into Selwyn Rd. Grumpy's NZ Garden is 1st gate on left.
Phone: 0-3-366 7774
Fax: 0-3-366 0448
Email: hobbs&co@xtra.co.nz
Open: All year, by appointment
Fee: $5 per adult; $4 pp for groups
Size: Large – 4.2ha (10½ acres)
Terrain: Flat

Grumpy's New Zealand Garden was designed in 1992 by Christchurch's well-known landscape architect, Robert Watson. The concept comprises 20 different gardens all planted in natives or New Zealand raised varieties of exotics. The design is semi-formal bordered with 1.5 kilometres of green totara hedges, ponds both formal and informal such as the camellias pond, lawn with formal planting of rimu, and Oamaru stone seating. Previously a horse paddock, Grumpy's was planted in poplars and tree lucerne for shelter from the cold easterlies in spring and the nor'wester in summer. Within this shelter podocarps, a beech forest, a young kauri forest, and wetland, lowland forest are developing. A sizeable shadehouse is home to New Zealand ferns and orchids and there is also a large formal grass garden, a rose garden, a New Zealand border and a long canal. In spring the camellia garden features 400 varieties grouped in flower styles, and then the colour-coordinated rhododendron garden with its 400 varieties takes over, along with the deciduous azaleas, magnolias, cherries, irises, peonies and primulas. In summer the lilies and fuchsias are joined by perennials of New Zealand-raised varieties of dianthus, lavenders and others. The foliage of the cherries, magnolias and maples is an autumn feature followed by the hellebores in winter. Further gardens are planned including moss, bonsai and alpine.

WILLOW TREE COTTAGE
Weedons

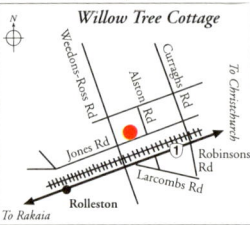

Owners:
Priscilla and Jeremy Palmer

Willow Tree Cottage

Address: Jones Rd, Weedons, R D 5, Christchurch
Directions: From Christchurch take SH 1 south to Templeton. Continue, then turn right into Weedons-Ross Rd. Cross railway line, then turn right into Jones Rd. Garden on left.
Phone: 0-3-347 9379
Fax: 0-3-347 9373
Website: friars.co.nz/gardens/pages/willowtree.html
Open: Nov.–April, daily, by appointment
Fee: $5 per adult;
$3.50 pp for groups 20+
Size: Small – 0.3ha (¼ acre)
Terrain: Flat
Teas: Herbal teas served on request
Nursery: Dried herbs, fresh lavender
Shop: Scented shop selling fragrant & culinary gifts

herbal, on request

Willow Tree Cottage, Lavender and Herb Gardens was laid out and planted in geometric beds in 1994. Priscilla specialises in lavenders, 30 different varieties featuring in her garden. Her favourite herbs also include fragrant bergamot, silvery-foliaged artemisias, and old-fashioned roses, which are really herbs too! Jeremy loves the perfume of lemon verbena. Colour-coded and labelled according to herbal usage, the beds border the courtyard in front of the shop. Categories include grey-foliaged, scented, lavender, medicinal, formal culinary and tea gardens, as well as dye, and bee and butterfly gardens. A small ornamental pond is established in one corner, planted with medicinal irises. The most recent additions are the Medieval and Biblical Gardens. Priscilla arranges the beds in colours, with the lavenders colour-coordinated. Purple and ochre seats and urns provide accent. Honeysuckle emerges in early spring, accompanying the blossom trees which include almonds, apples, apricots and olives. The long-bracted European stoechas lavenders and French *L. dentata* bloom in spring with the irises, valerian, catmint and early roses. Willow Tree peaks in summer, with the English spiky lavenders, complemented in January with bergamot, salvias, catmint, artemisias, elderberry and the grape walk. In February the hops and annual herbs flower, with late roses continuing into autumn.

THE GUMS
Darfield

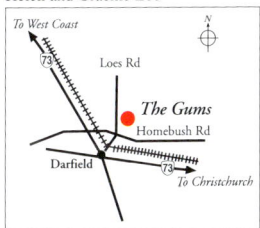

Owners:
Helen and Graeme Loe

Address: Loes Rd, Darfield, R D,
Central Canterbury
Directions: From Christchurch, take
SH 73 west to Darfield. Continue,
then turn right into Homebush Rd.
Cross railway line, turn 1st left into
Loes Rd. Garden on right.
Phone: 0-3-318 8373
Fax: 0-3-318 8373
Open: October to April, daily,
by appointment
Groups: By appointment, as above
Fee: $3 per adult
Size: Medium – 0.8ha (2 acres)
Terrain: Flat with banks
Nursery: Some plants available

   by arrangement

Set in the vast Canterbury plains, The Gums is encircled by a perimeter of trees and raised banks providing a strong design for the lush plantings within. Paths ambling over the banks, offer visitors inviting vistas of the garden. Roses, peonies and perennials are massed below the west bank, with the tennis court beyond enclosed with climbing roses. An immaculate lawn bordered by azaleas and rhododendrons leads to a pergola hung with wisteria by the house. Past a waratah, scarlet in the spring, a narrow pathway winds round to a new rose garden and on to a rhododendron dell where the pastel shades of 'Naomi', 'Lems Cameo', 'Pilgrim', 'Lady Dorothy Ella' and many others glow in the dappled shade of mature trees. The east bank provides further vistas with walks past climbers including the fragrant peach-coloured old rambling rose 'Albertine', the pink-flowering bower vine, *Pandorea jasminoides*, and plumbago, to more rhododendrons and roses flowering beneath dogwoods and cherry blossoms, underplanted with annuals and perennials. The reflective waters of the swimming pool mirror the surrounding evergreen shrubs with an occasional splash of colour from rhododendrons, fuchsias, roses and clematis tumbling over a fence or climbing a tree. Seasonal colour has been planted at The Gums since 1970.

TUDOR ROSE
Coalgate

![Tudor Rose garden]

Owners:
Katrina and David Mitchell

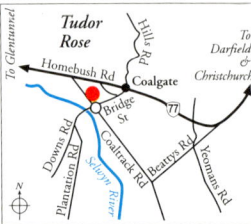

Address: 15 Coaltrack Road,
Coalgate, R D, Canterbury
Directions: From Christchurch take
SH 73 south to Darfield (30 mins).
Continue south on SH 77 for 11km to
Coalgate. Turn left into Bridge St,
then right into Coaltrack Rd. Tudor
Rose garden on right.
Phone: 0-3-318 2799
Fax: 0-3-318 2705
Mobile: 025 264 1699
Open: October to February, daily,
by appointment
Closed: Winter
Groups: As above
Fee: $3 per adult
Size: Medium – 0.4ha (1 acre)
Terrain: Mainly flat on slight rise
For sale: Hand-painted ceramics

by arrangement

Tudor Rose is an English-style semi-formal garden surrounding a neo-Tudor house, half an hour south of Christchurch. The house was built in 1985 and most of the garden planted five years later. Tracey Ower landscaped the garden with its rock walls, rock garden, formal box hedging and architectural structures complementing the style of the house. Katrina obviously loves roses, with climbers over archways, peach-coloured 'Phyllis Bide' on the blue gazebo, trellis work laden with more roses, 'Iceberg' and miniature white agapanthus disguising the swimming pool fence, and lots of her favourite David Austins. A rose circle adjacent to the driveway is edged with buxus and contains 45 roses. An avenue of hornbeam creates an axis with the gazebo and a lavender parterre at the cross-axis. An urn provides the focal point for the formal parterre, filled with angustifolia species and the delicate 'Marshwood' and also edged with buxus. Beside it is a white, yellow and blue garden, in harmony with the pastel colour scheme of the garden. Roses and peonies provide pinks to accompany the blues. Clematis climbs a fence behind blue delphiniums, silver foliage plants, white 'Margaret Merrill' and yellow 'Graham Thomas' roses. A clipped pittosporum hedge leads to the gazebo and a row of conifers separates the parterre from the pool. A potager is planned next.

HOMEBUSH
Darfield

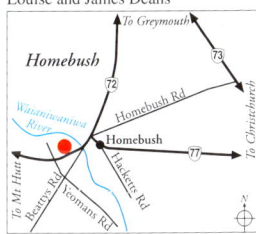

Owners:
Louise and James Deans

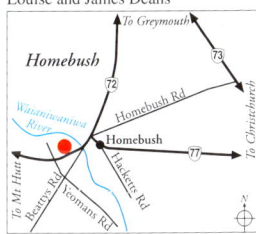

Address: Homebush Rd, Darfield,
R D 1, Canterbury
Directions: From Darfield take SH 77
for 8km. Cross Waianiwaniwa River
& pass Homebush woolshed on right.
Then turn right into drive to garden.
Phone: 0-3-318 2785
Mobile: 025 233 5920
Fax: 0-3-318 1671
Email: deansbush@xtra.co.nz
Website: friars.co.nz/gardens/pages/
homebush.html
Open: September to April, daily,
10am to 4pm, by appointment only
Fee: $5 per adult
Size: Large – 3.4ha (8½ acres)
Terrain: Flat
Museum: In historic stables
Shop: Souvenirs, jerseys, books, pottery
Café: $5 pp teas, $13 pp full lunch

by arrangement

The long driveway at Homebush is lined with *Cedrus atlantica* leading to the historic homestead and garden. The Deans brothers, William and John, farmed the run from 1850, when many English trees were planted. Homebush has been in the Deans family now for six generations, Louise gradually restoring the garden to its former glory. The Waianiwaniwa River flows through the garden, edged with yellow irises and crossed by a bridge to the orchard and bush walk. The circular orchard of apples and pears is enclosed in a holly hedge planted circa 1860. A semi-formal rose garden and lavender is planted within the orchard. The woodland walk is lined with rhododendrons and leads to a "cathedral" of mature tree trunks, featuring English beech, oaks and three Wellingtonias. The homestead is surrounded with trees which provide autumn colour and attract the birdlife, including bellbirds. Nearby is a pond which ices over in winter for skating. Spacious lawns adjacent to the river feature specimen trees such as a black poplar planted in the 1850s, a huge copper beech planted in front of the house in 1910, oaks, beeches, rowans and redwoods. The daffodil lawn, bluebells, camellias, cherry blossom and an azalea walk all bloom in spring. A walnut avenue has a statue of David for a focal point and other long vistas end at a Lutyens-style seat and a Burelli pot. Louise has converted the old stables into a museum and shop.

MARSAL PAEONIES
Dunsandel

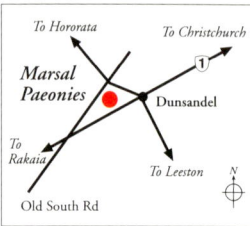

Owners:
Julie and John Allan

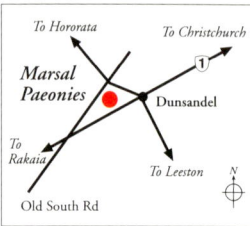

Address: Old South Rd, Dunsandel, Christchurch
Postal Address: R D 2, Leeston, Christchurch
Directions: From City, take SH 1 south for 45 mins to Dunsandel. Turn right into Hororata Rd & left into Old South Rd. Travel 1.5km to garden on left.
Phone: 0-3-325 4003
Fax: 0-3-325 4222
Website: friars.co.nz/gardens/pages/marsalpaeonies.html
Open: Labour weekend (end October) to mid December, or by appointment
Groups: Open weekends from mid Nov.–mid Dec. or by appointment
Fee: $3 per person for groups & buses
Size: Large – 2ha (5 acres)
Terrain: Flat
Nursery: Peonies & perennials

by arrangement

The name "Marsal" is a combination of two of the Allan children's names, and "Paeonies" is the botanical spelling of peonies. Julie likes propagating all plants, but tree peonies, "the king of flowers" in ancient China, are her prime love. These flower early, just before Labour weekend (late October), followed by the herbaceous peonies, starting with the corals then white 'Miss America' at the beginning of November and reaching a peak towards the end of the month. Julie is also interested in the new intersectional hybrids, which are disease-resistant and feature a tree peony top with herbaceous roots. John's favourites are the trees, particularly maples, along with oaks and a few special birches. Companion plants include daffodils in spring, lilies and roses in summer and many unusual perennials such as the hostas that are predominant throughout the garden, adjacent to the peony field. A small native area was planted in 1986. Panoramic views have been retained to the Southern Alps, but the peonies seem to thrive in windy conditions, enjoying the cold, frosty winters and hot, dry summers. Contrary to popular opinion, certain early peonies can also be grown in warmer climates, providing they are planted close to the surface to maximise the cold in winter.

WENDRUM
Southbridge

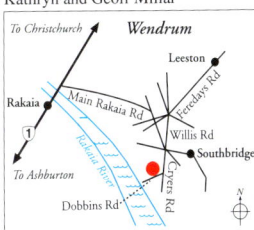

Owners:
Kathryn and Geoff Millar

Address: Dobbins Rd, Southbridge
Postal: R D 3, Leeston, Canterbury
Directions: From SH 1, turn east into
Main Rakaia Rd. Turn right into
Cryers Rd. Then turn right again into
Dobbins Rd. Wendrum on right.
Phone: 0-3-324 2511
Fax: 0-3-324 2511
Email: wendrum@paradise.net.nz
Open: October to late May, daily,
by appointment
Fee: $3 per adult; discount for
horticultural societies
Size: Medium – 1ha (2½ acres)
Terrain: Flat
Farm tours: By request, $3 per person
Nursery: Unusual perennials
propagated from garden
For sale: NZ-raised rhododendron &
azalea book, co-authored by Kathryn

by arrangement

Starting with only two original trees, Kathryn has developed this woodland garden since 1970, under-planting with her favourite species that love the coolness, especially trilliums. Rhododendrons now predominate, providing spring colour along with deciduous azaleas, unusual woodland plants and blossom trees, including the delicate pink *Kolkwitzia* by the house. Kathryn grows many unusual plants and is interested in colour effects, combining blues and yellows and planting lots of whites, such as foxgloves and lupins, that glow in the evening. She uses green extensively during the hot, dry Canterbury summer, when roses she planted in 1975 bloom among the peonies. Summer also brings a distinct contrast to the soft informality of the green garden, with the formal borders in the summer garden closely planted in roses, lilies, Turkscap martagons, select perennials and Kathryn's salvia collection. The lilies and salvias offer inviting gimpses of colour through the trees until late autumn, with the foliage of mollis azaleas, maples, cercidiphyllum, claret ash and two ginkgos providing brilliant colour. The form and structure of the garden become apparent when the deciduous leaves fall, a time Kathryn likes best. A small family museum of farm collectables is an added attraction. *Beyond the Rubicon*, a rhododendron handbook co-authored by Kathryn is for sale.

SUZETTE GARDENS
Rakaia

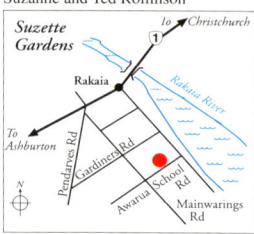

Owners:
Suzanne and Ted Rollinson

Address: Awaroa School Rd, Dorie
Postal: R D 11, Rakaia, Central Canterbury
Directions: From Rakaia, take SH 1 south for 2.8km. Turn left into Pendarves Rd, then left again into Mainwarings Rd. Travel 9km & turn left into Awarua School Rd. Travel 500m to garden on left. From Ashburton, take SH 1 north for 25 mins. Turn right into Pendarves Rd.
Phone: 0-3-302 0864
Fax: 0-3-302 0865
Open: All year, daily, by appointment
Fee: $5 per adult
Size: Large – over 2ha (over 5 acres)
Terrain: Slightly undulating
Accommodation: B&B by arrangement

   by arrangement

In 1983, Sue landscaped and planted a large paddock, while Ted made the retaining walls and structures, such as the rose pergola featuring 'Wedding Day', 'New Dawn' and a white banksia rose. The viburnum walk and lilac walk provide colourful fragrant avenues in spring, while a David Austin walk features the lovely English roses in summer, complemented by old-fashioned and formal rose gardens. Other predominant areas are the camellia bed which includes miniatures, the rhododendron garden, and the woodland area underplanted with spring bulbs. A white camellia garden and separate blue and white, pink, and pastel beds are colour-coordinated. A rockery constructed with rocks from the Rakaia Gorge surrounds a small pool. Magnolias and over 30 flowering cherries blossom in spring, with clematis climbing the trees. Each summer Sue plants 5,000 annuals including her favourite Livingstone daisies, asters, petunias, pansies, violas and dwarf phlox. These complement massed perennials such as catmint, daisies, phlox and salvias. Other summer delights include peonies, lilies and dahlias, and the garden is enlivened with peacocks and white and fantail pigeons. A clever way to hide the clothesline is to enclose it with a hedge of native olearia as Sue does. She also offers bed and breakfast accommodation by arrangement.

TROTTS' GARDEN
Ashburton

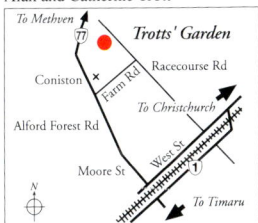

Owners:
Alan and Catherine Trott

Address: Racecourse Rd, R D 6, Ashburton
Directions: At the north end of Ashburton, turn west off SH 1 into Racecourse Rd. Continue for 3km to Trotts' Garden on left.
Phone: 0-3-308 9530
Fax: 0-3-308 8568
Email: trottsgarden@hotmail.com
Open: All year, Mondays to Saturdays, 9am–5pm, or by appointment
Closed: Sundays, or by appointment
Groups: Welcome by appointment
Fee: $8 per adult, school children free
Size: Large – 3ha (7 acres)
Terrain: Flat
Nursery: Full range including rare trees & shrubs; giftware
Functions: Function centre for meetings or gatherings, catering on request, toilets available

The Trotts' Garden is a combination of woodland planting and formality. Many rare trees and shrubs feature in the garden together with extensive collections of rhododendrons and acers. Other predominant trees include magnolias, beeches and birches. Camellias and trilliums also provide spring interest, followed by perennials throughout the summer months. A stream edged with water-loving plants leads to a bog garden and pond. Foliage plants are a real feature in the garden, and some interesting bark trees are an added visitor attraction. Garden structures include arbours, a gazebo, chapel and belvedere. The belvedere lookout provides views over the garden to the mountains beyond, and bridges the transition to the formal garden. This is introduced by the wrought iron gates (pictured above) which open into a broad grassy walkway between twin herbaceous borders 110 metres long. Within the formal garden is a box-edged rose garden with 16 varieties of roses in 16 separate beds. The formal garden is enclosed in a neatly trimmed macrocarpa hedge. A historic chapel, built in 1916, has been moved, restored and placed in the formal garden, where it is a focal point and popular venue for weddings. Trotts' Garden is open to visit all year, with its variety of botanical features making it a garden for all seasons.

CONISTON
Ashburton

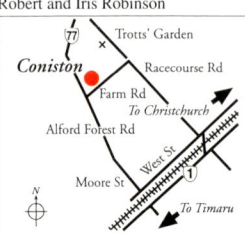

Owners:
Robert and Iris Robinson

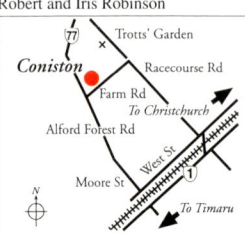

Address: Alford Forest Rd, Ashburton
Directions: At the south end of Ashburton, turn west off SH 1 into Moore St, then continue on Alford Forest Rd (SH 77) for 3km to Coniston garden on right.
Phone: 0-3-308 6221
Fax: 0-3-308 6213
Open: October to December, daily, by appointment
Groups: By appointment, as above
Fee: $5 per adult
Size: Large – 2ha (5 acres)
Terrain: Flat

         mostly

Originally established in 1890, Coniston is now a woodland garden, developed by the Robinsons since 1956. Gigantic turn-of-the-century wellingtonias, Lombardy poplars, oaks, elms, ashes, cedars, picea and thuja form a shelter belt around the perimeter of the garden and line the curving driveway. A canopy of old pear trees provides dappled shade for rhododendrons, azaleas and perennials. Favourites are the tree-like rhododendrons, especially mauve and blue shades, underplanted with groundcovers. In early spring, daffodils accompany camellias, then flowering cherries and dogwoods blossom. Early magnolias bloom with the rhododendrons and golden and apricot mollis azaleas established in 1965, now underplanted with blue ajuga and forget-me-nots. Two years earlier, a natural riverbed gully was transformed into a lake bordered with weeping willows, maples, conifers and swamp cypresses. Cherry blossom, colourful azaleas and Kingcup calthas are mirrored in the still waters among waterlilies, while other moisture-loving plants crowd the banks. Tea roses and climbers take centre stage in summer, when the woodland is brightened with *Cardiocrinum giganteum*. Autumn colours deciduous trees established in the 'sixties and a range of conifers provide contrast, with natives including evergreen beeches and a 12-metre kauri that Bob planted in 1936.

214

STONEHAVEN
Ruapuna

Stonehaven

Owners:
Warren and Liz Scott

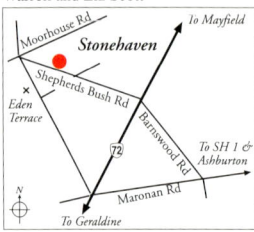

Address: Shepherds Bush Rd, Ruapuna
Postal: Ruapuna, R D 5, Ashburton
Directions: From Tinwald turn right
into Maronan Rd. Turn right into
Barnswood Rd. Cross SH 72 into
Shepherds Bush Rd. Continue 2km to
Stonehaven garden on right.
Phone: 0-3-303 6108
Fax: 0-3-303 6008
Email: wscott@voyager.co.nz
Open: Open Days, Mondays &
Tuesdays, mid October to mid
December, 10am–5pm; other times
from October to April by appointment
Fee: $5 per adult
Size: Medium – over 1ha (3 acres)
Terrain: Flat
Nursery: Groundcovers, perennials,
alpines, bulbs, primulas, gentians

mostly
by arrangement

Liz has used local stone from the abundant heaps in nearby paddocks, since 1975, to build the low stone walls that separate Stonehaven into garden rooms. A raised alpine rock garden features lewisias and Liz's favourite blue gentians. A formal malus avenue, underplanted with irises, leads to double perennial borders in blues, whites, yellows and apricots, incorporating a rustic old woolshed. The verandah of the century-old house is draped with purple wisteria, harmonising with the border below. Rose pergolas lead beyond spacious lawns to wandering paths among species rhododendrons such as *R. roxieanum*, combined with old roses. Groundcovers from adjacent beds stud the stone-edged pathways meandering through deciduous trees to arrive at the pond hidden in a sea of bluebells beneath rhododendrons. Cherry trees drop white petals around the stony perimeter among primulas, irises and hostas. Elsewhere, a woodland garden is carpeted with honesty, bluebells and forget-me-nots. Woodland paths lead to a bog garden where astilbes and primulas contrast with lush hostas, gunneras and *Cardiocrinum giganteum*. A bank of silver pears tones with *Stachys lanata* beneath. Rose pergolas and tennis-court netting clad with clematis and roses create windows to paddocks of specimen trees and spring bulbs, with snow-capped mountains beyond.

SOUTH CANTERBURY,
NORTH OTAGO AND DUNEDIN

South Canterbury stretches from Geraldine to Waimate in the south. It incorporates Mt Cook National Park, featuring New Zealand's highest mountain, Mt Cook, and a number of beautiful glacial lakes, with ski-fields a major drawcard. The clear waters of typical South Island rivers with their shingled banks are crossed in travelling to many of the 18 gardens featured in these regions.

Near Temuka is Newlands Rock Gardens specialising in low-growing plants and campanulas. On the Orari River is Orari Estate with its historic woodland garden. North of the City of Timaru is Ranui, with roses and views to the alps as well as a woodland garden with historic trees. Also in Timaru are Ethridge Gardens designed in English style with high brick walls, and Timaru Botanic Gardens with parklands of specimen trees surrounding two large ponds and many endangered plants from around the world. Overlooking the shores of Lake Pukaki is Braemar Homestead Garden, with views of Mt Cook. Between Lake Benmore and Lake Ohau is Omarama where The Briars offers accommodation as well as garden visits. The formal design of this garden is based on circles, framing panoramic mountain views. Nearer the coast, at Waimate, are two more gardens, both historic. Te Waimate Hitorical Tours take visitors through the early buildings as well as the garden with topiary trees and other original features. Centrewood Estate has a lake for a focal point, surrounded by mature trees, rhododendrons and a formal rose garden. There is quality accommodation also available at Centrewood, by arrangement.

North Otago includes the main city of Dunedin on the east coast, and begins at Oamaru, famous for its soft pale limestone so easy to carve and build with, making it a useful structural addition to many gardens. In Oamaru are the Oamaru Public Gardens sited in a natural gladed stream valley and featuring a beautiful marble fountain just inside the main gates. South of Oamaru at Maheno is Joan Elder's Garden with water features, which provides inspiration for Joan's paintings. Then further south at Waianakarua is Glen Dendron, a two-hectare valley planted with a variety of wodland trees, shrubs and flowers.

There are five gardens in the main city of Dunedin, which is known as the Rhododendron City because of its annual Rhododendron Week in October. The well-known Dunedin Botanic Garden comprises a lower almost level formal garden and the top steeper informal garden, separated by a stream and extensive rock garden. In Abbotsford, south-west of the city, is Wylde Willow with its creek throughout as a focal point for garden lovers and children alike.

There are three gardens on the Otago Peninsula, the first being the well-known historic Glenfalloch Woodland Garden featuring many mature trees and rhododendrons. Next is the equally renowned Larnach Castle Garden surrounding the historic castle. Past Portobello is Hereweka Garden and its adjoining nursery in a valley featuring the only extant stand of rimu on the peninsula. The coastal roadway leads to the only mainland Royal Albatross colony in the world.

The main road to Central Otago leads south of Dunedin to Milton and continues past Garvan Homestead where a historic Alfred Buxton garden has been restored round the old homestead which also provides meals and accommodation by arrangement.

BEN OHAU RANGE

49
Lake Pukaki

79
Geraldine
Fairlie
44
45
8
Pleasant Point
Temuka
Rangitata River
8
Twizel
46
Lake Ohau
47 Timaru
50
Lake Benmore
48
THE HUNTERS HILLS
Omarama
83
Lake Aviemore
Otematata
52
51
Waihao River
Kurow
Lake Waitaki
HAWK DUN RANGE
82
Waimate
83
Waitaki River
Danseys Pass
Naseby
53
Ranfurly
Maheno
54 Oamaru
Herbert
Kakanui
KAKANUI MTS
85
55
Hampden
Middlemarch
Palmerston
87
Waikouaiti
1
Karitane
Warrington
Lake Mahinerangi
Waitati
56
59
OTAGO PENINSULA
Mosgiel
Outram
60
57 58
Allanton
Lawrence
Brighton
DUNEDIN
8
61
Milton
Taieri River
N
Balclutha
Scale
Kaitangata
0   50km
Clutha River
Cartography by Terralink Ltd

ORARI ESTATE
Geraldine

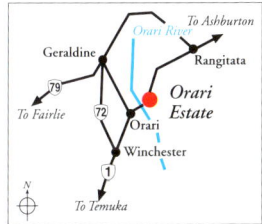

Owners:
Rosie and Ian Morten

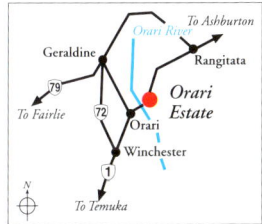

Address: SH 1, Orari
Postal: R D 22, Geraldine
Directions: Take SH 1 south of
Ashburton or north of Temuka.
Garden entrance at Rest Area just
north of Orari River.
Phone: 0-3-693 9058
Fax: 0-3-693 9058
Email: orariest@voyager.co.nz
Website: friars.co.nz/gardens/pages/
orari.html
Open: All year, daily, by appointment
Groups: By appointment, as above
Fee: $5 per adult
Size: Large – 2ha (5 acres)
Terrain: Undulating

  x2 partial

  by arrangement

Orari Estate has been in Rosie's family since the time of the first settlers, with trees planted back in the 1850s providing a mature woodland. Rosie's grandparents began building the homestead in 1912; a pink kalmia from that era still thrives, with a pear orchard, nut walk, and original main lawn. Rosie's mother began revamping the garden in the 1970s, creating three new garden areas. Sycamores are being progressively culled to open up the woodland, and Rosie is planting old roses. Predominant spring features are the rhododendrons, then in summer cardiocrinum lilies bloom with perennials including irises, delphiniums and groundcovers such as ajuga. A dozen different magnolias announce the arrival of spring, followed by camellias, mollis azaleas, the rhododendrons, a michelia and a spectacular kowhai. Two creeks flow through the property, one dammed to create a pond which is enjoyed by a white swan. Bridges cross the creeks, edged with pink primulas, ligularias and yellow Kingcup calthas. An old water-race now forms a pathway and drifts of blue forget-me-nots carpet the ground under mature conifers, including an unusual weeping Douglas fir. In autumn the deciduous trees and azaleas feature, while winter highlights the structure of the trees and the garden. Peacocks are an additional attraction.

NEWLANDS ROCK GARDENS
Temuka

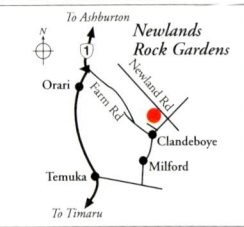

Owners:
Bev and Peter Davidson

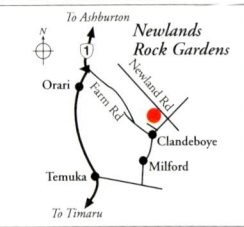

Address: 1036 Newland Rd,
Clandeboye, Temuka
Postal: "Newlands", Orton, R D 26,
Temuka
Directions: Take SH 1 south through
Rangitata. Before Orari turn left into
Farm Rd. Travel 11km to Clandeboye.
Turn left into Rolleston Rd, then left
into Newland Rd. Garden on left.
Phone: 0-3-615 9828
Open: Spring to autumn, daily
Groups: By appointment
Fee: No charge
Size: Medium – 0.6ha (1½ acres)
Terrain: Flat
Nursery: Specialises in all low-
growing plants, bulbs & shrubs (most
less than 30cm high). Free catalogue
available; mail orders taken.

individuals
only

on lawn

Devonshire
by arrangement

Peter's mother planted the large trees round the
perimeter of the garden in 1960 and Peter's sister
established the first rock garden. This has been extended
to accommodate Bev and Peter's favourite alpines –
gentians, dwarf narcissi, dwarf irises and, more recently,
peonies. Spacious lawns with seating provide a tranquil
setting, the Davidsons' private garden adding to the display
garden. Waterlily ponds feature Japanese irises and Peter
has developed a rose garden. Early spring is welcomed by
the crocuses, dwarf narcissi, cyclamen and aconites. Deep
blue gentians and pulsatillas predominate, accompanied
by adonis, sanguinaria, scillas, erythroniums, trilliums,
wood anemones, muscari, saxifrage, dianthus, and *Primula
auricula*. Other spring features include prunus and cornus
blossom, weeping maples clothed with new foliage,
rhododendrons blooming and lots of clematis. In summer
Peter's roses take over and rhodohypoxis adds to the
colour. Bev and Peter specialise in the campanulas which
feature from late summer through the autumn months
when they are joined by crocuses, colchicums,
schizostylis, and the colourful foliage of deciduous trees
such as the maples, liquidambars and dogwoods. In winter
the cyclamen and narcissi feature with witch hazel and
wintersweet trees providing colour for the bare branches.

RANUI
Timaru

![garden photo]

Owners:
Margaret and Kevin Cosgrove

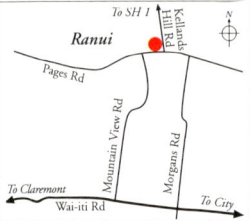

Address: 5 Kellands Hill Rd, Timaru
Directions: From north, turn right into
Washdyke Flat Rd. Turn left into
Kellands Hill Rd. Garden at end on
right. Or from Timaru, turn left into
Wai-iti Rd. Turn right into Morgans Rd,
left into Pages Rd & right into
Kellands Hill Rd. Garden on left corner.
Phone: 0-3-686 1288
Fax: 0-3-686 1285
Email: ranui@timaru.com
Website: friars.co.nz/gardens/pages/
ranui.html
Open: Spring to autumn, by
appointment only
Fee: $3 per adult
Size: Medium– 0.6ha (1½ acre)
Terrain: Flat
Nursery: Perennials from garden
Accommodation: Bed & breakfast

 by arrangement

The garden at Ranui has been planted since 1987 on a historic site, with many of the trees dating back to circa 1920. Located on the north-west boundary of Timaru, Ranui is semi-rural with views over farmland to the Southern Alps and Mount Cook. Shelter belts had to be planted around the perimeter of the garden, but Margaret was careful to use only low-growing perennials and roses round the lawn in order to retain the view. The garden changes quite dramatically with the seasons. In spring the woodland garden along the driveway is the greatest feature. The established English trees such as the oaks, flowering cherries, weeping maple and elm provide the shade for Margaret's woodland plants. She loves the brick pathway through the 140 rhododendrons, hostas, Chatham Island forget-me-nots, violets and hundreds of spring bulbs. In late spring the delphiniums and irises flower. Then in summer the newer garden around the house takes the limelight, with 200 roses and perennials. Margaret's favourites are the old roses and David Austins. She uses mainly pastel shades of blues, pinks and whites, with a touch of red such as 'Dublin Bay' with 'Iceberg' around the swimming pool where it is more sheltered. The clay soil has had to be built up with many bales of pea straw, newspaper, sawdust and compost. Then in autumn the historic trees along the driveway change colour.

        © Friars' Guide to New Zealand Gardens Open to Visit

ETHRIDGE GARDENS
Timaru

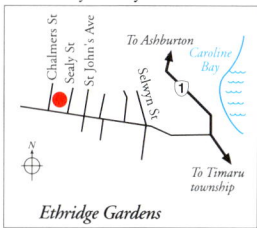

Ethridge

Owners:
Nan and Wynne Raymond

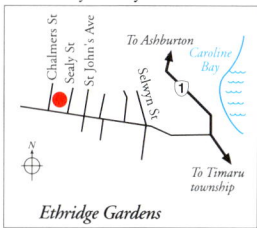

Ethridge Gardens

Address: 10 Sealy St, Timaru
Directions: Take SH 1 to Timaru.
Turn west north of the town into
Wai-iti Rd. Travel 2km to Sealy St.
Garden on left.
Phone: 0-3-684 4910
Fax: 0-3-684 4910
Open: September to May, daily,
by appointment
Groups: By appointment, as above
Fee: $5 per adult
Size: Small – 0.3ha (¾ acre)
Terrain: Flat
Nursery: Perennials eg *Cerinthe major*,
Alchemilla mollis, cynoglossum
Functions: Weddings, cocktails,
receptions, by arrangement
Accommodation: By arrangement

   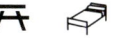

by arrangement

This English-style garden, named after Nan's English great-grandmother, was inspired by Sissinghurst and Hidcote. In 1984 it was virtually a blank canvas. Nan designed high brick walls to divide it into a series of rooms and vistas, with grassy axes leading from one colour scheme to the next, each carefully coordinated throughout the changing seasons. A century-old oak dominates the front lawn, fringed with rhododendrons, camellias and roses. The driveway border in yellows, blues and whites features 'Maigold' roses climbing the high trellis fence. In summer the herbaceous red, blue and lime-green border is full of red roses and lilies, with blue irises, delphiniums and lime-green euphorbias and alchemilla. Further long borders overflow in pinks, mauves, purples, whites and silver, with a 'Mary Rose' walk edged in box, contrasting with a semi-circle of silvery, blue- and plum-coloured foliage, surrounding a silver pear as focal point. A cross-axis takes the eye to a statue of Atlanta. The first of many archways leads into the formal courtyard centred around a pond and fountain framed with 'Iceberg' roses. A landscaped swimming-pool area in bright yellows and blues ends at the rose gazebo where red 'Dublin Bay' climbs to the Marseilles-tiled roof, matching the 1911 house, and over the wall into the potager.
Accommodation is also available at Ethridge Gardens.

TIMARU BOTANIC GARDENS
Timaru

Owner:
Timaru District Council

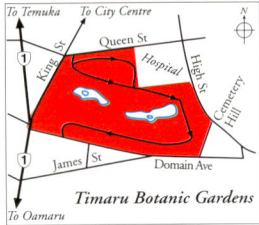

Timaru Botanic Gardens

Address: Corner of King St (SH 1) &
Queen St, Timaru
Postal: P O Box 522, Timaru
Directions: Take SH 1 to Timaru.
Turn east into Queen St. Gardens on
right. Entrance from Queen St to one-
way drive through Gardens to
Domain Ave.
Phone: 0-3-684 8199
Fax: 0-3-684 2203
Email: bills@timdc.govt.nz
Open: All year, daily,
8am to dusk
Fee: No charge
Size: Large – 19ha (47½ acres)
Terrain: Flat to undulating
Children: Playground available
Refreshments: Shop opposite Gardens

Two large ponds are focal points at Timaru Botanic Gardens, originally established in 1864. The ponds are home to ducks and other water fowl and water loving plants. Pathways edge the ponds and a footbridge was gifted by the Friends of Timaru Botanic Gardens in 1993. The ponds can be viewed from the driveway throughout the Gardens, surrounded by parkland set with mature specimen trees, mostly deciduous English varieties providing autumn colour. On the slope overlooking the ponds is a species rose collection featuring a rose pergola. There are over 30 other collections within the Gardens, such as the adjoining Legume Border, and the adjacent Canary Islands Border. There are also camellia and maple collections, and many flowering borders. Backing the ponds is a woodland area containing mostly black and red beech, and native kowhai and ribbonwood. The Gardens are renowned for preserving endangered species from around the world, with a bed of indigenous threatened plants above a garden of native species found in the Canterbury region. The Graeme Paterson Conservatory and Fernery also features plants grown in varying conditions. A Herb Garden is located near the bowling green and several interesting trails have been developed such as the Shakespeare theme walk, Trees of the World, and a historical walk. An aviary, band rotunda, statuary, and playground are added attractions.

BRAEMAR HOMESTEAD GARDEN
Lake Pukaki

Owners:
Carol and Duncan Mackenzie

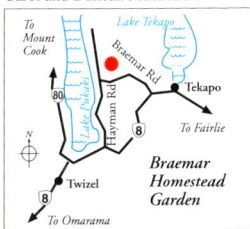

Address: Braemar Station, Lake Pukaki
Postal: P O Box 62, Lake Tekapo
Directions: From Twizel, travel 15km on SH 8 to Lake Pukaki. Turn left into Hayman Rd. Travel 20km to Braemar on right. From Tekapo, travel 5km west on SH 8 & turn right into Braemar Rd. Continue 24km to garden.
Phone: 0-3-680 6844
Fax: 0-3-680 6854
Email: (pending)
Open: Oct.–April, daily, by appointment
Fee: $5 per adult
Size: Medium – 1ha (2½ acres)
Terrain: Varied – hilly
Nursery: Occasional perennials & roses from garden
Gallery: Art & photography
Accommodation: 2 cottages available, sleeping 8 & 14 guests respectively

flat areas

by arrangement

When Lake Pukaki was raised 38 metres in 1976, it flooded the Mackenzies' former home, forcing their move to a hilly paddock overlooking the lake, with spectacular views to Mt Cook. Although advised to grow only hardy natives on such an exposed site, the Mackenzies planted the perimeter in shelter trees, and huge moraine rocks were moved on to the garden. Carol grows clematis, old rambling roses and rhododendrons in the sheltered courtyard, where pots of lewisias in sunrise colours love the heat and tolerate the cold. As well as the alpines and natives that are suited to the conditions, Carol finds her favourite old roses – particularly the rugosas and musks – tough enough to survive. She colour-coordinates different areas, with creams, pinks, whites and apricot roses along the driveway, contrasting with lemons, blues and golds on the slope below. Yellow irises and blue aquilegias combine elsewhere, while splashes of red provide accent throughout the garden. A natural stream opens into a pond in a sheltered glade, reached via a grassy avenue. Spring bulbs naturalise under the trees and pulsatillas seed freely. Rose-clad archways lead into a cottage garden where peonies feature among foxgloves, delphiniums, lilies and gentians. Two accommodation cottages provide a good base for outdoor pursuits such as tramping, boating and fishing, or Braemar's nine-hole golf course at Lake Pukaki.

THE BRIARS
Omarama

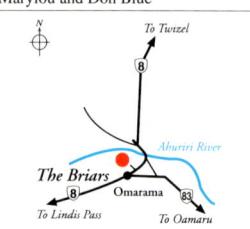

The Briars

Owners:
Marylou and Don Blue

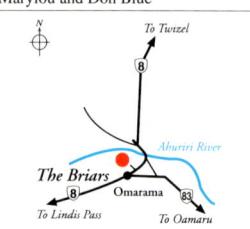

Address: SH 8, Ahuriri Heights, Omarama
Postal Address: Ahuriri Heights, Box 98, Omarama
Directions: On SH 8, travel south 25km from Twizel, or north 2km from Omarama to Ahuriri Heights. Turn west and continue 300m to The Briars garden on left.
Phone: 0-3-438 9615
Fax: 0-3-438 9655
Email: info@mtcook.org.nz
Open: All year, daily, 10am–4pm
Groups: As above
Fee: $5 per adult
Size: Medium – 0.8ha (2 acres)
Terrain: Flat, terraced and steep
Accommodation: B&B available, by arrangement

   partial

by arrangement

Since 1990, the Blues have transformed a hillside of rabbit burrows and briar roses into a formal garden designed in circles, with even a circular carpark. The Briars is named after the wild sweet-briars beyond the garden, contrasting with the old roses that Marylou has planted within. A long pergola walk features 18 pink climbing roses edged with lavender, and a white garden mixes modern and old-fashioned rose varieties. The roses continue into autumn when the purple and white borders bloom. Spring bulbs and trilliums announce the end of winter. Because of the panoramic mountain views, Marylou has planted the lower gardens in bold lines, with hardy perennials that will survive the harsh climate. Silver birches, gums, oaks and red-leafed malus provide shelter, with dry stone walls adding to the structure of the garden, and pergolas shading the seats placed strategically throughout. Many urns are used to accentuate the walkways and steps. A square herb garden contrasts with a traditional circular herb garden featuring a large sunken trough. This opens into Don's potager with its high pergola and four silver pear trees trimmed into topiary balls. The potager leads into a box-edged square garden, in greens and whites, where the historic font from the Omarama church is a focal point. A new cloister garden is dominated by a 1.5-metre Oamaru stone statue overlooking four paths which form a cross.

TE WAIMATE HISTORICAL TOURS
Waimate

Owners:
Jan and Mike Studholme

Address: Gorge Road, R D 9, Waimate
Directions: From Timaru, take SH 1 south to SH 82. Turn right & travel into Waimate. Continue south on Gorge Rd over Centennial Bridge. Opposite Kitchener Park, garden on left (1.8km from town centre).
Phone: 0-3-689 7199
Fax: 0-3-689 7855
Mobile: 025 228 9608
Email: mjstudholme@xtra.co.nz
Open: All year, daily, by appointment
Groups: Welcome, by appointment
Fee: $6 pp; groups of 10+ $5 pp
Size: Medium – 1.6ha (4 acres)
Terrain: Flat
Teas: $5 pp, by arrangement
For sale: Cards & postcards
Tours: $5 pp historical group tours

  by arrangement

Te Waimate has been in the Studholme family since 1854 when the first European dwelling in Waimate was built. This "cuddy", made from a single totara tree and thatched with flax-bound snowgrass, still stands in the garden today. Two years later the woolshed was erected, one of the oldest still in working order, and in 1860 the garden was planted, incuding the oaks that line the kilometre-long driveway. The first homestead burnt down in 1928, but tours of other historic features at Te Waimate take in the stables, built in 1888, the brick creamery behind the cuddy, and the "phutta" or food storehouse in the garden, as well as the four topiary yew trees, cut to the shape of the family bell brandmark. Nearby is the sundial placed there in 1904, backed by a large rose garden. 'Old Blush' was planted by Effie Studholme in 1860, and David Austins have been added to the original rose plantings. Other predominant species are the blackwoods, magnolias and rhododendrons in the spring, and the bulbs in the extensive woodland garden thriving under the canopy of mature trees. Pittosporum, hebes and other natives are scattered throughout the woodland garden too. The cottage garden and roses take centre stage in summer, then in autumn the English trees turn, and along with the foliage of the oaks, dogwoods, maples, flowering cherries and deciduous azaleas provide colour.

CENTREWOOD ESTATE
Waimate

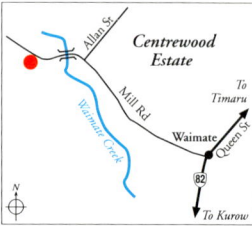

Owners:
Anne and Jamie Sutherland

Map showing Centrewood Estate, Allan St, Mill Rd, Waimate Creek, Queen St, To Timaru, To Kurow, route 82

Address: Mill Rd, R D 8, Waimate
Directions: From Timaru, take SH 1 south for 35km. Turn right into SH 82. Continue to Waimate into Queen St. Turn right into Mill Rd. Cross Garlands Bridge to Centrewood Estate which is 4th house on left.
Phone: 0-3-689 7465
Fax: 0-3-689 7464
Email: jhmsuth@voyager.co.nz
Websites: friars.co.nz/hosts/centrewoodestate.html *and* www.voyager.co.nz/~jhmsuth/
Open: September to May, by arrangement
Closed: June, July & August
Fee: $5 per adult; $4 pp for groups 20+
Size: Medium – 1.6ha (4 acres)
Terrain: Undulating

 by arrangement

Centrewood Estate is set in an extensive established garden in the centre of mature English trees, some of which are over a century old. Built in 1890, Centrewood has been home to five generations of the Sutherland family. Designed in triple brick by the French architect Maurice Duval, this historic homestead is sited on a sheep farm and the first Australasian Charolais cattle stud. The almost two-hectare (four-acre) grounds include a formal rose garden designed by landscape architect C.H. Reese and a large pond where visitors can feed the white swans and ducks. The first deciduous trees were planted in 1892 by Jamie's great-grandparents and now provide strong autumn colour and a haven for birds. Jamie's aunt planted the rhododendrons which are the predominant species at Centrewood, and imported deciduous Exbury azaleas from England. Anne learnt to propagate them for their now defunct nursery and had to plant the rhododendrons on top of the clay soil for drainage. She has softened the garden by reducing the rosebeds, adding perennials and edging with railway sleepers. Anne has also softened the colours by replacing reds with pinks and whites, which she prefers to pick for the house. Her favourite areas include the hellebores and snowdrops in the gully in spring and the new softer wild area. Quality accommodation is available by arrangement.

OAMARU PUBLIC GARDENS
Oamaru

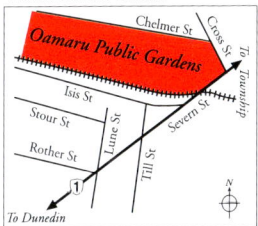

Owner:
Waitaki District Council

Address: Chelmer St, Oamaru
Postal: Parks Department, Private Bag 50 058, Oamaru
Directions: From Timaru, take SH 1 south to Oamaru. Turn right before bridge into Cross St. Turn left into Chelmer St. Travel 200m to main carpark on left. Or from Dunedin, take SH 1 to Oamaru. Turn left after bridge into Cross St. Then as above.
Phone: 0-3-434 1658
Fax: 0-3-434 1144
Open: All year, daily, dawn to dusk
Groups: Guided tours by appointment
Fee: No charge
Size: Large – 13ha (32½ acres)
Terrain: Flat, valley
Tours: Clydesdale wagon tours by arrangement

The Gardens are set in a natural gladed stream valley, close to the town centre. After the opening in 1876, Oamaru Stream was straightened, and the old stream bed transformed into a number of wildlife ponds. From this beginning, the Gardens have evolved and matured into a series of interconnected spaces, each with its own ambience. The framework is provided by large trees – especially elm and English beech – planted soon after the Gardens were established. The main gates were built in 1912, opening on to the formal Front Lawn, which is dominated by the beautiful Craig Fountain, carved from Italian Carrara marble in 1915. During the 1920s, other gardens were established, notably the Rose Garden, the Azalea Lawn and the Rhododendron Dell. In 1928 the bronze Peter Pan statue, now the centrepiece of the picturesque Wonderland Garden, was sculpted by Thomas Clapperton in London, and presented by a former Mayor. Also in 1928, the Great Garden Fête was held, providing funds for a number of developments, including the first Display House, children's playground, lawn tennis courts and croquet lawn. It also funded the construction of the Japanese Red Bridge, which now provides access to the latest Gardens development – the Chinese Garden. This was begun in the early 1990s, and opened by the Chinese ambassador in 1995.

JOAN ELDER'S GARDEN
Maheno

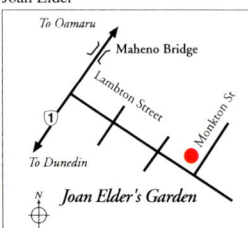

Owner:
Joan Elder

Joan Elder's Garden

Address: 1 Monkton St, Maheno, Oamaru
Postal: Maheno, R D 6-O, Oamaru
Directions: From Oamaru, take SH 1 south 9km to Maheno. Turn left into Lambton St, then 3rd left into Monkton St. Joan Elder's Garden 1st on left.
Phone: 0-3-439 5859
Open: Spring & summer, daily, by appointment
Groups: By appointment, as above
Fee: $4 per adult; groups $3 pp
Size: Small – 0.3ha (¾ acre)
Terrain: Flat
Paintings: Joan's watercolours, oils & miniatures of the garden & floral still-life for sale

Joan has established her garden since the mid 1950s, featuring favourite roses and rhododendrons, including 'White Pearl' which was planted in 1965 and is now trimmed like a tree. Other predominant species include hostas, meconopsis, trilliums and *Primula auricula*. With an artist's eye, Joan has designed her garden for all-year colour, providing inspiration for her paintings. In spring, early rock rhododendrons flower, along with dog-tooth violets and bulbs including a winding narcissi path. Joan plants for colour blends as well as line, incorporating complementary colours, such as lavender under yellow rhododendrons. Red rhododendrons provide strong accents, with various hybrids emerging at different times to maintain the impact of red. Further spring features include dogwoods, kalmias, magnolias, and hybrid clematis such as *C.* 'Jackmanii' flowing over an archway with the old rose, salmon rambler 'Phyllis Bide'. A rose bed adjacent to the house continues the red highlights with climbing 'Birthday Present' and other sunset colourings, joined in summer by dahlias. Then in autumn the red and golden maples, prunus and oaks are really colourful. Water features include three small goldfish ponds with mat-forming sagina and moss-like *Scleranthus biflorus* edging them in green. During spring the sunken water garden is lush with the hostas and other bog plants.

GLEN DENDRON
Waianakarua

Owners:
Anne and John Mackay

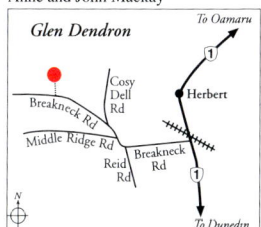

Address: 284 Breakneck Road, Waianakarua, North Otago
Postal: R D 9-O, Oamaru
Directions: From Oamaru, take SH 1 south for 25km to Waianakarua. Turn right into Breakneck Rd & travel 2.84km to garden on right. Or from Dunedin take SH 1 north for 90km.
Phone: 0-3-439 5288
Mobile: 021 615 287
Fax: 0-3-439 5288
Email: anne.john.mackay@xtra.co.nz
Open: August to May, by appointment
Closed: June & July
Fee: $4 per adult; groups of 10+ $3 pp
Size: Large – 2ha (5 acres)
Terrain: Flat & hilly
Nursery: Perennials, trees & shrubs
Accommodation: Farmstay available

by arrangement

Glen Dendron is a large informal country garden, set in a two-hectare (five-acre) valley. Anne, a floral artist, and John, a tree lover, who had previously established a two-hectare garden in West Otago, transplanted a large collection of plants to their new site in 1995 and began again on the bare hillside. They started planting with clear goals of utilising the natural contours and enhancing the panoramic views of the Waianakarua River and Herbert Forest to the ocean beyond. They have developed a variety of distinct areas incorporating elements of surprise, within the aim of creating a restful haven for humans and birds alike. The predominant species are maples and rhododendrons, as well as perennials. The cherry walk is underplanted with daffodils in spring and the silver birch woodland is carpeted with bluebells. There is also a conifer woodland and exotics are planted throughout the garden. Summer features daisies, roses, lilies and the dahlias which flower into autumn accompanied by lavender. Other plantings include peonies, irises, proteas and leucadendrons, with new plants being added all the time, limited only by the clay soil and droughts. Anne has a yellow, blue and silver garden in the courtyard for summer entertaining and other colour schemes are evolving. A bog garden and small pond will be followed by a larger water feature and plans include the building of archways and a summer house.

DUNEDIN BOTANIC GARDEN
Dunedin

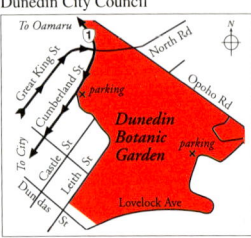

Owner:
Dunedin City Council

Address: Lovelock Ave, Opoho Rd &
Great King St, North Dunedin
Postal: P O Box 5045, Dunedin
Directions: From City, take Great
King St north. Carparks on
Cumberland St & Lovelock Ave.
Phone: 0-3-471 9275 or 0-3-474 9649
Fax: 0-3-477 8052
Open: All year, daily, dawn to dusk;
Information Centre/shop: 10am–4pm;
closed Christmas Day
Restaurant: 9.30am–4.30pm
Groups: Guided tours book at
Information Centre phone 471 9275
or fax 471 9928
Fee: Guided tours $3 per person for
groups of 10+
Size: Large – 28ha (70 acres)
Terrain: Flat to steep; good paths
For sale: Garden books & gifts; plants

   mostly

restaurant

The first botanic garden in New Zealand was begun in 1863 in Dunedin. It was relocated to the present 28-hectare site in 1867. The Garden has two distinct areas – the formal almost level Lower Garden and, separated by Lindsay Creek, the informal bush and woodland areas of the steeper Upper Garden. The latter includes the Native Plant Collection, which displays an Alpine Scree, Wetland Garden, and many rare and endangered New Zealand indigenous plants. Also in the Upper Garden is the four-hectare Rhododendron Dell, established in 1914, and now containing over 3,000 rhododendrons. Nearby, the Geographic Borders display plants from several regions of the world, including the Australian Plant Collection which surrounds a large modern aviary complex. Sited on the bank above the creek is one of the largest rock gardens in New Zealand. Construction began in 1904, and today includes alpine trees and shrubs as well as traditional diminutive rock garden plants. Centrally located in the Lower Garden is the restored Winter Garden, housing cacti, succulent and tropical plants. Built in 1908, this Edwardian public conservatory was one of the first in Australasia. Other features in the Lower Garden include the Camellia Collection, Rose Garden, Thematic Borders, Herb Garden, Water Garden and Herbaceous Borders. The Information Centre, shop and restaurant can also be found there.

GLENFALLOCH WOODLAND GARDEN
Otago Peninsula

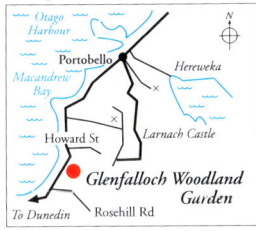

Owner:
Otago Peninsula Trust
Manager: Bruce McCormick

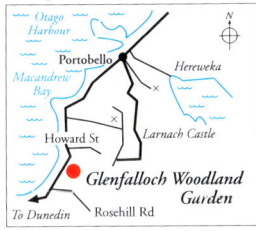

Address: 430 Portobello Rd, Otago Peninsula
Postal: P O Box 492, Dunedin
Directions: From City, travel to Otago Peninsula. Follow Portobello Rd for 11km to Glenfalloch on right, just before Macandrew Bay township.
Phone: 0-3-476 1775
Fax: 0-3-476 1137
Email: bruce@albatrosses.com
Open: All year, daily, dawn to dusk and evening meals at restaurant
Fee: By donation
Size: Large – 9.8ha (24 acres)
Terrain: Flat and steep
Restaurant: Licensed; restricted hours in winter
Groups: Bookings for dinner

   partly

at restaurant on site

Gaelic for "Hidden Glen", Glenfalloch is situated in a coastal valley overlooking the harbour. Developed as a private garden by Phillip Barling in 1917, Glenfalloch was bought by the Otago Peninsula Trust in 1968 to ensure public access. Sheltered by a ring of pines and eucalypts, Glenfalloch features original European trees from 1872, underplanted with sizeable azaleas and rhododendrons, including many unique hybrids and large-leafed species. Daffodils announce the arrival of spring, followed by tulips blooming beneath flowering cherries, magnolias and chestnuts. Native clematis climb the trees under which peonies and lilies flower in summer. Mature maples and silver birches provide spectacular colour in autumn. Then the early camellias bloom, including a Women's Year planting of white camellias, established in 1993 and interspersed with native hebes. A 45-minute bush walk leads past an ancient matai where birdlife includes tui, bellbirds and native pigeons. Russell Creek runs through the garden, bordered by massed azaleas under a woodland canopy. Perennials and moisture-loving plants include gunneras, hellebores, aquilegias, Solomon's seal, bergenias and hostas. Drifts of bluebells, ajuga and cerise primulas carpet the stream banks in spring. Other features include a 1945 "Peace Arch", Otago Herb Society Herb Garden, and a studio selling pottery.

LARNACH CASTLE GARDEN
Otago Peninsula

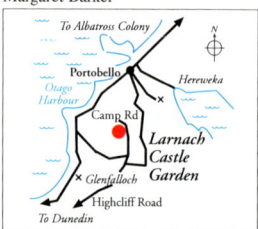

Owner:
Margaret Barker

Address: 145 Camp Rd, Otago Peninsula
Postal: P O Box 1350, Dunedin
Directions: From City, take Highcliff
Rd along top of Peninsula. Turn left
into Camp Rd. Castle on left.
Phone: 0-3-476 1616
Fax: 0-3-476 1574
Email: larnach@larnachcastle.co.nz
Website: www.larnachcastle.co.nz
Open: All year, daily, 9am–5pm;
during daylight saving 9am–7pm
Groups: Guided tours by arrangement
Fee: $6 per adult, $2 per child
Size: Large – 5ha (12½ acres)
Terrain: Mostly flat
Nursery: Rhododendrons, perennials,
woodland plants, alpines, bog plants
Tearooms: 9.30am–4.30pm daily
Accommodation: Lodge available; with
dinner in castle by arrangement

The gardens surrounding Larnach Castle have been recreated from 1967, incorporating 120-year-old trees. An expansive lawn in front of the castle is formally designed, with conifers symmetrically placed on the perimeter around the central focal point of a marble fountain from Pisa. A great laburnum arch underplanted with spring bulbs leads to a square pool with a view between immense conifers over the harbour 300 metres below. Alice in Wonderland figurines by Tenniel adorn the lawn border, with the Cheshire cat in the boughs of the original old cedar encircled with daffodils next to the historic glass cupola. A rhododendron dell features beyond the original holly hedge and on the opposite side of the castle is the restored rock garden. Azalea and heather gardens in front of the ballroom provide spring and autumn colour. The alpine garden also features in spring and the lath-enclosed perennial garden peaks in summer, when the damp garden near the driveway entrance flowers. Behind the ballroom, a box walk leads to an original copper beech by the wishing well. Beyond, Margaret's rainforest garden of native ponga, beech, kauri, rimu, totara, rewarewa and cabbage trees is interplanted with species rhododendrons, the colourful flame creeper *Tropaeolum speciosum*, and cardiocrinums. Accommodation is available in the adjacent Lodge, with dinner by arrangement in the Castle.

HEREWEKA GARDEN AND NURSERY
Portobello

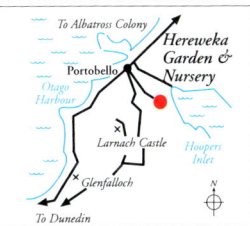

Owners:
Dr Peter Cooke and Anna Moore

Address: 150 Hereweka St,
Portobello, Dunedin 9004
Directions: From Portobello, turn
right into Hereweka St. Continue
500m then follow steep gravel road
1.4km through bush to garden.
Phone: 0-3-478 0165 or 0-3-478 0880
Fax: 0-3-478 0600
Open: All year, most weekends, other
times by appointment
Groups: By appointment
Fee: $5 per adult; refund on purchase
from nursery
Size: Large – 2ha (2 acres of garden
& 3 acres bush walks)
Terrain: Hilly
Nursery: Rare old perennials eg
Barnhaven double primulas, 'Pink
Sensation' delphiniums, *Gladiolus
tristis*, species aquilegias, irises,
penstemons, campanulas, heliotropes,
meconopsis, choice dwarf bulbs

Hidden in a valley of native bush, including the only extant stand of mature rimu trees on the peninsula, Hereweka looks out to hills and the inlet beyond. In 1985 the steep slope in front of the house was bulldozed into two levels, dry stone walls built, herbaceous borders planted and ponds established. Peter's walls overflow with blues and yellows – a favourite colour combination of Anna's – such as weeping rosemary, blue aquilegias, purple aubrietia, and lilac *Thalictrum aquilegifolium* contrasting with drifts of lemon *Gladiolus tristis*. A bed of creamy rhododendrons underplanted with daffodils is shaded by a kanuka tree, with a rare native *Clematis foetida* climbing to a tiny rifleman bird-box. Anna prefers scented species in soft muted lemons, yellows and creams, rather than hot colours. Early spring begins in September with flowering cherries and bulbs including miniature narcissi and a bed of pink tulips. *Convolvulus mauritanicus* adds to the blues in summer, when the perennial bed peaks with delphiniums, drifts of gypsophila, peonies, old roses and lilies. The sloping lawn leads to a stone and kanuka arbour, draped with white wisteria and old roses. Peter has planted the largest southern collection of over 25 bamboo species.

WYLDE WILLOW GARDEN
Abbotsford, Dunedin

Owners:
Fran and Mike Rawling

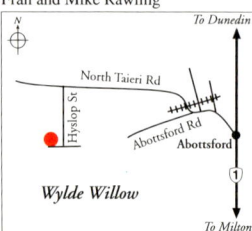

Address: 132 North Taieri Road, Abbotsford, Dunedin
Directions: From City, take SH 1 to Abbotsford. Turn right into Abbotsford Rd. Take 3rd right over railway line into North Taieri Rd. Travel 2km to end of road. Turn left into Hyslop St & right into Wylde Willow Garden.
Phone: 0-3-488 3988
Open: September to April, by appointment only
Closed: May to August
Groups: By appointment, as above
Fee: $3 per adult
Size: Medium – 0.8ha (2 acres)
Terrain: Mostly flat
Nursery pending: Plants grown in garden, mostly perennials
Children: Welcome – children's activities in garden

♟ partial   🍲 by arrangement

Abbots Creek, which flows through Wylde Willow Garden, has always been an attraction for local children. Back in the 1940s it was the site of a coal mine and adjacent sand mine. Then in the 1950s it became a whippet track for locals. In 1990 Fran began developing the area into an extensive garden, establishing different areas little by little. The woodland and creek walk is the central focus of the garden, with a new reflective pond and island added for birdlife, and recent parkland area of trees chosen for spring and autumn interest. The oldest part is the summer cottage garden with hundreds of heritage roses and perennials. White roses climb round the barbecue area and roses also line the driveway, edged with catmint. Visitors drive over the narrow bridge that leads into Wylde Willow, with further little bridges and crossings over Abbots Creek. The woodland is full of rhododendrons and underplantings of hostas, foxgloves, aquilegias and honesty. Thousands of daffodils carpet the orchard which features apples, plums, apricots and nut trees. Fran selects fairly monochromatic colour schemes in mostly pastel shades, as she feels these colours suit the southern light best. Wylde Willow Garden welcomes children, with available activities including a garden treasure hunt, creek exploration, and handling the numerous friendly animals and poultry.

GARVAN HOMESTEAD
Milton

Owners:
Hazel and Brian Marsh

Address: SH 1, Lovells Flat, Milton
Postal: SH 1, Milton, R D 2, South
Otago
Directions: 45 minutes south of
Dunedin. Take SH 1 to Milton.
Continue another 12km. Garden on
right. 12.5km north of Balclutha.
Phone: 0-3-417 8409
Fax: 0-3-417 8429
Email: garvan@xtra.co.nz
Open: All year, 11.30am to 6pm,
Tuesdays to Sundays
Closed: Monday
Fee: No charge
Size: Large – 2.4ha (6 acres)
Terrain: Mostly flat
Accommodation: Quality
accommodation by arrangement

 by arrangement

Garvan Homestead is set in a historic Buxton garden, designed and constructed by the well-known Christchurch landscape gardener, Alfred Buxton, in 1915. This English-style woodland garden has been restored since 1987. The original rhododendron plantings are still the predominant species, underplanted with huge drifts of violets, lily-of-the-valley and hellebores, and set amid a large collection of mature trees, mainly English oaks, elms and birches. Other Buxton features that are still apparent include the sweeping drive lined with assorted hollies and *Crataegus* (hawthorn), the tennis court, hazelnut walk, pond and the weeping trees that Buxton so often used. The pond was rediscovered and edged with massed white and pink primulas, silver astelias and deep blue *Iris sibirica,* in Monet-like effect. Primulas were also used with ligularias, gunneras and other bog plants to beautify the bog garden created from a boggy part of the front lawn. Camellias and spring bulbs accompany the cherry blossom, followed by colourful perennial borders and old English roses that adorn the garden and house. The roses continue into autumn when the the Virginia creeper turns scarlet and the maples and English trees colour up, in contrast with the conifers and evergreens. Planned plantings will transform a disused open-cast coal mine area. Quality accommodation is available upstairs in Garvan Homestead.

SOUTH AND CENTRAL OTAGO, AND SOUTHLAND

Inland from Dunedin is Central Otago with its cold winters and hot, dry summers producing wonderful stone-fruit. Beautiful glacial lakes backed by Aspiring National Park make this a favourite area for winter sports and summer sightseeing. Set in the stark beauty of the Maniototo is Clachanburn, with a stony creek flowing through the garden. Arahura is a new garden at Wanaka, with water features, stone terracing, woodland areas and a Celtic knot garden. Arahura also offers quality accommodation. Two further gardens at Wanaka have views to the lake and mountains beyond. Stuarts Wanaka Garden and Seeds is planted round streams, and Ashdon Garden, although small, features many rhododendrons. At Lake Hayes is the Rosedale Chapel and Water Garden where weddings are celebrated.

Inland at Tapanui is Blue Mountain Nurseries, specialising in double azaleas, with a range of hardy trees and plants. At Lawrence is The Ark, providing accommodation set in a cottage garden. Further south, at Stirling, just north of Balclutha, is Nagol Garden full of roses, with ponds and an adjacent nursery.

Southland is a rich farming region at the southern tip of New Zealand. To the west is the extensive Fiordland National Park and south, across Foveaux Strait, is Stewart Island. Invercargill, the southernmost city in New Zealand, is sited on open plains at the centre of the Southland grasslands. Like Dunedin, it was settled by Scots and the speech of locals incorporates the Scottish burr, undampened by the cooler temperatures experienced at such a southerly latitude. Many of the regional names and garden names also reflect this origin.

In the Gore area there are three public gardens worth visiting. The first, located in Gore township itself, are the Gore Public Gardens featuring century-old English trees and a number of unusual conifers. Gore's Rhododendron Festival is held in these Gardens every October. Nearby is Bannerman Park set in a picturesque valley intersected by streams and ponds bordered with bog plants. Just west of Gore is Dolamore Park with 95 hectares largely in native forest. Walking tracks provide access to the birdlife and an Education Centre has recently been established. Mature rhododendrons feature in spring, and every February a country music festival is held in the Park.

To the west of Gore is Winton. En route south to the City of Invercargill, the traveller passes through Lochiel. Here is located The Hideaway 201, with its garden rooms connectd by rustic archways and a giftshop tucked away behind high hedges. Nearby is Tudor Park, with lots of old roses as well as ponds and architectural features. Quality accommodation is also available at Tudor Park. North-west of Invercargill, at Northope, is Belle Fleur, specialists in dahlias which flower in summer, and north-east, at Glencoe, is the Hosta Garden featuring over 350 varieties for sale and hostas planted throughout the woodland garden. Just north of the City is Anderson Park, well-known for its art gallery set in extensive lawns and gardens. And, finally, in the City of Invercargill itself is Queens Park, planted since 1911, with a range of gardens radiating from the central band rotunda.

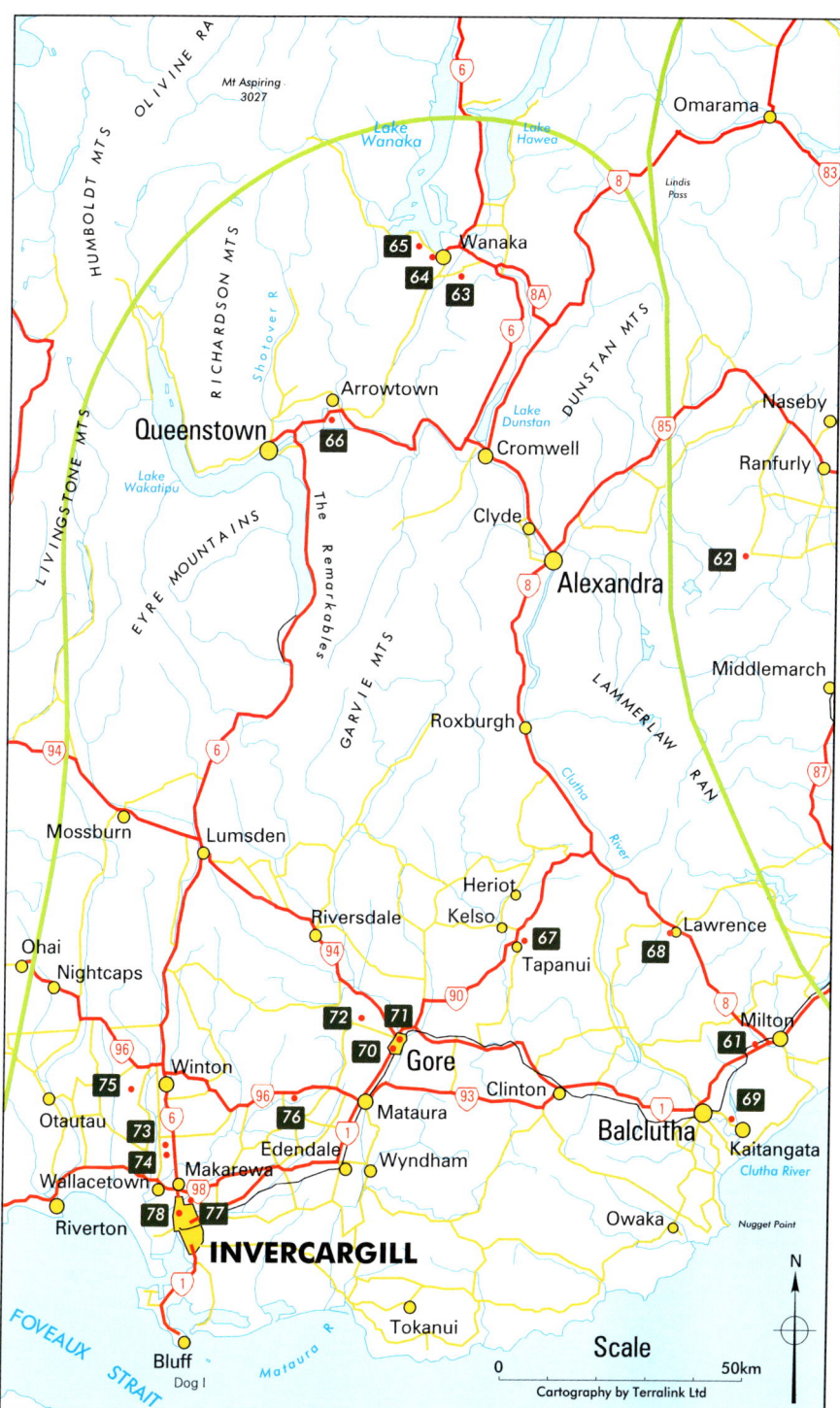

CLACHANBURN
Ranfurly

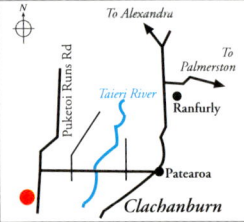

Owners:
Jane and Charles Falconer

Address: Puketoi Runs Rd, Patearoa
Postal: Patearoa, R D 4, Ranfurly
Directions: From Ranfurly, travel
18km south to Patearoa. Garden
signposted. Cross Sowburn Bridge,
continue 0.5km, then turn 1st right.
After 200m take 1st turn left. Cross
Taieri River & continue to T junction.
Turn left into Puketoi Runs Rd.
Continue 3km to garden on right.
Phone: 0-3-444 7501
Fax: 0-3-444 7044
Email: clachanburn@xtra.co.nz
Open: October to March, by
appointment
Groups: By appointment
Fee: $5 per person
Size: Medium – 1.6ha (4 acres)
Terrain: Flat to undulating

mostly

by arrangement

Clachanburn is Gaelic for the "Stoney Creek" which flows through the property. Poplars, pines, willows, prunus and an *Acer negundo* were the original plantings in the 1920s, but Charles and Jane have extended the garden since 1977, when they moved into the homestead, designing a new area each year. Despite the harsh Maniototo climate, with its hot, dry summers and freezing winters, Jane manages to plant for seasonal colour. Spring blossom is accompanied by drifts of daffodils, primulas, trilliums, fritillarias, aquilegias, forget-me-nots and hellebores. Then wisteria, clematis and peonies bloom, followed in summer by roses and perennials. A large formal rose garden of old-fashioned and modern roses is bordered by a low hedge of *Buxus sempervirens*. The deciduous trees provide the rich autumn colours of Central Otago, and its schist stone features in walls throughout the garden. White Pekin ducks swim in a natural stream-fed pond edged with water irises, hostas and astilbes and featuring a curved stone bridge and waterfalls created by boulders lining the stream. Jane is landscaping a second pond which has at its water's edge a boat shed and kauri clinker boat. She is carefully retaining the northern vista of the vast Maniototo plains to the hills beyond. Jane sells a range of pickles and preserves as well as house and garden craft. Her beloved donkey, Jacob, lives adjacent to the garden.

ARAHURA
Mount Barker, Wanaka

Arahura

Owners:
John and Tricia Carr

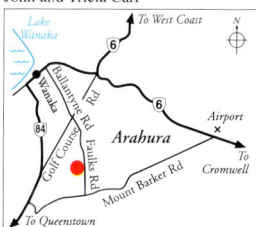

Address: 142 Faulks Road, Mount Barker, Wanaka
Directions: From Cromwell, take SH 6 towards Wanaka. Opposite airport, turn left into Mt Barker Rd. Travel 5km & turn right into Faulks Rd. Continue 1.5km to Arahura on left.
Phone: 0-3-443 7439
Fax: 0-3-443 6503
Email: relax@arahura.com
Open: October to mid May, by appointment only
Closed: Mid May to October
Fee: $3 per adult for charity
Size: Large – 2.8ha (7 acres)
Terrain: Flat on 2 levels
Accommodation: As in *Friars' Guide to NZ Accommodation for the Discerning Traveller 2001*
Functions: Weddings by arrangement

Maori for "path of discovery", Arahura was built in 1991 on a scenic spot with views to the Southern Alps. Designed by Wanaka architect Sarah Scott, Arahura offers quality accommodation, each guestroom opening to the almost three-hectare (seven-acre) landscaped garden. Water features include a waterfall feeding the small lake bordered by a laburnum walk leading to a nuttery circle, as well as an ornamental pond edged with a bog garden. There is also a heated swimming pool and rose-clad tennis court. A full-size croquet lawn is surrounded by a young photinia hedge with four golden rain trees and a herbaceous border backed by a woodland area. A focal point in front of the house is the Celtic knot garden with its box hedging. Spring is full of colour as the deciduous trees come into leaf and blossom, and the wisteria flowers. Summer brings the roses into bloom and the lavender bank. The bog garden and herbaceous border complement the shrub garden throughout the summer months. Many exotic trees have been planted with the emphasis on vibrant autumn colours. A large area has also been devoted to native planting, with a cabbage tree walk leading from it interspersed with indigenous flaxes. Paths connect the two garden levels, with stone terracing and steps down to the walkway around the lake. Arahura has a weddings licence and welcomes garden weddings.

STUARTS WANAKA GARDEN AND SEEDS
Wanaka

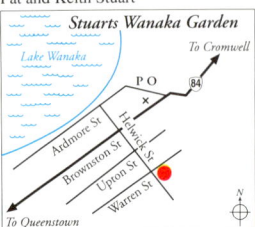

Owners:
Pat and Keith Stuart

Address: 32 Warren St, Wanaka
Directions: Take SH 89 from Cromwell to Wanaka. Turn left into Helwick St. Continue past Warren St. Garden entrance on left. (Nursery entrance from Warren St.)
Phone: 0-3-443 8866
Fax: 0-3-443 7846
Open: September to May, daily, by appointment
Groups: By appointment, as above
Fee: No charge for individuals; bus trips $2 pp
Size: Medium – 0.53ha (1⅓ acres)
Terrain: Gently sloping
Nursery: Specialists in rare & unusual plants; seed available from many specialist plants grown in garden

  by arrangement

In 1985, the Stuarts converted an acre of peat bog into garden, diverting springs to form streams meandering through a series of waterfalls into Bullock Creek. The creek-banks have been landscaped with blossom trees, cornus, maples, gunneras, rodgersias and *Peltiphyllum*. Drifts of phlox, Japanese irises, astilbes and azaleas tumble over rocks, which also edge the clear water, enhancing the plantings of hostas and primulas. Bridges cross the water-ways to paths edged with purple violas, leading past red native astelia and peonies canopied by dogwoods, parrotia and maples. Early spring features a collection of hellebores with carpets of *H.* 'White Magic' and many new hybrids. These are followed by primulas, meconopsis, alpines and bulbs. A woodland path leads to an azalea bed with bright-coloured companion plants. Further spring highlights include groups of rhododendrons, camellias, and enkianthus underplanted with trilliums, wood anemones, primroses and *Primula auricula*. White wisteria hangs from the house balcony, while another climbs high into a red silver birch. Summer and autumn feature herbaceous gardens and a rosebed punctuated by schist rock columns. Maples, stuartia, cornus and other deciduous trees display brilliant autumn colour. The New Zealand cedar gazebo provides a lake view against a backdrop of snowcapped mountains.

ASHDON GARDEN
Wanaka

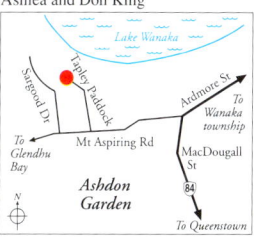

Owners:
Ashlea and Don King

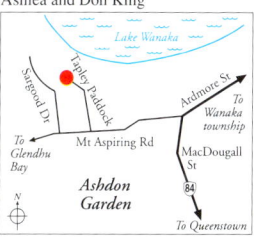

Address: 8 Tapley Paddock, Wanaka
Directions: From Wanaka, take the
lakeside road, Ardmore St, into
Mt Aspiring Rd. Turn right into
Tapley Paddock. Ashdon Garden at
end of road on right.
Phone: 0-3-443 8067
Fax: 0-3-443 8077
Email: avakwanaka@clear.net.nz
Website: friars.co.nz/gardens/pages/
ashdon.html
Open: September to April, daily,
by appointment
Groups: By appointment, as above
Fee: $4 per adult
Size: Small – 0.08ha (⅕ acre)
Terrain: Flat

Ashdon Garden, its name a combination of Ashlea and Don's names, has been developed since 1980, adjacent to a bush reserve leading to Lake Wanaka and Wanaka Station Park. This was part of the original Wanaka Station homestead, featuring historic oaks and cedars and provides a borrowed view for the Kings, making their garden appear much larger than its fifth of an acre. Rhododendrons are Ashlea's favourite species, over 100 featuring in the garden, such as 'Sarita Loder' beneath the montana clematis cascading from a sycamore tree. Camellias beside the house colour the early spring, and a white wisteria drips from the verandah. Further spring features include tulips, the cornus 'Eddie's White Wonder' and several species of crab-apple that provide spring blossom, summer fruit and autumn colour, as well as attracting the birdlife. A rosebed features old roses with climbers and ramblers on the fenceline accompanied by lots of summer perennials. Don constructed a rockery and stone walls which form low terraces planted with ferns, ericas, pieris and weigela. The path to the front door is bordered by malus, pink azaleas and white camellias underplanted with lush bergenias. The pieris and rhododendrons shade peonies and drifts of blue forget-me-nots.

ROSEDALE CHAPEL & WATER GARDEN
Lake Hayes

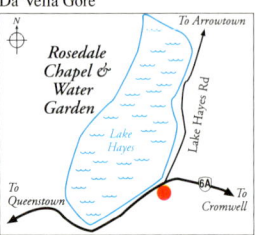

Owner:
Da'Vella Gore

Address: SH 6A, Lake Hayes
Postal: Eden Postal Agency,
Frankton, Queenstown
Directions: From Queenstown, take
SH 6A. Travel to "T" junction with
Lake Hayes Rd. Garden on right.
Phone: 0-3-442 1343
Fax: 0-3-442 1358
Website: friars.co.nz/gardens/pages/
rosedale.html
Open: Nov., Feb.–April, most
afternoons, or by appointment
Groups: Mornings, by appointment
Fee: $3 per adult
Size: Medium – 1.2ha (3 acres)
Terrain: Sloping on hillside
Painting workshops: Spring & autumn
For sale: Da'Vella's paintings & books
Tours: Historic house tour $8 pp
Accommodation: B&B available

   limited
by arrangement

Rosedale Chapel & Water Garden is just 10 minutes from Queenstown overlooking Lake Hayes, with a backdrop of snowcapped mountains. Historic ruins of a gold-mining hotel form the entrance, now clad with old-fashioned roses. The garden covers more than a hectare (three acres) and features streams, ponds and waterfalls. Set in a vineyard is a Gothic-style wedding chapel, an art gallery and the house built with materials from two historic Catholic churches. Trees planted since 1993 include weeping silver pears, maples and conifers. Springtime features cherry blossom trees, daffodils and bluebells, followed by drifts of mauves, pinks and purples on a carpet of snow-in-summer. The autumn colours are brilliant with the foliage of maples, liquidambars and oak trees. This is a scenic venue for weddings with its chapel, soft colours and panoramic views. Da'Vella is a marriage celebrant, artist and author, with her paintings and books for sale displayed in her art gallery. Da'Vella has created her garden for everyone to enjoy and visitors to the Rosedale often call it a "Garden of Eden".

Accommodation in Da'Vella's Gothic-style home is also available by arrangement. House tours can be arranged and painting workshops are held in the spring and autumn months. All visits to Rosedale are by appointment: phone 0-3-442 1343 or fax 0-3-442 1358.

BLUE MOUNTAIN NURSERIES
Tapanui

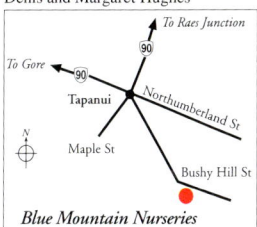

Owners:
Denis and Margaret Hughes

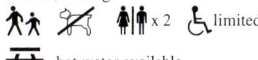

Blue Mountain Nurseries

Address: 99 Bushy Hill St, Tapanui
Directions: From Gore or Raes
Junction, take SH 90 to Tapanui. At
crossroads, take Bushy Hill St east
to Blue Mountain Nurseries on right.
Phone: 0-3-204 8250
Fax: 0-3-204 8278
Email: hughesc@esi.co.nz
Website: www.bmn.co.nz
Open: All year, Mondays to Saturdays,
9am–5pm
Closed: Sundays
Groups: By appointment
Fee: No charge
Size: Large – over 6ha (16 acres)
Terrain: Flat
Nursery: Hardy trees & shrubs, alpines,
perennials, climbers, rhododendrons
& azaleas, specialising in double
azaleas; catalogues available

🚶 🚫🐕 👫 x 2 ♿ limited

⛩ hot water available

Denis' father began the bulb and perennial nursery in 1932, then Denis and Margaret developed the trees and shrub side of the business in 1966. Denis' favourites include the deciduous azaleas that he began in 1972, raising his own double hybrids, with the fragrant white 'Pavlova' the first to be released, followed by the apricot 'Sunray'. The most recent release is the creamy pink 'Softlights'. The azalea beds also provide lovely autumn colour, along with the maples and over 20 different viburnums, some of them fragrant. The nursery features an extensive rhododendron shadehouse, where Margaret breeds the popular compact *R. yakushimanum* hybrids. Ivy cultivars climb the poles of the shadehouse, the Hughes holding the national ivy collection. A glasshouse displays the extensive collection of pleione orchids that Denis loves, in whites, yellows and cerise, including rare varieties selling for $200 per bulb! Denis is also keen on tree peonies, and other spring highlights include a bed of trilliums with three main varieties for sale. In summertime the 15 *Eucryphia* trees bear white and pink flowers. A comprehensive range of conifers provide winter colour, as do the berries on the rowan trees, until the snowdrops emerge. Other interesting features include the spiky variegated yuccas and native flax-like astelias.

THE ARK
Lawrence

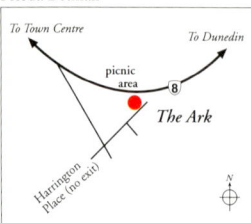

Owner:
Frieda Betman

Address: 8 Harrington Pl, Lawrence
Directions: From Dunedin, take SH 8 towards Lawrence. Just at the "Welcome to Lawrence" sign, garden immediately on left. Parking in No Exit road, Harrington Place, behind The Ark.
Phone: 0-3-485 9328
Email: lawrence.infocentre@xtra.co.nz
Website: www.thearknz.homestead.com
Open: November to March, daily, preferably by appointment
Fee: Gold coin
Size: Small – 0.2ha (½ acre)
Terrain: Flat
Nursery: Some perennials from garden for sale
Accommodation: By arrangement

 in park across road

 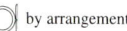 by arrangement

Frieda has created a florist's cottage garden as a setting for her restored turn-of-the-century house dubbed "The Ark", situated in the old gold-mining town of Lawrence. Frieda's favourites are cottage perennials such as the abundant phloxes, bergamots and penstemons. She worked with the contours of the garden, planting in whites through to pinks, lavenders and blues, with a touch of gold such as the bog primulas interplanted with deciduous azaleas and masses of delphiniums by the wee bridge which crosses the pond. A stick bridge and curved brick wall provide further structure and a pergola is engulfed in blue wisteria in spring. Blossom trees include 'Mt Fuji' cherry, 'Eddie's Wonder' dogwood, *Magnolia stellata* and viburnums. White daisy-like *Anthemis cupaniana* begin flowering in October and continue through to March, and rhododendrons start blooming in November. Peonies, summer perennials and a few roses follow, with catmint and Lady's mantle (*Alchemilla mollis*) making wonderful borders. Native ponga trunks edge damp areas that favour Solomon's seal, hostas, *Primula auricula*, astilbes, phlox, filipendulas and astrantia. A huge weeping willow on the fenceline provides shade, other trees including eight maples, a walnut, beech, golden ash, four claret ashes, silver birches and a medlar tree. Frieda's inseparable fox terrier, Holly, is an added attraction, and accommodation is available.

NAGOL GARDEN
Balclutha

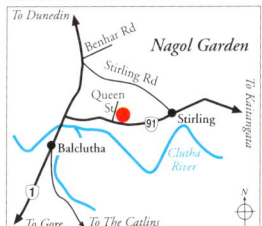

Owners:
Chris and Russell O'Hara

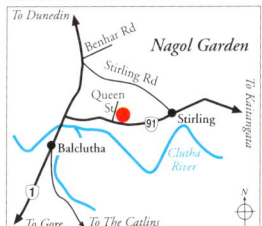

Address: 261 SH 91, Stirling, Sth Otago
Directions: From Milton, take SH 1 south towards Balclutha. Turn left at north end of Balclutha bridge, into SH 91. Travel about 3km & turn left into Queen St. Garden on right.
Phone: 0-3-418 2867
Mobile: 025 229 8816
Fax: 0-3-418 2869
Open: October to March, 10am to 5pm
Closed: April to September
Fee: $3 per adult, refundable on nursery purchase
Size: Medium– 0.53ha (1⅓ acres)
Terrain: Flat
Nursery: Annuals, perennials, shrubs, trees & roses for sale from Queen Street Nursery

Named after Chris and Russell's late son, Logan, the original garden was extended after 16 years in 1994 into the adjacent paddock. The new area is predominantly roses, with over 750 of Chris' favourite varieties. Visitors can walk through the large square beds of David Austin roses edged with *Lonicera nitida* hedging. Architectural structures include a rose pergola covered with the apricot 'Paul Transom' and the single red 'Dortman'. Archways lead into different garden areas, the sundial on a brick dais is encircled with flowers, and the gazebo forms a quiet garden retreat. A bridge crosses the goldfish and waterlily pond, designed as a raised "L" shaped water feature constructed from railway sleepers. Gunneras grow beside the bridge, with irises, primulas, hostas and drifts of pink and white heucheras. A further pond in the house garden incorporates a well, with a mature golden elm, gum and silver birch surrounded by elders. Spring features include bulbs, camellias and prunus and malus blossom. Chris found the conditions to be too wet for rhododendrons, but the roses thrive. Annuals and perennials accompany the roses through summer and into autumn when the prunus foliage colours up. Future plans include installing a three-tier fountain in the pond area, which Chris loves. And she also plans to expand the number of plants available from her Queen Street Nursery.

GORE PUBLIC GARDENS
Gore

Owner:
Gore District Council

Address: Fairfield St, Gore
Postal: P O Box 8, Gore
Directions: From Main St, turn west
into Irk St or Medway St. Turn into
Fairfield St to Gore Public Gardens.
Phone: 0-3-208 9080
Mobile: 025 382 542
Fax: 0-3-208 9087
Email: gbailey@goredc.govt.nz
Websites: friars.co.nz/gardens/pages/
goregardens.html *and*
www.mataura.com *and*
www.goredc.govt.nz
Open: All year, daily, daylight hours
Groups: Guided tours – 5 days notice
Fee: No charge
Size: Medium – 1.5ha (3¾ acres)
Terrain: Flat
Festival: Rhododendron Festival held
annually in October

The land was originally set aside in 1874, but not laid out until 1906 by David Tannock of Dunedin. The present design is based on this historic layout and incorporates many mature trees such as the gigantic wellingtonia and horizontal elms planted at that time. Among the exotic trees and shrubs are a number of rare and unusual specimens including those in the extensive conifer border. Spring bulbs are accompanied by the camellias, magnolia and enkianthus trees flowering. Then Gore's Rhododendron Festival is held each year in the Gardens in October complemented by the spring bedding display of annuals. Tree peonies are a feature, the peony border being spectacular in November. This is followed by the roses, modern varieties making an impressive display through the summer months when the eucryphia trees blossom. Further annuals continue into the autumn as the deciduous foliage begins to turn on the maple trees, the enkianthus becomes a bright red and red berries appear on the sorbus trees. Winter features include the witch hazels which bear yellow flowers on bare branches after the yellow autumn foliage drops. And hawthorns (*Crataegus*) produce red berries through the winter after the white blossom finishes. The conifer border is also a winter attraction and the Winter Garden complex is open all year. An added feature is the aviary, especially in spring.

BANNERMAN PARK
Gore

Owner:
Gore District Council

Address: Crewe St, Gore
Postal: P O Box 8, Gore
Directions: Signposted from SH 94.
Or from Gore Public Gardens, take
Ardwick St north. Turn left into
Martin St or Crewe St to gardens.
Entrances from both Martin St &
Crewe St opposite Gore Cemetery.
Phone: 0-3-208 9080
Mobile: 025 382 542
Fax: 0-3-208 9087
Email: gbailey@goredc.govt.nz
Website: friars.co.nz/gardens/pages/
bannerman.html
Open: All year, daily, daylight hours
Fee: No charge
Size: Large – 6ha (15 acres)
Terrain: Hilly
Car access: Drive through park in
spring & summer

tables

limited to main pathways

Bannerman Park was named in 1977 in honour of Mr R.B. Bannerman whose foresight helped procure extra land for the park. Known as the Hidden Valley, the land dates from the 1870s but was full of gorse and broom until cleared in the 1960s. Grass was then sown and the springs drained. Extensive plantings of rhododendrons, conifers and silver birches were established at that time and a deer park was also created. Twenty years later the creek beds were developed with bog plants, and since then herbaceous perennials have been extensively planted. Today, streams meander throughout the valley bordered by sealed pathways. Early spring is announced by the daffodils, meconopsis, camellias, cherry blossom and magnolias. The rhododendron collection includes large beds of *R. yunnanense, R. decorum* and *R. spinuliferum* all grown from seed gathered in the wilds of the Yunnan Province in China. In November the streams and ponds are lush with gunneras, hostas, irises and candelabra primulas. Native ferns, astelias and Chatham Island forget-me-nots also edge the streams. Peonies, daylilies and ajuga groundcover add to the colour as summer progresses. The deciduous foliage provides brilliant autumn colour from the weeping maples to the oaks, twisty willows and silver birches shading the picnic tables. Then winter brings the hellebores into flower. Most of the plants in the park are named.

DOLAMORE PARK SCENIC RESERVE
Gore

Owner:
Gore District Council

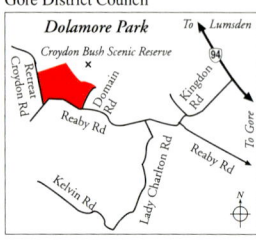

Address: Retreat Croydon Rd, Gore
Postal: P O Box 8, Gore
Directions: Signposted. Or from
Bannerman Park, take Reaby Rd north
for 11km. Turn right into Retreat
Croydon Rd. Gardens on right.
Phone: 0-3-208 9080
Mobile: 025 382 542
Fax: 0-3-208 9087
Email: gbailey@goredc.govt.nz
Website: friars.co.nz/gardens/pages/
dolamore.html
Open: All year, daily, 8am to dusk
Fee: No charge; campers $5 per adult
Size: Large – 95ha (237½ acres)
Terrain: Flat & hilly
Picnic ground: Electric 50 cent BBQ
Children: Playground
Festival: Country music festival each
February
& camping

limited to picnic ground

D olamore Park is named in honour of the Dolamore family whose gift allowed the camping area to be developed. The land was originally bought by the Gore Borough Council in 1940 to establish a public picnic area and provide access into the adjacent Croydon Bush Scenic Reserve in order to maintain it as a wildlife sanctuary. Walking tracks enable visitors to view the native birdlife, such as wood pigeons, fantails, bellbirds and tui especially in spring when the kowhai and flax flower. This native forested area forms a green backdrop for the park and is the largest lowland broadleaf podocarp forest in the region, featuring substantial stands of southern rata and rimu, totara and matai over 500 years old. The Waimumu Stream and Whisky Creek running through the park are home to trout, eels, crayfish, ducks, geese and native shags, herons and kingfishers. Extensive lawns are bordered by stone wall terracing. In spring the mature rhododendrons feature, followed by the red rata flowers in summer. Fine selections of conifers can be seen in the Bert Newman Arboretum and the Ian Gilchrist Conifer Collection. The park includes a children's playground and is popular for picnics, parties, barbecues and camping. A country music festival is held here each February. An Education Centre is open by appointment, displaying interactive information which shows the balance of biodiversity in native forests.

THE HIDEAWAY 201
Lochiel

![garden photograph]

Owners:
Joanne and Wayne McCallum

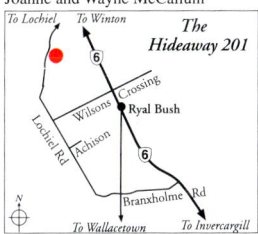

Address: 201 Lochiel Branxholme
Rd, Lochiel, R D 1, Winton
Directions: From Invercargill, take
SH 6 north towards Winton. At Lochiel,
turn left into Lochiel-Branxholme Rd.
Travel 2.01km to garden on left. From
Winton, take SH 6 south for 6km to
Lochiel. Turn right, then as above.
Phone: 0-3-221 7176 or 0-3-221 7364
Mobile: 025 322 875
Fax: 0-3-221 7364
Open: Garden: Nov.–March; cottage
shop: all year; both: weekends, 1pm
to 5pm, other times by appointment
Fee: Gold coin
Size: Medium – 1.5ha (almost 4 acres)
Terrain: Flat – easy levels
Nursery: A few plants from garden
Cottage shop: Sells quality gifts

 for booked groups only

Tucked behind high hedges of native manuka, with
very old macrocarpa hedging in front, The Hideaway
is a garden of separate rooms created from bare paddocks
in 1987. Apart from a large elm tree and the 120-year-old
oak by the rustic cottage shop, built the same year, all the
trees have been planted by the McCallums. Blossom trees
include an avenue of 'Pink Perfection' cherry trees, the
walkway leading to a sunken waterlily and fishpond area,
with adjacent rustic gazebo. Paths and rose-covered
archways link the various garden rooms, the arches
known as "bungies". A laburnum walk through four of
these archways leads to the cottage where quality
giftware is displayed. Tasman poplars provide height,
behind a dovecote, with lavender and buxus hedging
beneath manuka arches forming a long vista. Ponga
pergolas and a native garden surround the sunken
conversation pit with its wooden outdoor furniture. The
spacious lawns on different levels create a peaceful
country atmosphere, with birds attracted to the specimen
trees, which provide shade in the summer. Joanne uses
pastel colours in the cottage garden round the house,
including spring bulbs and roses, with highlights of red
contrasting with the green grass on the west side. The
barbecue area features white 'Iceberg' roses and blue and
white catmint.

TUDOR PARK
Invercargill

![photo of Tudor Park house and garden]

Owners:
Joyce and John Robins

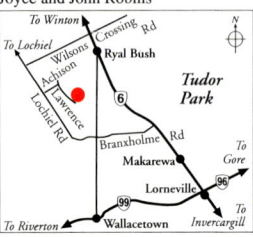

Address: 21 Lawrence Rd, Ryal Bush,
R D 6, Invercargill
Directions: From Invercargill, take
SH 6 north for 6km. Turn left into
Branxholme/Makarewa Rd. Travel
7km & turn right into Achison Rd.
Travel 1km & turn right again at "T"
junction. Tudor Park garden 1st on left.
Phone: 0-3-221 7150
Mobile: 025 310 031
Fax: 0-3-221 7150
Email: tudorparksouth@hotmail.com
Open: August to May, by appointment
Closed: June & July
Fee: $3 per adult
Size: Medium – 1.8ha (4 acres)
Terrain: Flat & gently sloping
Meals: By arrangement
Accommodation: See *Friars' Guide to
NZ Accommodation 2001*

 by arrangement

Set in almost two hectares (four acres) of tranquil gardens, Tudor Park is only 15 minutes north of Invercargill City, near the Southern Scenic route. This neo-Tudor home offers quality accommodation with garden views. Teas and meals are also offered, alfresco in the garden in summer. The garden is a blend of formal and informal, with an English influence to complement the style of the house. Although it was established by the original owners in the 1980s, Joyce and John have expanded the garden since 1995, bringing loads of plants from their previous home. The extensions have been carefully planned to retain the vistas to the surrounding mountains and also within the garden, with plenty of seats and rose arbours for enjoying the views. Two large pergolas support rambling roses, and a formal rose rondel features repeat-flowering old roses and is enclosed by a hornbeam hedge. The architectural structures, including a belvedere, are designed to harmonise with the landscape. Bridges cross a small pond close to the house and a larger pond at the far end of the garden, edged with irises, ligularias and other perennials, and willows and swamp cypresses. Rhododendrons and bulbs provide spring colour, with a wealth of over 300 old roses in summer, followed by autumn foliage and shrubs bearing berries and heps until June. Joyce plants creams, golds, oranges and blues in one area, with pinks, mauves and blues in another.

BELLE FLEUR GARDENS
Northope

Belle Fleur

Owners:
Walter and Kathleen Jack

Address: Drain Rd, Northope
Postal: Northope, R D 4, Invercargill
Directions: From City, take SH 99 for
13km to Wallacetown. Continue 5km,
turn right into Oporo-Northope Flat
Rd. Travel 15km & turn left into Drain
Rd. Garden 2nd on left. From Lumsden,
take SH 6 south. Turn right into SH 96.
Take 1st left & turn right into Drain Rd.
Phone: 0-3-236 8523
Fax: 0-3-236 0594
Website: friars.co.nz/gardens/pages/
bellefleur.html
Open: Feb.–April, daily, dawn to dark
Groups: By appointment
Fee: No charge
Size: Medium – 1ha (over 2 acres)
Terrain: Flat
Nursery: Dahlia specialist; hardy
pot-grown tubers @ $5–$8 each

hot water available

Belle Fleur, French for "beautiful flower", is the home of Oreti dahlias which the Jacks breed. Begun in 1976, when gums, silver birches and rhododendrons were planted for shelter, the dahlia garden now features over 700 different varieties. The shaped display beds are arranged in different types; some are colour coordinated and others feature companion planting. Dahlia sizes range from the tiny dwarfs which are ideal for border displays, to the giant 40-centimetre dahlias planted in exhibition beds. Kathleen and Walter find that red, lavender and purple dahlias sell well, while the yellows, oranges and whites are not as popular, so they have a demonstration bed of red dahlias interplanted with yellow and white to show how these colours bring the red out. Colour combinations change each year, with many of the beds edged in annuals such as the fluffy blue ageratum bordering lemon and yellow dahlias in one plot, and pink dahlias in another. Dahlia foliage varies from green to a rich black, with one plot devoted to the black-leafed varieties. Lavenders and ageratum edge the garden by the bridge which leads to a trial garden, where new dahlias are assessed by the National Dahlia Society, along with a public voting system. Walter and Kathleen's dahlia video, selling for $17.50, features over 150 dahlias. A mail-order catalogue is available for $2.50.

HOSTA GARDEN
Glencoe

![Hosta Garden photograph]

Owners:
Gaynor and Chris Miller

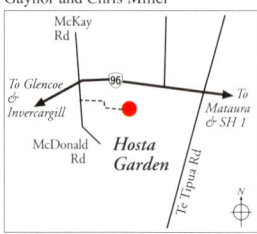

Address: 111 McDonald Rd, Glencoe
Postal: Roslyn Downs, R D 2,
Glencoe, Invercargill
Directions: From Gore, take SH 1
south to Mataura. Turn right into SH
96, then travel to McDonald Rd on
left. Take 1st left to Hosta Garden.
Phone: 0-3-230 6144
Fax: 0-3-230 6144
Open: Garden: October to December
during nursery hours;
Nursery: 1 October to 31 March,
Wednesday to Saturday, 9am–5pm
Groups & tours: By appointment
Fee: $3 per adult
Size: Large – 2ha (5 acres)
Terrain: Undulating with levels
Nursery: Specialists – over 450 hosta
varieties & new releases from USA;
daylilies; mail-order catalogue

  mostly

Established in 1965, this woodland garden is heavily underplanted with hostas which thrive in the moist sheltered conditions. A wide range of hosta species features, with many new cultivars and hybrids mainly derived from *H. fortunei*, *H. montana* and the blue-leafed *H. sieboldiana*. Structure is provided by brick pathways, rocks, retaining walls and steps Chris made from sleepers, creating various levels and heights. A bog dell is planted with native ferns, primulas and gunneras complementing the hostas, and a creek crossed by a bridge is edged with rocks and further hostas, and runs into a large pond. A thatched manuka belvedere overlooks the Douglas firs, gums, native ponga and deciduous oaks, ashes, prunus, birches and maples, including some new and rare varieties. Gaynor uses white and blue with the bright spring colours of rhododendrons, edged with large drifts of unfurling hostas. The texture and form of hosta foliage cools the summer, when peonies and roses provide splashes of colour. Indigenous plantings include native cedars, kauri, totara, pittosporums, ponga ferns, pseudopanax, grasses and some groundcovers. Gaynor has developed a rustic shade arbour, with species clematis climbing over it and a hosta display around a central urn. Beyond is a silver birch grove. The Hosta Hut sells hand-made crafts such as designer rabbits and sculptural ceramics including terracotta earth-mothers.

ANDERSON PARK GARDENS
Invercargill

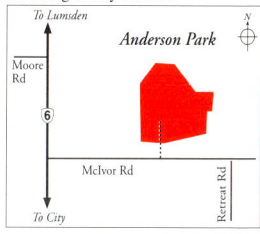

Owner:
Invercargill City Council

Address: McIvor Rd, Invercargill
Postal: Private Bag 90 104,
Invercargill
Directions: From Invercargill, take
SH 6 north towards Lumsden. Travel
7km, then turn right into McIvor Rd.
Gardens 900m on left.
Phone: 0-3-217 7368 (gardens);
0-3-215 7432 (gallery)
Fax: 0-3-217 5358
Open: All year, daily, daylight hours
Fee: No charge
Size: Large – 24.8ha (62 acres)
Terrain: Flat
Gallery: Anderson Art Gallery on site;
open every afternoon 2–4pm;
tours by arrangement; NZ art
collection established since 1951;
annual spring exhibition in October

 & in bush

Anderson Park is well-known for its art gallery, established in 1951 when the homestead was gifted to Invercargill by the late Sir Robert and Lady Anderson. Designed in neo-Georgian style by Christchurch architect Cecil Wood, the homestead was completed in 1925, when the gardens were developed. The driveway winds through native bush, opening at the Gallery set in extensive lawns and backed by native and exotic trees. Springtime feaures mature rhododendrons and azaleas bordering the duck pond. A colourful display of thousands of annuals is complemented by perennials and the two rose gardens which are the main summer attraction. These incorporate a laburnum walk and a miniature rose garden. Deciduous foliage provides autumn colour, while conifers are a year-round attraction, the most significant specimen being a Monkey puzzle tree (*Araucaria araucana*). There is a well-formed walking track through the interior of the native bush, suitable for wheelchairs. Indigenous species include the white pine (kahikatea), rimu, thin-barked totara, matai, miro and pokaka. Behind the gallery is a replica Maori Wharepuni or Whare Whakairo, carved in Rotorua. In 1932, one of the Andersons' daughters, Kathleen, was married in it. The spacious grounds at Anderson Park also include the picnic pavilion and wedding areas, as well as the children's playground.

QUEENS PARK
Invercargill

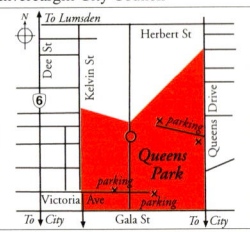

Owner:
Invercargill City Council

Address: Gala St & Queens Drive, Invercargill
Postal: Private Bag 90 104, Invercargill
Directions: From the City, take SH 6 (Dee St) north. Turn right into Victoria Ave & continue to garden entrance. Or travel north on Queens Drive, turning left into gardens at entrance.
Phone: 0-3-217 7368
Fax: 0-3-217 5358
Open: All year, daily, daylight hours
Fee: No charge
Size: Large – 80ha (200 acres)
Terrain: Flat
Refreshments: Kiosk & Museum café
Children: Wonderland Castle, playground & splash pool
Sporting attractions: 4km fitness trail, 18-hole golf course, hockey turf, tennis courts, cricket pitch, pétanque court, bowling green, & croquet lawn

Eighty hectares were originally set aside in 1857 for Queens Park. It was sown in English grasses and planted with radiata pine and macrocarpa shelter belts, then in 1900 the 18-hole golf course was established. By 1911 the first ornamental plantings were in place and the impressive Feldwick Gates at the Gala Street entrance were erected in 1924 in memory of John Feldwick whose bequest greatly aided the development of the Park. Today there are pathways throughout, radiating out from the band rotunda in the centre to the various gardens, ponds and other attractions. The predominant species are the rhododendrons, roses and New Zealand native plants. The first to emerge in spring is the camellia bed, followed by the rhododendron dell and azalea garden. The main summer feature is the formal rose garden with brick-pillared pergolas. Here the Jessie Calder Rose Garden displays a collection of old-fashioned bush roses and the Henry Edginton Rose Garden shows a range of modern roses from bush to standards and climbers. The deciduous foliage on the established English trees is the main autumn attraction, although there is much year-round interest, including the glasshouses in the Winter Gardens, the recent Japanese garden, the New Zealand native section, the rock garden, the duck ponds and bog garden, and the animal enclosures including the new aviary.

NORTH ISLAND GARDENS INDEX

NORTH ISLAND GARDENS INDEX

NORTH ISLAND OWNERS INDEX

NORTH ISLAND OWNERS INDEX

SOUTH ISLAND GARDENS INDEX

SOUTH ISLAND OWNERS INDEX

Other Guides by Denis and Jillian Friar

Friars' Guide to New Zealand Accommodation for the Discerning Traveller – 2001

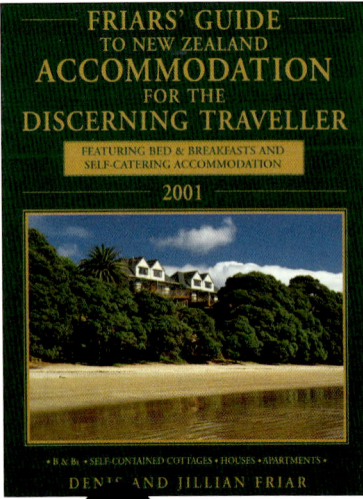

$24.95 RRP

— Offering B&B or self-catering, this showcase guidebook features —

- 280 full-colour pages
- 257 top accommodation places
- 4 exclusive tours
- B&B or self-contained information
- exterior & interior photographs
- directions & street location maps
- all tariffs displayed
- bedrooms & bathrooms detailed
- facilities & activities available
- North & South Island colour maps
- 210mm x 275mm
- http://friars.co.nz

— Offering dining, this showcase accommodation guidebook features —

- 216 full-colour pages
- 187 top accommodation places
- 3 exclusive tours
- dinner offered at every place
- exterior & interior photographs
- directions & street location maps
- all tariffs displayed
- bedrooms & bathrooms detailed
- facilities & activities available
- North & South Island colour maps
- 210mm x 275mm
- http://friars.co.nz

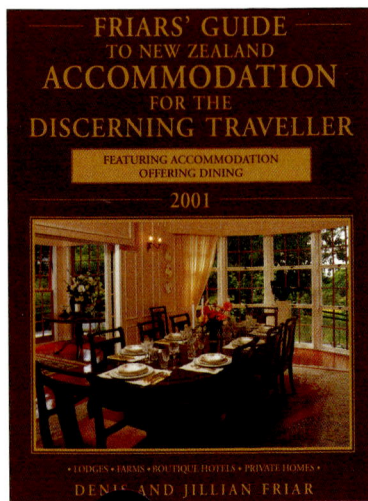

$24.95 RRP

ON SALE AT ALL GOOD BOOKSHOPS